METAMODERN LEADERSHIP

A HISTORY OF THE SEVEN VALUES THAT WILL CHANGE THE WORLD

JAMES SURWILLO

PAGE PUBLISHING, INC.
New York, NY

First originally published by Page Publishing, Inc. 2017

ISBN 978-1-63568-219-9 (Paperback)
ISBN 978-1-63568-220-5 (Digital)

Printed in the United States of America

To my grandfather for the wisdom of the past and
my daughters for the possibilities of the future.

CONTENTS

INTRODUCTION

METAMODERN LEADERSHIP

In recent years, leadership has become an industry, a discipline, and a philosophy that uses a mix of character and skills to encourage motivation to comply with a vision. Business school leadership curriculum has guided dry tutorials to apply to positions and insert into organizations. The leadership industry has thousands of "thought leaders" who have gained key universal insights of personal experience and expertise. Organizational culture has embedded leadership within its teachings and applications, which always prescribe static and eternal methods of success. The entire understanding of the constructs of modern-day leadership was developed and tested within the span of one small cultural era, which has no method to project the inevitable and drastic transformation of generational leadership change. As the current generation of the post-war baby boomers, who dominate our ideas of leadership, begin to retire, a new generation of leaders will begin to fill in the voids with completely new ideas and values. The way we understand leadership assumes that these new humans will assume the old roles without questioning its constitution. For the sake of continuity and progress, we must dig deep to fully understand the state of affairs that has formed our youth. The near universal mistake of the leadership industry is attributing past success to future standards, especially as it relates to a starkly different category of human beings.

Generation Y, or the millennial generation, are the adults who have come of age after the new millennium. They are the largest and most diverse generation in American history with ideas that contrast with the leadership status quo in nearly every manner. Most of the dialogue regarding this generation attempts to apply their current behaviors to current realities but are usually viewed through the context of a different era. Without question, their leadership models will be the status quo within a decade. The expertise of technology is always skewed toward the young. As the exponential pace of technology change increases, leadership in the near future will shift from experience to competence. Culture at large, consisting of all conceivable and inconceivable institutions and organizations, will transform in the image of a generation of new decision makers. Thus far, there has been no sincere interest or intellectual pursuit to understand this generation besides occasional articles that attack character or relegate their skills into obscurity. They have not engaged in a power struggle because they are an innately optimistic and pragmatic generation who understand that time is their only vehicle for change within existing structures. In their youth, they remain relatively apolitical. They were raised in a world where the individual has gained more power in nearly every aspect of their lives while simultaneously losing power politically. Twenty-five years ago, generational theorists William Strauss and Neil Howe predicted the "awakening" period indicative of the power of the youth of the 1960s, which would inevitably swing toward a "crisis" period, where power would be inaccessible to the youth by the second decade of the new millennium. The role of youth today is, instead, tending to institutions in new ways. Therefore, transparency and democratization of leadership as a means to power and progress will be their legacy.

In *The Bed of Procrustes,* Nassim Nicholas Taleb said, "Since Cato the Elder, a certain type of maturity has shown up when one starts blaming the new generation for 'shallowness' and praising the previous one for its values." Fareed Zakaria's *In Defense of a Liberal Education* recounts that the Greek poet Hesiod called the young cal-low and morally unserious around 700 BC. Xenophon and Plato would later comment on the decaying virtues of youth. It may seem in fashion to highlight how the values of youth are out of touch with mainstream society, but it has gone on for at least 2,700 years. We always forget that the values and events of the past are directly connected with the present and future. Beliefs and experiences of a generation will be embraced or rejected based on the amount of truth perceived by the latter. Eventually and inevitably, worldviews develop, which define a generation. To a lesser extent, cultural norms, which define eras, have been changing at an exponential pace. The period of late modernism, for instance, was understood to be the one hundred years of industrialization from roughly 1850 to 1950, underscored by great cultural and technological progress. The postmodern period, a strange illiberal trance of decadence in the post-industrial decades, lasted from sometime in the 1950s to around the turn of the millennium. Generational periods remain unchanged in length, although cultural period timeframes are diminishing. This rarely studied phenomenon makes generational change in our current environment even that more drastic. Never before has the speed of cultural era been in competition with the static pace of generational change. Simultaneously, the largest generation in American history, which has shaped the country in their image, will begin to relinquish their leadership roles to an even larger generation.

Millennials, it is said, are unserious, lazy, entitled, and ignorant to the workings of the world. It is my attempt to refute these charges by explaining their origins, defining their values, and contemplating their possibilities. They just happen to be a generation at the right time and place to possess and act upon the great wisdom of the ages. The greatest generational power shift in America's history is on the precipice, yet it has not been acknowledged because their power in the current context is nearly irrelevant. This is the great human interest story of our times, yet we are distracted because they seem more narcissistic than the Baby Boomer Generation, who were the original narcissists in their youth, or more coddled than Generation X, who were left to their own devices as children in the staunchly adult culture of the 1970s. Of course, the "micro-aggressions" of language, "trigger warnings" of unsuitable material, and "safe spaces" for psychological comfort are alarming. As I will uncover, these are the remaining pieces of the postmodern hyper individualistic dead ends that have been the cultural trajectory since before this generation was born. As our young adults mature, they are primed to gain a stoic nature that uses pragmatism to guide their idealism. In 1917, John Dewey taught the virtues of "practical idealism," which has been defunct for generations. The grand idea of its return is best defined by Dewey as "aligning what is right with what is possible."

Our youth is the most educated generation in American history and among the worst educated in American history in relation to the rest of the world. They are the first to literally compete with the entire world at the inception of their career. They have new and more requirements to be successful than any generation previous. They have, at once, more reasons to be happy and more barriers to happiness than ever before. Average in America was once successful to the world. Because of the displacements of jobs due to globalization and technology, starting wages and median wages are falling in the United States and rising in the rest of the world. This is less due to government policy and more due to the fact that the United States infrastructure has been built for decades and the possibilities for infrastructure throughout the developing world are much greater and much easier thanks to modern technology. The space in between is developing a generation of innovative and creative individuals who can solve the big issues, which have gridlocked organizations for years and now decades. Our most educated generation has within them the greatest repository of knowledge any group of humans ever has known. They also possess a device in their pocket, which may attain nearly every objective fact on earth. The ability to decipher truth in new ways is an exercise in creativity. Creativity leads to innovation, which is the cornerstone of every industry in the twenty-first century. Innovation gives us greater productivity, which translates economically to freedom and progress. That freedom is a virtuous cycle of purpose and passion, which allows us to embrace even more creativity.

In other words, the virtues of a liberal education, thought to be for most of the twentieth century an exercise in futility to display elitist knowledge in an intellectual capacity void of any progress or productivity, is actually the foremost requirement for everything, from science, technology, engineering, and math (STEM) disciplines to art. A liberal education is an exercise in being "the complete man," which allows freedom from ignorance. It is the ancient tradition of learning disparate knowledge to apply to the future. Psychologist Barry Schwartz calls it practical wisdom, in the vein of Aristotle, which happens to be in demand. The twentieth century had mostly been geared toward ever more specialization and skills based learning, which ran in contrast to the practical, varied, and project-based curriculum taught by our early twentieth-century visionaries such as William James and John Dewey. Famed biologist E. O. Wilson has said, "We are drowning in information, while starving for wisdom. The world, henceforth will be run by synthesizers, people able to put together the right information at the right time, think critically about it, and make important choices wisely." Tony Wagner, an expert in twenty-first-century education and skills, sees the main issues as society still valuing the knowledge worker in the information economy. The *knowledge worker* was coined in 1959 by management visionary Peter Drucker, yet knowledge can now be searched for by anyone. Acquiring facts has no relationship to innovation. Acquiring wisdom by knowledge of various disciplines has the far better likelihood of innovation.

The original intention of the liberal arts was to become the "experienced navigator" in Plato's analogy of the philosopher as leader in *The Republic.* Only the person who had knowledge of the ship, the weather, the water currents, the stars, and capabilities of the crew should have access to governance of the ship. In other words, a broad base of knowledge is ideal in order for action to have more truth. There are great social implications when power is bestowed at the hands of the ignorant. America's founding fathers took Plato's advice by separating political powers and electing representatives to prevent the "tyranny of the masses," which Plato had feared. The great liberal tradition championed educating the masses for the advancement of culture. Thomas Jefferson once bragged, "Ours are the only farmers who can read Homer." Nearly a century later, Victorian England still found itself mired in the social hierarchy mostly absent from American life. In the years after the American Civil War, educational reformer Matthew Arnold wrote *Culture and Anarchy* as a means to push society forward in the great liberal tradition of progress for all. To Arnold, education was the development and balance of human potential, accessible to all society. For nearly one hundred years, into the 1960s, the great liberal tradition of the pursuance of self-development in education for riddance of egocentricity, selfishness, and narrowmindedness for the greater good was the mark of education well done. The humanities, social sciences, and civics, however, eventually gave way to generations of facts and skills-based learning, which separated the great liberal trajectory of the west. The disciplines of STEM as presently administered were never rooted in culture as Arnold prescribes. Anarchy, in modern culture, is the narrowmindedness of the pursuance of a single discipline at the expense of the enlightenment possible by understanding all.

The breakdown of our institutions, organizations, and communities has risen in direct conjunction with the economic requirements for singular mastery of a subject. Schwartz says there is a "collective dissatisfaction" in nearly every facet of our society stemming mostly from most people knowing very little except what they know. In a slightly less complex world, most breakthroughs, whether they be in art or science, would be in that particular field or at least a direct adjacent. In today's world, as told by Tim Harford in *Why Success Always Starts with Failure,* Cesar Hidalgo, a physicist, created a connected system of networks which outline capacities to grow in various economies. He used information seemingly unrelated from migration patterns to medical records to determine economic opportunities hidden to economists, and gaps certainly beyond the comprehension of anyone dictating public policy. Our next generation will have in their grasp counterintuitive breakthroughs that span the disciplines to enact solutions that seem impossible even by today's advanced standards. Knowledge embedded inside our vast information systems has barely scratched the surface for mining new applications never before considered. Progress in the 1970s was a postmodern issue, which turned conservatively to skills-based learning and efficiency. Progress today is more in the realm of the grand narrative of human progress and wisdom rather than artificial manipulations of momentary economics.

The possibilities are endless, yet the judge and jury of the reputation of the next generation of leaders require some self-reflection of their own. Our mostly baby boomer leaders have taken politics from the middle to the extremes, and extremism as a whole in the world is growing under their watch. Science, the only perpetual consensus, is being doubted. Democracy, as the one and only great social order, is dying; the natural world is being destroyed; inequality is drastically rising, and risk aversion is making us safe and conservative at a time when releasing the fear of failure should be valued more than all. The 24/7 news cycle mixed with social media personalization leaves us scared and angry rather than optimistic and grateful. Complexity has caused our experts to be among the worst predictors at their subject matter. Imagination has no economic value even though every CEO begs for their employees to be more creative. Statistics, which helps the human mind understand degrees of certainty for the future, is lost in favor of algebra, which only helps the rational mind explain what is present. US debt is skyrocketing and personal debt is increasing as education costs at once rise and become more of a necessity. Personal wealth and long-term savings are nonexistent. The generation mostly casting aspersions has let all of this happen since they have reached adulthood. Their economic livelihood, however, which includes pensions, social security, and Medicare, rests with the success of the generation they attack and which they have never invested any meaningful possibilities of an economic future.

Leadership is as old as time itself, yet its modern constructs adhere to the rational and eternal. It has never needed to answer to its new multidisciplinary masters, living in what has been referred to as the metamodern period. Many twenty-first-century philosophers have come to understand that a new period in human cultural evolution has taken place within the past two decades. It can broadly be described as a reassemblage of the fragmentation of the postmodern. The worldviews of current leadership in every facet of our lives have been in place before the cementation of these new foundations. Therefore, the metamodern is and has been a place of reality; it is just not accessible to the vast majority of the powers that be. As science fiction writer William Gibson has said, "The future is already here—it's just not very evenly distributed." The future mainstream is still disregarded as childish and immature, but that does not discourage its inevitability. Granted, there is a substantial population of youth that needs to align their values with their potential, a requirement of maturation, but that can be said about every generation since Cato the Elder. So leadership, as a discipline, concerns itself with capability, but the cutting edge of leadership thought should concern itself also with probability. August Comte said a century and a half ago, "From science comes prediction, from prediction comes action." I base my entire theory on the fact that my science of generational change is a foregone conclusion of demographics. I ask the same question as Comte, "What would be the action?"

I began the journey searching the principles of metamodern leadership through researching proper education and training of current industry standards. With the incorporation of leadership as a key understanding of success and progress, I wanted to know the cornerstones, which included trust, goodness, and accountability. Through moral psychologists, I learned that morality underlying the same idea may be widely interpreted. This led me to the ethics of Aristotle, in which adherence would land you in jail for child abuse, and the morals of Nietzsche, which questioned the very understanding of goodness itself. Leadership is thus mostly an incantation of the times. A leader in the truest sense has no power over the individual. She only speaks the language compatible with the internal motivation of the individual that had been absent or improperly communicated. In chapter 5 of J. B. Bury's 1921 masterpiece *The Idea of Progress*, he identifies the reality that progress is the trajectory of the history of the world, yet since human existence, it has not always been strictly linear in every facet. The overarching themes, however, are that science, technology, and the collective devices of mankind can initiate a social progress that benefits the circumstances of humanity at large.

Problem-solving in recent decades has been limiting not because of our capabilities but because of what French sociologist Pierre Bourdieu would call habitus. The hyperindividualism of the postmodern period has caused socially internalized dispositions. Physical and psychological stimuli act to reinforce the habitus of the individual. He claims we have been socialized in a very individual manner, which limits the actual shared potential of mankind. The various ideas of capital and power, which include prestige and reputation, allow for more cultural and social access into a new and various arrays of economies hidden to the generations of the past. The habitus of the postmodern period, which negated progress, never attached itself to the millennial generation. Cheap technologies and connection capabilities give every individual equal opportunity to access infinite ideas and surmount the limitations of the habitus from just a generation ago. Breaking free and expanding our views to include a heterogeneous composite of partners will be a requirement. The metamodern world will be one of endless choices where the inevitability of choice must end anxiety or progress stalls. It must also be where humans begin to use their technology for sustainability as a means to progress. Leadership, even in the short term, will need to answer drastically different questions than the present. There have been but five hundred generations since man learned how to plant a seed and only fifteen who have called themselves Americans. Generational change is something to be embraced with optimism and openness for the good of the future as inevitability. Winston Churchill said, "For myself I am an optimist. It does not seem to be much use being anything else."

Just as I believe the future of leadership requires a strong understanding of the various disciplines of the liberal arts, I have designed this book as an anthology into the far corners of subjects which, without the science of big data, would have no correlation. Big data is the metaphor for the synthesis of information thought impossible just a decade ago. Part 1 is concerned with the philosophical framework as well as the genres that most closely apply for a complete history of our present generations. Part two identifies the seven values, which my research indicates applies to the essential requirements of the next generation of leaders. In this section, I complete the genealogy began in the first section, yet I add the seven corresponding values that are vital to the identity of the metamodern leader. These seven comprehensive proficiencies go beyond a learned skill set to involve a fundamental change of worldview. They include participation as a new understanding of ownership and accountability and partnership, which is a way to reorganize existing social structures. Personalization discusses the psychological findings of motivation. Pedagogy explains the shift necessary in education and learning. Purpose describes a new way to understand the next iteration of capitalism most potable to the young. Through myth, I illustrate the power shift inevitability, and planetary shift outlines the next evolution of human connectedness and consciousness. Ultimately, the goal is to shed light on the universal truths behind the disciplines and highlight a path forward for the future. Leadership, then, cannot be just another discipline to learn but a melding of all the virtues of human knowledge. I use the double-faced symbol of Janus of ancient Roman mythology, looking opposite directions, to symbolize leadership in the metamodern world. It is a symbol of the duality indicative of the present state of humankind because finally, the grand narratives of the past can solve the great problems of the future.

PART I

THE GENEALOGY OF A GENERATION

CHAPTER 1

GENEALOGY AND ETHICS

The usefulness of philosophy in the modern world has been abandoned. What was the center of the ancient world and the arrow of progress for the Enlightenment has been relegated to an obscure theoretical discipline. The prerequisite for truth for thousands of years has become embedded in an unrecognizable fashion into our culture. Its value, once concrete and proactive, has been replaced with the anti-intellectual empiricism of reaction. The wisdom for which philosophy has always searched became fragmented. The history of the twentieth century was, in essence, a conscious departure from the power that philosophy had over the human life. The circumstances of the early twenty-first century require a new history, one that concludes that philosophy has never left; it was just hidden in new priorities. Philosophy itself was banished to the immeasurable metaphysical realm. It was clouded in the apathy of complexity and is only now emerging in its new material form. The ethical virtues of philosophy, which include wisdom, morality, unity, and progress, had been frozen in time by a modern world that needed to prepare itself for a new era. Virtuous philosophy acts rather than theorizes, but it must also be conscious to be impactful.

Ethics is the branch of philosophy concerned with the concepts and principles that govern and describe human values. What began as the meta ethics, which had governed all of human behavior in the ancient world, has become blurry deconstruction into various fields of disciplines, from the role of bioethics in medicine to machine ethics in artificial intelligence. The earliest philosophers were concerned with ethics as it refers to virtue. Socrates believed that virtue and knowledge were indistinguishable. Every criminal act and evil inclination is a result of ignorance in one form or another. Only through self-awareness and knowledge of the physical world would we leave our ignorance behind and evolve into a state of full potential. This state, called Eudaimonia, equated with happiness to the ancient philosopher. Aristotle added to Socratic virtue by aligning Eudaimonia with the way of nature. Goodness is embedded in self-awareness but also self-realization of the individual. These ideas are the basic structures for the argument of goodness living inside the notion that the quest for human progress is the infinite virtue. Aristotle wrote *Nichomachean Ethics*, for which Christianity would eventually refer to construct its moral code, but the immediate legacy lived in the sensibilities of the Stoic philosophers.

The story of philosophy as we know it begins with the tension of the rationality of Plato, who believed that our senses fail us and we must seek an objective truth, and the empiricism of Aristotle, who believed that the only way to truly collect evidence was through the senses of the individual. No single philosopher synthesized these disparate concepts for two thousand years until Immanuel Kant published *A Critique of Pure Reason* in 1781. The futility of the speculation of the relationships between the two forms of historical knowledge was not leading to progress. Kant found himself as possibly the arbiter of a period of time defined by progress itself. The west had shed the stagnation of one millennia of "Dark Age" inertia. He had consolidated the ancient wisdom in a form that laid the path for further progress. It was well believed that the rational and the empirical had never joined hands by a single philosopher. Even the modern world of Kant, however, may not have fully respected the cultural impact of ancient philosophy. It was not a vocation or a discipline; it was a way of life. If one is to live according to philosophy and if true knowledge draws from empiricism and rationalism, then Kant's ideas were a manufactured construct of the ideals of the ancient world.

The philosophical schools of ancient Greece were many. Often, ideas from the Skeptics would overlap with those of the Cynics or the Epicureans. The ideas of Stoicism, however, endured as the power structure of the western world transferred from the Greeks to the Romans. The practicality of Stoicism was a natural fit to the Roman world, which placed a higher value on politics and engineering than their Greek brethren of mostly pure ethics and remedial science. Virtue was always the goal of the Greeks, who practiced Stoicism, but the Romans turned it into a psychological self-medication as well. The Roman Empire, sometimes compared to modern America, excelled in the window of the Pax Romana, or the time of "Roman peace." Nineteenth-century French novelist Gustave Flaubert described it as thus: "When the gods ceased to be, and Christ had not yet come, there was a unique moment in history, between Cicero and Marcus Aurelius, when man stood alone." In the decades before the birth of Christ to near AD second century, man had become enlightened by displacing the gods with reason. The story of Christ, however, was soon to arrive and transform, but it followed with a thousand-year stagnation of every aspect of life. That unique moment in history that Flaubert described was characterized by the Stoic ideal. The Renaissance and the Enlightenment restored progress, but the embodiment of the modern Stoic was relegated to a Kantian version of theoretical progress.

The Roman Enlightenment was more than a philosophical mediation of the genesis of human knowledge as Kant describes. Much of the Stoic tradition, especially that of its last great forbearer, Roman emperor and philosopher Marcus Aurelius, is the duty to "live as nature requires." This was, no doubt, borrowed from Aristotle but also the Hedonist philosopher Lucretius of the Epicurean school of philosophy. His work in 49 BC, *On the Nature of Things*, was a direct result to the divine humanism of the progress of the natural world to the likes of which was unmatched in history. According to Matt Ridley in *The Evolution of Everything*, a copy of his work was uncovered in Germany in the year 1417 and copied fifty times. This one act may have spurred the six hundred years of progress in the west. Thomas Jefferson was said to have kept five copies of the book himself. The philosophy of the Enlightenment picked up where the major pre-Christianity philosophy, Stoicism, had left off, but it still failed to reintegrate the constructs of pure Stoicism. The world was still not ready for its ancient virtue. Instead, philosophers were building constructs of the world of its own modern rendition.

By the eighteenth century, sensibilities and structures were changing, but it wasn't until the Industrial Revolution matured in the mid-nineteenth century that technology had begun to change the quality of life of man. The modern world, born of reason and rejection of the suffering of the middle ages, left the early philosophical realm and entered a new modern era. Dating back to the fifteenth century, the ideas of progress and enlightenment brought about a new consciousness. It was not until well into the nineteenth century, however, that a new modern period developed. It wasn't just the ideas of progress that were changing but, increasingly, the material world itself. What came to be known as the Great Divergence was a new realization that the restraints to growth in all facets of life were disappearing. Culture was no longer either erudite or lowly. Around the middle of the nineteenth century, a new and distinct cultural era was emerging. After centuries of the simmering of the Enlightenment, an inflection point of progress proved tangible results in all that could be measured. This transformed the societies of the west. A social class that was the precursor to the modern middle class was developing its own sensibilities.

Prior to the new modern period, the learned scholar had guided our rational and spiritual north. As higher level needs of the masses began to be met, a new bourgeois establishment intertwined with the emerging bohemia, which had displaced the mythology of the middle ages and the metaphysical of the Enlightenment. A new world stability born of politics and economics gave the world the preconditions for one hundred years of the best art that the world had ever seen. The great world cities of London, New York, and Berlin were second only to Paris, which became the center of the culture of the modern world. Art rose in tandem with economic interests of society.

The modern ideal, however, was to break from the new conservative bourgeois "middlebrow" in the midst of rapid progress. The bourgeois had too closely embraced their middle-class bohemian contemporaries. The rational and mechanical world of science that had brought about the preconditions for modernism to excel was being subverted. The mantle of the spirit of liberalism lived only through the aesthetics of the new cultural disruptors. Theophile Gautier exclaimed, "Everything that is useful is ugly." Oscar Wilde's purpose was to show the world beauty absent realism. There was a common sentiment that defined the new world order as an obligation to overthrow the subtle oppressions of normalcy.

Enlightenment had grown stale and rigid. Holbrook Jackson surveyed the mood of the 1890s and noticed that the common descriptor was the word *new*. Ezra Pound exclaimed it most profoundly by the simple utterance of the prevailing tide, "Make it new." Intentional disruption, the mark of heresy itself, was the method of the modern artist. Lord Byron exclaimed, "There is something pagan in me that I cannot shake off." This separation from the sensibilities of the mainstream guided all of modernist art, from the musical innovation of Stravinsky to the avant-garde prose of Joyce or the artistic possibilities of Picasso. Whatever the medium, the method for progress was transcendence with the understanding that the middle-class sensibilities may not be ready, but they would soon comprehend. Culture and progress, however, seem to always circumnavigate the logical inevitabilities of an era. Philosophy, always united under the banners of art (hitherto religion) and science, had separated into disparate beings. Philosophy as a coherent worldview had already dissipated like the definition in an impressionistic piece of art. The abstract of cubism told us more truth than a snapshot.

Philosophy as a discipline was in tatters. The world looked to a burgeoning American republic to inform philosophy, the most trusted conduit of human knowledge. Kant had split and synthesized rationalism and empiricism, but the modern world required something beyond epistemological theory. While the modernist intention began as lifting up culture to progress, it increasingly attempted to transcend it. Amid the cultural struggle, a new form of philosophy emerged in academic America. The romanticism of Victorian modernism, which discouraged the complacency and gradualism of the pragmatic ethics to live within the requirements of the current era, sought to shock culture along in an increasingly avant-garde fashion. These late modernists were concerned with the ideal of the immeasurable and sublime rather than the more mundane realism of progress. So Pragmatists wanted to understand truth and Modernists wanted to transcend it. Both camps were eschewing the perceived limitations of the centuries of Enlightenment—the Modernists with romance and the Pragmatists with a new form of reason.

Rationalism was the method of progress for hundreds of years. The supreme understanding of rationalism is that truth is an innate and static human understanding, without sentiment and regardless of time and space. From this perspective, the whole of human progress can be calculated with a definite ending point. Rationality seeks to find the perfect logic of the human being by using the supreme cognitive powers of the human brain in a vacuum. The limitations of this idea was the ire of the Modernist but also, strangely, the Pragmatist. To the Pragmatist, truth is temporal rather than eternal. A critic of Pragmatism may argue that Pragmatic ethics is a version of temporal cultural relativism. What is true in one era may not be true in another. This is not because there is no innate hierarchy of virtue in the human condition but because empiricism, which updates human knowledge through experience, dictates truth more closely than logical rationalism, which can only revert to past human experience and understanding. Pragmatists capture the hope of progress through some of the same perceptions of the Modernists; however, their prescription is a concrete path to infinite enlightenment rather than subscription to the dogma of the rationalists or the immeasurable aesthetics of the modernists.

The rational world would conclude that the Pragmatists stand for nothing because truth is fleeting. In reality, however, the Pragmatist can reach the same degree of certainty as the cold rationalist, just through different methods. Men have rationalized some of the greatest atrocities in history by calculating prior events, and the logic may have been sound for the time and place. The great

Pragmatist William James said, "Truth lives, in fact, for the most part on a credit system." Our thoughts and beliefs "pass" so long as nothing challenges them. The lesson of history is always that time challenges, culture challenges, and inevitable new truths of human progress challenge. The great rationalizations of evolved men seem to be just a pursuit of a yet unrecognized ideal. James concludes that we live forward and understand backward, yet the great majority of humanity never picks up on that subtle distinction in the collection of our greatest repository of knowledge. Philosophy, as James states, "bakes no bread." It spent the majority of two thousand years seeking to codify religion or pointing to scientific truth. Only Pragmatism broke the spell of the timeless and theoretical questions and replaced them with the real and temporal.

Eras were shortening and compressing. We were wild creatures for millions of years before we were hunter-gatherers for tens of thousands of years. The invention of agriculture brought us civilization ten thousand years ago. Writing brought us the Ionian Enchantment of the possibilities of human knowledge in the ancient world that lasted thousands of years from the first writings of the Sumerians to the centuries after the birth of Jesus and the fall of the Roman Empire. One thousand years of the Dark Ages built a moral foundation for which to catapult reason. Centuries of Enlightenment became one hundred years of Modernism. After the first few decades of the twentieth century, Pragmatism, which carried the mantle for the next great philosophic tradition, was wearing thin. Modernism, now in full avant-garde mode, had long since abandoned its role as the spiritual guide to any type of middle-class sensibilities. The artists of the extreme avant-garde turned to the grotesque and sadistic. Meanwhile, the late Pragmatic ideas held that the world is a system that we must continually try to update and understand. In one of his lectures, William James said, "It is easy to see the world's history pluralistically, as a rope in which each fiber tells a separate tale, but to conceive of each cross section of the rope as an absolute single fact, and to the sum of the whole longitudinal series into one being living an undivided life, is harder."

James was confessing that truth lay in that fiber, as a metaphor for the individual, but it was becoming more difficult to unfurl the surrounding fibers and still determine a truth. The rope is one just as the fiber is one. This was the next epoch in the cultural evolution of mankind. Pragmatism concluded that unity was the grandiose achievement of all intellectual philosophy. It was the opposite traditional philosophy in the sense that it subscribed to the antidogmatic theory that any means through human experience to conclude a truth was a viable conjecture. So Pragmatism is a vessel for all eras as long as the goal is progress. As the modern world became postmodern, the characteristics of progress seemed to change. All the known disciplines were investigated and researched rationally. It was as if an end had come to the possibilities of human progress. The meta ethic of Pragmatism had become indistinguishable from the new forms of knowledge. Even the antiphilosophy of Pragmatism had been enveloped in the tide of the preambles to the postmodern world. New and distinct disciplines of the early twentieth century, such as political science and sociology, were being subjected to a new cross-fertilization in academics as early as the 1930s. By 1948, Claude Shannon had submitted *A Mathematical Theory of Communication* that appeared in publications of nine different disciplines.

The "Renaissance man" of the past had become the "specialized man" of the twentieth century. By mid-century, however, Shannon's contributions, for one, seemed to show that immediate progress lay in combining the disciplines. There was room for an immediate breadth of knowledge as the new interactions of disciplines could then lead to another stage of depth of those outcomes. Even as the new promises of the return of the long-forgotten Renaissance man emerged, the only equivalent was the systems scientist. Whereas the great feat for the learned in the past was conclusively communicating the highest level truths of the few disciplines that existed, the new breed of the system scientist interpreted truth not as a higher echelon of reality but as a palatable interpretation of truth in a confusing world. In a philosophically material world, Leonardo Da Vinci could add to the knowledge of classical science by discovering properties of the mechanistic world. In a time when all the rationality had been discovered, we had no choice but to begin the empiricist journey of following our senses to discover the future. In the nonmaterial world, where the connections between the rational disciplines existed, science was becoming more difficult.

The basic form of science and philosophy is deduction of the properties of a whole. Plato's dialectic added the idea that the interaction of two wholes can introduce entirely new properties. In the course of conversation among two people, each may leave with knowledge that neither could have gained individually. Using rationalism and empiricism to understand these basic building blocks had always been satisfactory. In an increasingly complex world that continually introduced new systems, it became inevitable that the properties of the systems themselves, as well as the ramifications they produced, needed to be identified and studied. The rope, therefore, is James' metaphor for a system. It is both a single entity as well as a complex organization of single fibers with complex properties. A crowd may exhibit vastly different properties with the addition or subtraction of a single person. To system theorists, group changes lead to individual changes, which lead to further group changes. This is known as a feedback loop. This cyclical tendency is a phenomenon of physics. Duke engineering professor Adrian Bejan theorizes that all animate and inanimate objects follow what he calls constructal law, so that biology is not the driver of all natural systems but the energy that flows within and between every system on earth, from the human brain to the Internet, and is the world's driving force.

To a systems theorist, energy, rather than material, is the basic building block of life. During the Renaissance, this type of mind would belong to none other than Leonardo da Vinci who said, "Motion is the cause of life." Bejan was a modern engineer in the 1990s who subscribed to a very mystical idea of the role of physics in the world. He said physics and biology are the same, as they each constitute the basic building blocks of the world. In this theory, flow systems are alive. Simple movement is disguised in the complexities of the world. It would seem that Bejan was influenced by Fritjof Capra, who wrote *The Tao of Physics* in 1975. Later in his work *The Systems View of Life*, he described the stark difference of the world after Claude Shannon introduced his information theories in the late 1940s. The mechanical world was dead. In its place entered the networked world. In the mechanical world, one changed part in the machine may affect the rest of the parts, but the new part itself remains undisturbed. In the networked world, the new part is affected by the feedback of the system itself. This energy is the way of the world. This complex form of communication and its quantitative effect began to form feedback in the social networks of individuals. It came to be understood that the complex and the intangible and not the material was the nature of culture itself.

Bejan searched for the unifying idea of nature, which he had determined was flow. Capra believed the answer to be networks. William James said, "Unity in things is the sublimest achievement of intellectual philosophy." By the 1990s, these ideas of flows were producing new ideas of unified concepts of knowledge in academia. Julie Thompson Klein began researching the origins of the growing resistance to specialization and the insights that cross-fertilization of the disciplines could add to the long history of human progress. However, between the time of the great social scientists Mead, Boas, Dewey, and Veblen in the 1930s and the formal reemergence with the rational and conscious effort to progress in the 1990s, a strange period had taken place. The grand narratives, identified as the struggle for human progress in the material world, began vanishing in the surrealism of the late modernists. By the 1950s, the undercurrents of a great cultural disruption were quietly taking place. It was the beginning of the individual but, more so, the inflection point of the individual shouting amongst the new noise of the postmodern world. The systems of Bejan were being identified, but they were far from unified.

Cultural eras are famously nondiscrete and hard to define. Although the term *postmodern* has been dated back to the nineteenth century, the idea of structuralism, which generally defines the birth of postmodernism, can be dated to the 1950s. In 1927, Martin Heidegger outlined the building blocks of the entire understanding of the postmodern world. He identified the *hermeneutic circle* as the idea that we identify our surroundings as a baseline to what we experience. The truth of all phenomena lies in the way that we perceive all other phenomena that surround it. This is one of the first examples of the relationship trumping, or at least equaling the material form. From here, we meet the classification of theorists called Structuralists like Claude Levi-Strauss, who begin to apply these ideas of ill-defined truths in the cultural relativism of the fields of the social sciences. Up until this point, all scientific scrutiny would have empirically rejected the idea that a measurable quantity of material had any bearing on the relationship it had with another material.

Although the parallels of the subconscious are usually indicative of Sigmund Freud and the late modernist period. Philosophy, which sought to describe exactly this newfound cultural consciousness, was the new great unconscious of the postmodern world. In decades and centuries of recent past, the celebrity in culture would have been the philosopher spinning the intellectual struggle of the age. By the 1960s, rock and roll served the existential purpose of the philosopher. The philosopher's role, as well as his depiction of the realities of the world, had become inevitably illegible. What began as an illustration of new perspectives to add to established truths forgot entirely the hard-won infallibilities of the Enlightenment. Postmodernism is undoubtedly the most unclear era in all recent history. History's most precious documentarians have always been philosophers. This particular generation interpreted truth as a purposeful obfuscation of the times. The "spaces in between" the forms became the ultimate truth, yet none had developed an empirical method to prove it. As the postmodernists reached forward to the unfamiliar unknowns, they abandoned all which had been known. Perhaps this sin was ultimately a requirement for progress.

The "spaces in between the knowns" was the new realm of philosophy. These various philosophers were trying to find truth in ethics, but for the first time ever, culture was acting as a restraint for truth. Jacque Derrida took the hermeneutic circle and applied it to language. Words only had meaning when used in association with other words. Jacque Lacan said that words were only metaphors for true human intention. Words themselves were an injustice to truth. The role of language, for example, was never questioned as a vessel for human progress. According to Derrida, man was becoming constrained by language. The framework for everything in the post-modern world, which is loosely defined from the late 1950s to the late 1990s, is the idea of the poststructural. A new individualism replaced the objectivity of the author from the permanent subjectivity of the reader. The very essence of truth was being questioned, and the role of the postmodern philosopher was to explain how this was changing the world. The distinct—and sometimes connected—concrete hierarchal structures of the world were dissipating into the obscure truths beyond the realm and understanding of modern scientists. The theoretical subconscious of Freud acquiesced to a much more complicated notion of the exponential identifiability, the social unconscious.

The empirical truths of science were not telling the story. The only alternative to this power structure of the past is narrative. The answer to philosophers was social theory or critical theory by applying culture to science or vice versa. In academia, new cultural criticisms began to be examined such as women's studies, black studies, and American studies. The methods of literary criticism, which centered on the conversation of cultural phenomena, bared a closer resemblance to truth than the limitations of a discrete and testable hypothesis of a single cause. In this era, the empirical methods had no way to capture and define nonhierarchical and systems-based approach used to understand the new understandings of cultural reality. Even the social sciences, which had been the receptacle of the obscurity of the human sciences for decades, were forced to abandon the insights of these new social theorists because they were simply untestable. The goal of explanation was theory rather than fact. The mere attempt to locate fact automatically translated to a loss of truth. This was the great cultural shift from the midcentury values of the importance of objectivity to the new individual priority on the subjective. It is no coincidence that psychologists and sociologists equate the beginning of the postmodern world with a new consciousness of narcissism and selfishness. The actionable world of pragmatism was dying with the rhetorical and theoretical world of ideology.

So how do we interpret a world with no rules, a world where subjective opinion, unfiltered through the science of empiricism, breeds a culture of knowledge without the self-examination of individual bias? The only answer was to tell a story. In 1969, French postmodernist Michel Foucalt wrote *The Archaeology of Knowledge*, which was an encapsulation of this new transformative method. His belief was that all the study of history as it could be reported was never an accurate picture of reality. The depiction of history is more complex than anyone intends. Whereas twentieth-century philosopher Walter Benjamin claimed, "History is written by the victors," to Foucalt, history is written by the dominant ideology that exists within the mind of the storyteller. History is nothing but a reimagining of the past that we interpret through our own consciousness. Generally, the goal of history is to tell one linear story without contradiction or counterhistory. To Foucalt, even a complete and unabridged history over long periods of time will certainly clash with the interpretation of the author.

This idea was undoubtedly borrowed from Friedrich Nietzsche in his 1877 work *On the Genealogy of Morality*. Nietzsche's work may have been the first to put man's moral understandings into the continuum of time. This stark discontinuity in the philosophy of ethics makes him the grandfather of all postmodern thought. In 1971, Foucalt updated the idea of genealogical history with *Nietzsche, Genealogy, and History*. Foucalt described genealogy as a truer depiction of history by breaking with traditional methods and introducing what he called the history of the present. This new form of history does not seek one point of view but a series of complex narratives that paint a picture of a closer version of reality. Any depiction of universals in history is inaccurate and impossible to replicate. In traditional history, the prevailing ethic is accuracy. In genealogy, accuracy is already a fallacy. Therefore, the ethic in genealogical history is to explain the present. Recording history for posterity is useless unless the aim is to transform the present. Truth is invariably tied to contradiction. The only objectivity is the infinite subjective.

These various and concurrent dialogues that attempted to explain the postmodern world became increasingly pessimistic and, to many, incompatible with the centuries-old march of progress. The totality of the world sharing common stories and shared truths was dead, according to Jean-Francois Lyotard in 1979. Jean Baudrillard was concerned with language, signs, and technology that began to simulate reality beyond recognition. The grand Marxist narrative of the alienation of the individual throughout the nineteenth and much of the twentieth century had turned into the fragmentation of the individual. The nature of the postmodern world was taking its toll on the identity of the individual. Literary theorist Ihab Hassan believed that the deconstruction of identity led to the idea of identity politics through the various signals introduced by Baudrillard. The grand ideas of truth, liberty, freedom, justice, and humanity imploded into the subjective concerns such as of postcolonization, feminism, civil rights, and gay rights. The great western liberal tradition of progress stuttered over the micronarratives of identity. The mantle of progress itself had been splintered and increasingly divisive.

Meanwhile, the demand side Keynesian approach to economics which was nearly unquestioned since the Depression was being usurped by a libertarian notion called neoliberalism. Freedom of the market to behave as nature intended supplanted the centrally planned notion. A political tide of conservatism paradoxically calling itself new liberalism spread throughout the west. Ronald Reagan was embraced as a form of progressive. In Great Britain, Margaret Thatcher echoed the same realities of the postmodern philosophers, stating, "There is no society—only individuals." The lack of shared values and community as compared to the recent past was inevitably leading to a culture where the center wouldn't hold. The modern world, entirely based on the virtue and uplifting of the center, was quickly dying. The authenticity, spirituality, and sincerity that guided the 1960s began devolving into cynicism, irony, and nihilism by the 1990s. Complacency, in this realm, is the virtue. The great odyssey of Enlightenment had acquired incompatible goals. Fundamentalism and reaction governed the dominant ideology of narrative across every aspect of our culture. For decades this voice has been the Baby Boomer Generation, born en masse for nearly twenty years after World War II.

The postmodern period is infinitely complex and understood by few. The most important lessons of the period pertain to the way that our view of the most important values of human existence had changed. Because of the complex forces of nature, the psychological state of man exists as a subject of determinism rather than an individual agent of free will. Our cultural and historical circumstances dictate our identity, which leaves man powerless and armed only with a coy cynicism. For centuries, humanism had been at the center of progress, but mature postmodernism unconsciously relinquishes the very idea that liberty, freedom, and justice are even attainable. So we identify, then self-identify, then act from a place of irony where the act of choosing is never really a choice. A cultural theorist would identify this attribute most closely with what came to be known as Generation X, or the group born between the early to mid-1960s to the late 1970s. This fracturing killed the trust of truth and, with it, the hope of progress. The pragmatic notion of identifying injustice through human experience never intended for the hypersubjectivity of intense personal experience learned during the postmodern period.

The postmodern period is described through the intellectual lens of philosophy, but what it hoped to describe was a complex tangible culture, which was increasingly multifaceted. Lyotard described the condition of a new information revolution as an outsourcing of human knowledge. When humans cease to internalize truth and the methods to access it are incomplete and ambiguous, a malaise arises, directly connected to the trust in our information systems. Around the turn of the millennium, the critics, whom developed the narrative to articulate this cultural period, could sense that their stories were changing. Science, specifically computer science, was emerging to create a new digital world in rapid succession. Meanwhile a generation of size only comparable to the Baby Boomers themselves was entering classrooms. The Gen X heirs, named Generation Y or sometimes called millennials, have become pop culture pariahs for traits incompatible with all that was known and learned in the sordid period known as the postmodern period. While we have learned many lessons from this period, the most offensive residuum is that this is where we have all become the most comfortable.

Cultural periods like generational theory are unscientific. They are imaginary creations of critics and historians who interpret material forms and theoretical ideas that discretely break from the past. History is clearly continuous. In past eras, we have had millennia or centuries to digest discontinuity. The postmodern revolution coincided with the cultural revolution of the 1960s, which shocked the sensibilities of the past and came to terms with the world that it had created. Politically, this shock manifested itself into a long history of increasingly polarizing ideologies. Although critics agree that the postmodern world died nearly two decades ago, we can look to politics, for one, to identify that the trend of fragmentation fifty years in the making cannot be easily reversed. So it seems that the increasingly diminishing length of cultural periods has surpassed our ability to objectively learn the lessons that the period has taught humanity. So we have broken from the postmodern reality, but the applications of it are still administered by the leaders who spent their entire formative years embracing it. The only generation to acknowledge its conclusion is the generation who never fully experienced it. Therefore, we have learned that a cultural era may diminish in length, but it is destined to last a lifetime. The leadership of the millennial generation is the only option for a clean break from the postmodern world.

Jean-Jacques Rousseau, the eighteenth-century philosopher, was perhaps the arbiter of the notion of the prevailing liberalism that ultimately instituted modern democracy. He said, "Man is born free, yet everywhere he is in chains." The fight for freedom and progress to break the chains of society is a virtue. Education, first and foremost, should be deemed liberal, minus the political connotation, because it liberated us from ignorance. In the postmodern period, the grand narrative of human progress had been forgotten. It is often labeled a conservative era because the ethic relied on the fear of progress. The 1950s-era nostalgia, for example, may conclude this decade had been the height of human goodness. This detachment to the future meant that energy was exerted to replace the past. Action and progress was replaced by fear, anxiety, and fracture. Francis Bacon brought us the scientific method four hundred years ago. He warned of the four idols of intellect. It was here in the postmodern period that we forgot his lessons. The "idols of the tribe" returned as technology allowed redistribution of the like-minded so that human bias and prejudice no longer required examination. The "idols of the cave" caused us to prioritize and promulgate our own cause as the most correct. The "idols of the marketplace" abandoned all nuanced communication and interpretation, and the "idols of the theater" allowed politics, media, marketing, and public relations tactics to disavow truth and reason. In short, critical thinking itself was abandoned in the name of old idols in disguise within a new culture.

The postmodern period was not just the death of rationalism and empiricism in science but also the romanticism of the spirituality of progress. The medieval ethics of St. Thomas Aquinas defined *natural law* as an expression of God's will. Thomas Jefferson and his empirical teacher John Locke described nature as self-evident. The Marquis de Condorcet wrote *Sketch for a Historical Picture of the Progress of the Human Spirit* in 1795, which laid the assumptions for the idea of progress on a grand scale. The progress of humanity itself was the common good for all of humankind. He said that greater compassion, affluence, and freedom were the natural trajectory of humankind. The agent of the cause of natural law could be disputed, but what was universally unquestioned was that the nature existed and was evolving. A revolution in the natural sciences would inevitably bring progress in the social sciences and back again into an infinite virtuous cycle of progress. Eventually it would be clear, according to Condorcet, that "all epochs are fastened together by a sequence of causes and effects, linking the condition of the world to all the conditions which have gone before it." This great unity of learning was the propeller for advancement of the species. It is what biologist E. O. Wilson was describing in his 2012 work, *The Social Conquest of Earth*. In it he describes the loss of the liberal arts values of the Renaissance and Enlightenment over what he considered to be about the last forty years. Inevitably, the loss of the liberal arts will naturally repeal the will of progress.

Although many critics believe that the postmodern period has ended, most believe that its effects still control the majority of our culture. The idea of digimodernism, as described by Allen Kirby, believes that technology is the driver of supplanting the postmodern in favor a return to the grand narrative. However, because the return finds a society more impatient, more fanatical, and more conformist, the great intellectual traditions of modernism did not return with it. He describes old values returning to an immature society. He calls it a "fusion of the childish and the advanced, the powerful and the helpless." The good news is that action and, more specifically, interaction has returned as a necessary part of life. Social media, for example, requires an output from the individual. The advancements of web 2.0 have given the world the ability to create cheaply with their own individualized production. The passive television viewer and radio listener, who was the criterion for the condition of man for decades, has transformed into the requirement of engagement rather than aloofness. This is a much different narrative than the Baudrillard notion that man is powerless against the systems, symbols, and information in which the prior generation's technology offered. Although it appears that Kirby may not agree with the simplicity and short attention spans that inevitably accompany this new period, the possibility of a break from the stagnation of postmodernism seems to be possible. Man, the individual, is once again an actor rather than a subject.

The idea of a culture of digimodernism replacing the prior period introduces a new locomotion of the trajectory of the world. As Ezra Pound exclaimed "Make it new" as the modernist motto, Fredric Jameson decried "the end of . . ." as the postmodern sentiment. All forward momentum had ceased. Whether digimodernism is the vehicle for progress or the effect of this new version of progress is debatable. What most cultural theorists, literary critics, and philosophers engaged in the topic have come to understand is that a great and unprecedented change has occurred. What is clear is that no consensus has been able to offer a grand narrative to which any formidable return to a modernist period would beg. British artist Luke Turner and Dutch current affairs researchers Timotheus Vermeulen and Robin Van den Akker understand the era as metamodernism. In this view progress has, in fact, returned, but the state of man is such that the natural inclination is to return to the safe zone of irony.

Whereas irony and cynicism were once used to describe nihilism and desperation, they are now used as vehicles of the sincerity of progress. Metamodernism claims that one can be sincere and ironic at the same time. It is the belief that the human condition has reached the state of quantum mechanics. In the modern world, the arrow of progress pointed straight ahead. In the postmodern world, the arrows pointed in multiple directions. In the metamodern world, progress is once again inevitable hurling forward, but the arrow is at once reaching for the past while grasping for the future.

Oscillation is the term often used, like a pendulum reaching for the utopia of nostalgia while still acknowledging the hope of progress. Since philosophy was born, the understanding of nature has been monistic and eternal. Only the pragmatists declared that nature is only the circumstances and experiences of individuals. The diminishment of the length of cultural eras in history before our eyes speaks to the pragmatic truths dead since the age of Ezra Pound. In the year 2016, the average sixty-year-old was taught the idealistic values of the modern world, learned and applied them in the postmodern period, and leads in the metamodern period. The condensing and overlapping of cultural eras only adds to the confusion. Oscillation is the only string theory that can connect the disparate disciplines that define our lives. We are compressing more into less, which is an obvious metaphor to the power that technology has secured in our lives. The exponential pace of change that technology promises is destined to speed the pace of the revolution. Generations, once loose and gradual, are now concrete and discrete. The pace of cultural epochs have attenuated and aligned with generational change.

Therefore, the return to modernism is synonymous with the millennial generation. They alone will be responsible as the first generation of adults insusceptible to the malaise and atrophy of the postmodern. While they may recognize the oscillation in the pendulum of the metamodern period, ultimately it will be their responsibility to ensure the inevitable forward trajectory of the momentum of the pendulum. It would seem that the only phenomenon that technology cannot hurry is the value system of a generation. If the battle of society is fought within the arena of culture versus politics, today's youth overwhelmingly fight firmly within culture because it has no long-term stigma. Culture invariably catches up to the rising generation, while politics is an affront to the powers that be, in which resistance has significantly more consequences than in the past. In today's world, politics takes a backseat not due to priority but due to pragmatism. Idealism is the leadership recipe de jour. The grand oscillation of culture signals a return to spirituality and Romanticism. The grand narratives of truth, justice, and freedom, thanks to the postmodern period, are finally truly open to everyone. With the millennial, human consciousness has finally expanded beyond fragmentation. We have the opportunity to truly universalize the grand narratives rather than labeling them universal during the modern period.

I call the grand ethic millennial modernism as the precursor to understanding metamodern leadership. It is the idea that progress remains the cornerstone of all human intention. The ethic itself is referred to astutely as pragmatic idealism in David Burstein's book *Fast Future*. Although pragmatism and idealism are traditionally competing entities, Burstein, a millennial himself, is intuitively aware of the competing internal and external battle of modern youth. The embrace of oscillation is a cathartic experience unto itself. Vermeulen and Van den Akker illustrate this succinct generational distinction as the postmodern metaphor of Lyotard imagining the individual as the captain of a ship that can continuously sail to a conglomerate of islands, each with its own distinct and varied resources. The postmodern ethic states that no island need ever be chosen over the other. The return to modernism in the form of metamodernism suggests that the ship is sinking and an island must be chosen. No mathematical calculation exists to determine the correct choice, but the unconscious oscillation between the pragmatic and the idealistic encourages a sense of peace within the apparent ambiguity of the selection. What seems to be an irrational, caustic, and shallow existence is actually rooted in a philosophy deeper than we have experienced in decades.

Scientific researchers never adjust for cultural patterns, which may be one of the great lessons of the postmodern period. The trajectory of the happiness of society has been declining for decades, so naturally and inevitably, the younger generations will succumb to the patterns of the past. This almost never happens! Researcher Jean Twenge has found recently that millennials may be our happiest generation, which was inexplicable even to her past research. All signs pointed to an increasingly dissatisfied youth given the cultural trends. The oscillation of the metamodern is not an understanding neatly packaged by scientific observers, and it most certainly did not take into consideration generational changes, much less cultural epochs. There are two great philosophical traditions acting in tandem for today's young adults and tomorrow's world leaders. The young espouse an internal virtue ethic of idealism, which dictates progress without conceding but also replaces the external ideological dogma with pragmatism. It is a subtle and unconscious reality locked within the time and place of the millennial mind. A concurrent duality exists of gradualism and revolution, which angers the rational mind. Their progress is a natural phenomenon of a half of millennia of advancement, yet our natural complacency, bred in the postmodern period, resists the inclination. The mystique of millennial modernism is that it is inaccessible to most of the world, yet we must try to understand it.

Eudaimonia, which the ancients described as "happiness received through the art of goodness," has returned. Stoic Musonius Rufus described stoicism as the doctor for the mind. The prescription of the ancient arts of stoicism has curiously coincided with the modern science of positive psychology. A science with innumerable benefits and ancient origins has but two decades of scientific credibility. The desire for the Stoic "good life" became ill defined. Whereas it was once the mantra for the most important brand of philosophy and worldview in the western world, it had faded beyond recognition. "The good life" has returned in a scientific incarnation. Although the good life is a feeling, it is based on the rational view that all progress unites with faith rather than circumnavigates it. All intentions are good except for those that lead to fundamentalism, which stall progress. Devotion to faith is virtuous, provided it does not detract from the ordained path of progress. Therefore, tolerance of Islam, for example, is a virtue but only until its values are incompatible with the overriding sensibilities of an epoch. If freedom is universal, the natural systems override the dogma. This has been the nature of progress since Lucretius's manuscript was reborn six hundred years ago. It says that religion is not inherently good or evil, but the fundamentalism that displaces human empiricism of experience is troubling. Humanity is not above ceding the metaphysical to the spiritual, but the values of humanity are deserving of the earthly battle that had won them. Faith can supersede reason, but it cannot displace it.

Pragmatism died in the mid-twentieth century because the early Structuralists used its powers to advocate the notion of cultural relativism, an anthropological term that identifies space rather than time as an indicator of human progress. In other words, the moralities of distant and distinct cultures, regardless of the absurdity or archaic nature of their philosophies, are no better or worse than the modern civilized man. Albino killings in Tanzania, honor killings in Pakistan, and female genital mutilations in Ethiopia are not culturally relative; their immorality is self-evident in nature regardless of the rational doctrine that extols the acts as virtues. Thanks to Kant, the human mind is now rational and empirical. We have evolved culturally to determine right from wrong. If philosophy itself "bakes no bread," it can be maligned as but a framework which describes rather than acts. The revolutionary nature of Pragmatism suggested that action in philosophy was paramount for progress. By the time pragmatism aligned with structuralism, what was pragmatic evolved into inaction. The new version of pragmatism, however, aligns with a new sincerity and hope for progress in the twenty-first century. The idealism of the baby boomers, conceived in the modern world and filtered through the divisiveness of the postmodern period, has met its end. Virtue is once again the ethic of progress for the inner world with a renewed faith in Pragmatism to delivers its message for the outer world.

The notion of the hedonic treadmill has been around since the 1970s. The theory, which is a precursor to positive psychology research, identifies the tendency to always want more and better. Adaptation to the baseline of contentment is continuous and is considered the root of the decline of happiness in western civilization in recent decades. Consumerism and materialism as the basis of happiness was the trap of the postmodern period. The Roman Stoic

Seneca warned of placing too high a value on material things. The Greek Stoic Epictetus suggested that we should shift our desires from what we want to what we already have. Zeno the Stoic said, "The wise man is not enslaved by the feelings of fear or desire." Marcus Aurelius encouraged the serenity to accept things one cannot change through practiced perception and the will to take control of our own lives and circumstances while acting on behalf of the world at large. Traditionally, these ideas aligned more closely with the Eastern intuitive, irrational, and spiritual philosophic traditions. The tranquility that Stoicism prescribed has met truth in modern science. Positive psychology, which takes interest in human happiness through science, has laid bare the structure of Stoic joy. The avoidance of the negative tendencies of the internal, which are indicative of the postmodern period, can be overturned.

From the metamodern perspective of oscillation, a return to the postmodern period is a requirement to understand not just the present but the future. So I borrow Foucault's method of genealogical inquiry of narrative to interpret the present. As Foucault sought a return to Nietzsche, I seek a return to Foucault. We can now look back on the postmodern condition as a necessary dystopian progress. My genealogy uses his methods of complex narratives and apparent contradiction, but the goal is no longer regression and confusion of the present but searching the past for clues to the future. The "chaos of disciplines" leading to anarchy now seeks the unification of knowledge, which had no longer seemed possible. The story must be told from the perspective of the now. This is what Foucalt meant by "the history of the present." In this time in world history, the only generation that is fully mindful of solely the metamodern era as adults is the millennial generation. So I attempt to enlighten the world to their story while simultaneously enlightening them to the rest of the world. This would be sufficient as a history. Genealogy, in this case, uses systems thinking from the past to apply to the systems thinking of the future. The tendency of the oscillation of the metamodern always reaches back to push forward. That is the only method to tell the yet untold story of millennial modernism as the gateway to metamodern leadership.

CHAPTER 2

SOCIOLOGY AND INEQUALITY

Webster defines the term *consilience* as "the linking together of principles from different disciplines, especially when forming a comprehensive theory." In a simpler time, consilience was taken for granted as a natural system. In a world of complexity, consilience can seldom be found. True understanding of one discipline is now so time-consuming that synthesis from various fields is nearly impossible. Just 150 years ago, William Whewell was the Victorian authority on matters as diverse as philosophy, architecture, mineralogy, physics, theology, and astronomy. He was both a poet and mathematician. He was the epitome of the true polymath, a master of the arts and the sciences. Quite possibly, not since Da Vinci three and a half centuries prior had there been such a stark convergence between such remote disciplines in Europe. With the death of Whewell in 1866, however, the age of the Renaissance man abruptly ended. Consilience of knowledge yielded to increased specialization. According to American sociobiologist Rebecca Costa in her book *The Watchman's Rattle,* humans have hit a cognitive threshold. The evolution of the human brain is intensely slow; meanwhile, the evolution and complexity of culture is far more advanced. As her mentor and sociobiology founder E. O. Wilson has said, as humans, "We have paleolithic emotions, medieval institutions, and godlike technology." Our most complex problems are never solved but, rather, mitigated and passed on to future generations. No matter how civilized we become, we still have the same mental capacity as our Bronze Age ancestors. The great majority of our collective unconscious as a species of *Homo sapiens* has been scarcity, death, war, and tribalism. We have come to know a great deal collectively but much less individually, even though all the answers are now at our fingertips.

What we require is a generation that can understand the lessons of history and apply them to our future. Just a short time ago, we still invested in, rather than pillaged, our future prospects. In the last century, humans have gained more knowledge than in the last million centuries combined. This proliferation of information has inspired tribalism reminiscent of the hunter-gatherer society over ten thousand years ago. The evolutionary biologist recognizes that we humans always have clung to those to which we most identify. In modern social media culture, these groups are more identifiable and numerous. This leads to gridlock in our institutions, our organizations, and our communities. We have stopped investing in the broad view of humanity because it is much easier to recognize that the path to get there will be outside of our most basic rational interests. So our strategy has been to maintain and to convolute and to hope that someone in the future can figure it out, but we will never be able to move forward until we can learn about the past. So in the modern world, consilience brings order from chaos. It is the symbolic "back to nature" approach, which Henry David Thoreau declared when he published *Walden* in 1854. Thoreau chose to seek the true human condition by separating himself from society. E. O. Wilson opens his Pulitzer Prize–winning book, *The Social Conquest on Earth*, by introducing the nineteenth-century French painter Paul Gauguin. Gauguin left his Paris home for French Polynesia and adopted the primitive painting style of the native Tahitians. Here he painted his masterpiece "Where Do We Come from, What Are We, Where Are We Going"? These are the great questions that underlie every great philosophy, religion, and science since the beginning of time. Only by figuratively separating ourselves from the complex can we accurately tackle these issues.

As economist Angus Deaton outlines in his book *The Great Escape,* for the great majority of human history, progress was painstakingly slow and even. It wasn't until the maturity of the Great Divergence in North America and Europe in the nineteenth century that the masses would begin to escape the drudgery of ancient life. Thanks to technology and productivity, the West disconnected from the past and hurriedly propelled forward. The Industrial Revolution presented the first iterations of the conveniences that we know today. Tuberculosis, malaria, malnutrition, and diarrhea quickly went from the most common methods of deaths to diseases of poverty. Humanity had escaped the constant fear of death. We replaced our primitive fears of survival almost immediately with our modern fears of not succeeding. Enter the metamodern world. We live three to four times longer than our hunter-gatherer ancestors and twice as long as just a century ago. Our modern system of capitalism and democracy maximized our ancient propensity for sociality. Humans are blessed with the ability to collaborate and cooperate. This is what distinguished us from the rest of the animal kingdom millions of years ago. Commerce was the engine that lifted us from the doldrums of stagnation. For this we are grateful, but we must remain vigilant. As Costa has said, "Profitability has become the most powerful barometer of legitimacy." Most of our problems on earth have solutions; they are just not yet cost effective. Our grandparents' capitalism eschewed inequality; our capitalism embraces it.

We know an economic equilibrium exists. We have seen it before and not that long ago. We also know capitalism works. In 1976, biologist Richard Dawkins identified *The Selfish Gene.* The theory is that species evolve, preserve, and replicate out of pure selfishness. Looking out for ourselves and our family is not just a part of what makes us human; it is the essential component of our genetic makeup. Capitalism works so grandly because it is a natural economic manifestation of our ingrained selfishness. Communism worked so poorly because it was a system that disregarded the propensity of humanity. As Dawkins said himself, "We, alone on earth, can rebel against the tyranny of the selfish replicators." We may be genetically selfish, but we also have the capability to be intellectually and spiritually altruistic. Before we progress, we have to come to an understanding that what we did worked, and by doing the same under different circumstances, it will not any longer. A new consciousness is forming, just as it does during any new generation. Ideologues will be disappointed to find that it does not divide down party lines. It is not revolutionary, and it is not confrontational. It is a generation that understands selfishness better than any Ayn Rand devotee yet prides itself on openness, altruism, and diversity. It gently scrapes the surface of the powers that be, lying in wait for the cool mutiny of generational change. In the meantime, the structure persists. The living ecosystem that we call society is better off, we have found, when we divide labor and seek our own self-interest. Eric Liu and Nick Hanauer argue in their book *The Gardens of Democracy* that a slight tweak to co-invest in mutual interest, as we have in the past, may mean better well-being for us all. The realities of the world, and especially the modern world, mean that selfishness is a prerequisite to altruism. Before we can tend to the gardens of democracy, we have to be secure in our own situation.

Among the earliest and most universal questions in which we present ourselves is "What should I do with my life?" The advice possibly handed down from previous generations was to get a job with a good company. Then it became to go to college to get a job with a good company. This advice has just led to more questions in recent years. For instance, "What is a good company, and what does *a good company* mean?" The venerable companies of the past have become much leaner and much more selective. The young high-tech companies of the present have much more stringent paths to their front door. In the 1950s, we may have tried to go to work for America's largest employer, General Motors. In today's wages, assembly-line workers would have made as much as $35 per hour. Like GM in the 1950s, Wal-Mart is a very profitable company. It is also the new largest employer in the United States. An associate at Wal-Mart, the equivalent to the assembly-line workers of last century, will generally make a fraction of that salary, without benefits. Staking out good companies to provide large amounts of well-paying jobs does not work like it did in the past. That is not to say that Wal-Mart does not offer exciting and well-paid positions, but it best describes the extreme polarization in pay that has developed in the United States over the course of the last forty years. We, as a country, have found various ways to soften the blow of the deterioration of the golden age of American labor over those decades. This ever-increasing gap has little to do with increased nepotism or lack of hard work. Skills, education, training, talent, and experience have always been the gateway to our great organizations and opportunities. In recent years, there has been a sharp inflation in these areas from a variety of economic forces. Education is still the path for a better future, but the bachelor's degree, once a symbol of post-secondary success, has become in many cases the minimum requirement for many entry-level positions.

Great programmers, pharmacists, and senior managers can make a six-figure salary at Wal-Mart. There are many ways to find well-paying jobs in the new economy. In fact, there are more ways to find well-paying jobs than ever. Unfortunately, the assembly-line jobs, which sustained a large middle class throughout the middle of the twentieth century, now pay significantly less. Education is still the path to the American dream; it just so happens that the price of education has become inflated as well. So we find a generation of well-educated youth competing for the same salary range as those without education did a generation ago. The younger generations now enter the workforce five years behind their predecessors with thousands of dollars of student loan debt and little practical real-world experience. Instead of investing early for maximum time value of money benefits for retirement, they are instead borrowing. They are a complete generation who moved back in with their parents after graduation and have contemplated their future and their past. Never before have we questioned our choice to pursue education on a grand scale because it never left us reeling in a lifetime's worth of debt. This is the story of the millennials, and it is not over. It has been argued that this pattern is a conscious postponement of adulthood. It is a prolonged adolescence caused by a spoiled and entitled upbringing. As Anya Kamenetz points out in *Generation Debt*, it is "The new economic realities that are distorting the life paths and the relationships of the young." The millennial generation has the unique opportunity to renew the spirit of hope in the United States. As baby boomers begin to retire, this generation will eventually assume many leadership roles within our institutions and organizations. They are now the largest, and certainly the most diverse, generation in American history.

At this point, they have nearly all reached high school graduation age, meaning that they have, by and large, completed the same curriculum that most Americans have over the course of the last one hundred years. The value of that curriculum, which we still widely use, died when the last high-paying assembly line and factory jobs began winding down. The millennials were indoctrinated with a set of skills that have faded away in the memory of a bygone economy. The ones lucky enough to get their foot in the door at the mythical companies of the past are still led by those antiquated principles. Those same principles are now the competencies that get you hired as a sales associate at Wal-Mart. Those skills require following direction and the ability to do repetitive tasks. Essentially, they are the skills that Wal-Mart would like to automate should the proper technology arise. As technologist Jaron Lanier argues, "You are not a gadget." The future of work and the skills in demand should continue to separate us from what the capabilities of computers are and what they will be capable of in the near future. I set out to find out the exact policies and procedures that a generation would need to carve out of path of their very own in the metamodern world. I found out that it was not the details of your virtual resume, the length and depth of an essay you can dissect, your choice of degree, or your collection of certifications. It has nothing to do with your choice of industry or your IQ. Success in the future will be of a different variety. The paths that we once followed will become less traveled. This will require hard work and vigilance, but more than anything, it will require the agility to continue to move forward. We must make a concerted effort to separate ourselves from the machines of the future but also learn to manipulate and control their productivity. Most importantly, I found out that the policies and procedures did not exist. The panacea for the modern era is lifelong engagement and industriousness, not a road map. Essentially, it will be development and adherence to the values of the metamodern leader.

What we call the middle class had its origins in the middle of the twentieth century. The middle class was a phenomenon unfamiliar with the rest of history. In just a few decades, we have considered it a birthright. Most Americans would agree that a hardworking family that has always done their best and has been financially responsible should have the ability to gain access to this class. This is a sentiment uniquely American, borne from the entitlement of a century of unparalleled progress. By middle class, we mean the ability to afford health insurance, save for retirement, keep safe and updated living quarters, drive relatively new cars, pay for our children's education, and take a vacation once a year. In the past, the statistical distribution of the middle class in this country actually meant "in the middle," and many families could afford these relative luxuries. In today's economy, this standard of living would surely require a household income well above $100,000, which is way outside the spectrum of the middle as we once knew it. Globally, this amount would be even more skewed in the distribution. Statistically, the mean, or average, income in this country would be about half of that amount. The middle class were once the savers and the spenders. They were the drivers of the ever-expanding GDP. We still rely on this demographic to spend, as they are the heart of the economy, but we can no longer look to them to create wealth. The public and private benefits from the years of human capital investment assured generations that wealth building and entitlements would continue indefinitely. That sentiment has changed abruptly. The millennials will be the first generation, as a whole, that will not do as well financially as their parents on average in terms of wealth aggregation.

Striving for the median and mean income in the United States meant a standard of living of excellence here and anywhere else in the world. Striving for the median income in the United States today means a mediocre standard of living throughout the western world. It is also one of the few countries in the developed world where the burden for health care still lies on the individual. US healthcare is also the most expensive and overall, one of the least effective in the developed world. Healthcare in the U.S. Has been a very polarizing and debatable subject in recent years, but it is not up for debate that the American worker loses a competitive advantage in the world labor pool for requiring healthcare, where many other applicants may not. To put it in perspective, however, the American middle class is still many times the world median income. The pursuit of what we have come to know as the middle-class lifestyle is probably the most universal pursuit in the world. It has also become one of the most important, not for purely economic reasons but for the social implications as well. Social researcher Charles Murray has documented the proliferation of negative social behaviors that have mirrored the decline of a middle class that contained both college educated and non-college educated in 1960 America. His findings, when he compared the similar groups again in 2010, told a story of not only greater economic divide and increased unemployment but, in his opinion, a moral decline between the two groups. Two hundred years ago, Thomas Jefferson purported the benefits to citizenship that education could extol, and modern sociologists are finding scientific proof.

Throughout history, the physical labor of life combined with the scarcity of resources ensured the working class burned their calories before weight could accumulate. Once, the ability to exist in the state of being overweight represented health, wealth, and leisure. It was a physical manifestation of abundance in a time of scarcity. Times have changed. We now live in an era of abundance. The Indigents in the Depression era appeared malnourished and emaciated. When something broke, the only option was repair. This is still the mind-set of those who lived through that time. Today, in a disposable economy, we simply buy another. We take advantage of abundance, and food is no different. Higher earners can obviously afford more food, yet obesity actually declines with higher income. There are, of course, many factors that may explain this counterintuitive statistic. High caloric "junk food" is easier to locate and prepare and costs much less. It could also be the lack of education combined with effective marketing that sways this income bracket from healthy food to the subsidized sugars and grains. To contemplate this conundrum would be to miss the big picture. Science tells us that the state of being poor leads to bad decisions. The simplest among us would say that they are just not very bright and not very motivated. There is no reason to assume that they are not as smart as the rest of society, but it is safe to say that they are certainly less educated. We have known for some time that smoking is a detrimental habit. On the Center for Disease Control (CDC) website, it states that 6 percent of Americans with a postgraduate degree smoke while 45 percent with a GED smoke. The national average sits around 20 percent. Most large cities frown on smoking. New York has seen its level decline dramatically in recent years (up to 20 percent). There are, however, pockets in this country that still exist that embrace smoking as a social norm. Still, focusing on the continuation of smoking by the poor as an isolated event would be a mistake.

The lower-income population is more likely to be inattentive parents, to not keep steady jobs, to not take prescribed medication, etc. Essentially, they display a whole bevy of bad behaviors that seem to intertwine. Trash blights the poor neighborhoods of our smallest towns and largest cities. In the Arkansas and Missouri Delta, an area of deep poverty, one of the first things an objective observer would notice is a lack of trash cans in these small towns, even outside of gas stations and restaurants. In turn, people choose to litter. Litter begets more litter, like the "broken windows theory." This is a psychological phenomenon that succumbs to blight and slowly embraces it as a way of life. If a piece of trash blows away and lands on a mound of existing trash, the mind can easily justify not chasing after it. A massive campaign cleaned up New York City from its blemished dystopia of the 1970s, one broken window and one subway train at a time.

Deep-seated psychological perspectives shape these communities and perpetuate these behaviors. In Hayti, Missouri, for example, a full 37 percent here live below the poverty line and only 64.9 percent complete high school. Compare that with selected school districts in St. Louis County that may prepare 90–95 percent of students to be college eligible. A day in the life in Hayti, Missouri, would be a complete culture shock to most. The simplest answer as to the reason of poverty is the lack of opportunity. The conventionalist would claim that it is lack of motivation. That may be true also but still does not get to the root of the problem. The idealist may claim lack of choice, but should the opportunity of choice arise (e.g., a healthy meal), it is often overlooked for the unhealthy behavior. Is there, then, a thread by which to understand this behavior? A string theory of the underprivileged if you will. The most adroit hypothesis is given by Sendhil Mullainathan, a Harvard economist, and Eldar Shafir, a psychologist at Princeton. These researchers claim that scarcity, in general, creates a "tax" on the mind. Having to go without creates a cognitive blockage on our abilities to reason. The clearest example in a study is such. In a New Jersey Mall, random shoppers were classified between rich and poor. When asked about the circumstances regarding alternatives to a $150 car repair and then measured for cognitive control and fluid intelligence, the rich and poor fared evenly on the test. When replicated using a $1,500 repair, the poor group numbers declined significantly. The dip was enough so to equate to thirteen or fourteen IQ points, or the effects of going a night without sleep.

It could be that the state of destitution creates a type of tunnel vision that can only be understood when actually viewed through the eyes of scarcity. Planning for the future, an essential cognitive behavior for lifelong development, is almost nonexistent. This could answer the question as to why formerly poor professional athletes go broke after earning millions of dollars or lottery winners file bankruptcy shortly after a win. Indian farmers scored 25 percent higher on tests after the harvest when they were paid for their crops than just before. Their cognitive "bandwidth," as it has been described, is much greater when flush with cash. The act of collecting money without education is a good indication of the perpetuation of poverty. As compared to the poor from many other countries, our lower-income families have abundance but still the aura of scarcity. This understanding of scarcity does not allow for planning and will never lead to social mobility. It makes the middle class seem unattainable. If consilience at a high level is a path to greater understanding and knowledge, Hazel Rose Markus and Alana Conner, two self-described cultural psychologists, have outlined what this means in terms of inequality.

In late August 2005, Hurricane Katrina, one of the largest storms in United States history, was heading for the great city of New Orleans, known to have many areas where the elevation was more than six feet below sea level. The vast majority of the city fled for higher ground, but tens of thousands did not. Of these residents that stayed put, 93 percent were African-American, 57 percent had household incomes of less than $20,000 per year, 55 percent did not have a car or means to evacuate, and 76 percent had children under eighteen with them. Why would rational people of normal intelligence and the means of various forms of media warning of the dire circumstances not abide by the evacuation?

According to Markus and Conner . . .

Psychologists determined that the answer was mind-set. The particular individuals in this subset suffered from low self-worth. Their cognitive state is defined by outside forces, wherein control of the outside world has little to do with their individual choices. The motivation to evacuate requires internal decision making that has never been efficient in their lives. Life happens *to* them; therefore, they are helpless against a system greater than their abilities and capabilities. Their locus of control is external, and their internal responses are negligible or futile.

Sociologists and political scientists attribute the decision to their surroundings. In place of banks to keep their money, one would find check cashing and pawnshops. Lack of transportation out of the city is, of course, a problem to a population without sufficient income. Many of those who stayed required certain medical treatment only available near their home. Others feared that leaving home would cause their homes to be targeted by burglars, looters, and vandals and felt responsible to protect it. The circumstances of their living world dictate their decisions.

Anthropologists look at these people as humans with a distinct culture. To many living in these communities with limited resources, they have spent their lives relying on a specific set of family and friendships. The culture of poverty causes kin networks to organize in ways that is unnecessary for many. Deep religious faith assured them that God would spare them and their family. The city where they were raised and which many have ever known would never neglect or deny their safety. The ways and methods that they organized in this environment inform their actions.

Economists find the patterns in the way resources are distributed. The simple determinant in this case would be that those that remained in New Orleans to bear the storm simply did not have the resources to get out. Possibly, the access to knowledge of the dire threat was never completely or effectively communicated or accepted. An economist may also measure the financial implications of remaining in the city. Surely leaving would require a disruption of daily life. Transportation, lodging, and meals not cooked at home would be required. The financial incentive to stay may have outweighed the risk of not leaving, or financially, the evacuation was just not possible.

So who is correct in their astute series of intellectual theories? Does the anthropologist render the sociologist's theories false? The answer, of course, is that not every effect can be applied on an individual basis, but they are all correct. Truth can be found in each diagnosis. The aftermath of the storm was one of government and human failure. There was a breakdown of human decency stemming from despair and opportunity. This is a low point in our socioeconomic identity. Even the psychologists and the anthropologists would agree inequality of opportunity, whatever the root cause, is a mar on society as a whole. The mind-set of helplessness, hopelessness, and limitations does us no good. Poverty is a very rare goal for humanity. It is the fog of humanity where everyone searches for his or her own "Great Escape."

What we are truly striving for is mostly middle-class economic stability. In the modern world, freedom is tied to finances more than ever. We view the safety net that wealth brings as our ability to truly do what we would like. In other words, we believe that money is inextricably tied to happiness. The truth is that it is and it is not. Economist Justin Wolfers recently studied this question and found that wealthier countries are truly happier than poorer countries. Also, happiness and money are only positively correlated up to $75,000 per year. Seventy-five thousand dollars is above the mean and the median for the average income for the United States. Wolfers's data suggests that as societies get richer, they get happier. From an economist's viewpoint, the US happiness index could further be optimized as neither the mean nor the median has reached this benchmark The United States is a rich country with a lot of rich people. Opportunity was and is still plenty. Increasingly, however, there are much larger gaps between the rich and poor than we have ever seen before. There is a philosophic battle in economic circles as to what that really means. In their book *The Second Machine Age*, Erik Brynjolfsson and Andrew McAfee liken it to a broad and ancient battle over what they refer to as "bounty" and "spread." The future of the information age will only increase the spread of wealth to the rich because of more monopolization over the ability to collect the skills of the future. One side sees this as unimportant because technology will make the poor's lives increasingly more affordable and that any disruption to the free market economy is unfair to those that have already captured the most bounty.

The opposite viewpoint is that the spread skewing toward the rich in recent years is important. The fact that the vast majority of the bounty has moved to the upper classes and that social mobility is declining is a problem for the future of the United States and capitalism and democracy in general. The United States was founded on the rejection of the class system of Great Britain. The ideal of America has always been for everyone from anywhere to have the ability to pursue their dreams with meritocratic prospects. The twentieth century taught us unrealistic expectations of infinite progress. Now we find that life in America comes with half of the social mobility found in Nordic countries. We have become stagnant. We are locked in place, married to our birth status for life. This should be a fundamental rejection based on our founding principles. Social mobility must be based on spirit, drive, talent, and character but also equal opportunity, for which the classic American spirit barely need to contend.

So if it truly is happiness for which we seek, we should strive for lower economic inequality. Inequality leads to higher crime rates, which might account for our globally and historically high rates of incarceration. A 2011 *Time Magazine* article by Maia Szalavitz also outlines the fact the countries with higher inequality also see shorter life expectancy and poorer health. Stanford neuroscientist Robert Sapolsky eliminated the financial factor and focuses on stress in the animal world. He found that lower status baboons accumulate higher stress and poor health. In the United States, social hierarchy is financial hierarchy. It is no wonder then that health and well-being increase in more egalitarian societies. The inadequacy of being part of the working poor exists in modern-day America, second only to the inadequacy of unemployment and the loss of hope. What saves us is work. Voltaire proclaimed that it saves man from the three great evils—boredom, vice, and need. It is also a source of identity. When done correctly, not only can it provide for us and our family but a career can add real intrinsic value to our lives. To varying degrees, everyone wants the same things out of a career. We want a flexible, well-paying job with good benefits. We would like it to be engaging, meaningful, and rewarding. It should be in an exciting field with long-term growth prospects that align with our education and promulgate our best characteristics and natural proclivities while maintaining freedom and empowerment. These characteristics could broadly satisfy every job hunter for the past one hundred years.

Gallup began the World Poll in 2005 in an unprecedented attempt to poll every culture in the world about every issue in the world. When the data was sifted, it found that the one core theme that did transcend every culture was the need for a good job. In other words, the one thing that everyone can agree on throughout the entire world is the importance of work. Some may argue that it is the social value of most benefit in the twenty-first century. The latter half of the twentieth century in the United States spurred the greatest economy the world has ever known. As our hierarchy of needs increased in society, our needs evolved. Our attitudes about what is fundamentally required out of life changed. This is true even at work. Younger generations thrive on using their job to find meaning in their own lives, as well as finding the right places of work that reflect their own values. This prioritization is foreign to all other generations alive. Nothing acts as a stabilizer throughout communities, cities, states, countries, and the world as a good job. According to

Gallup Chairman and CEO Jim Clifton in his book *The Coming Jobs War*, a good job has reportedly become more important than religion and morality in the world because it has become what psychologist Fredrick Herzberg would call a "hygiene factor" for a happy life. Herzberg's original argument outlined a two-factor theory within the workplace focused on dissatisfaction. He claims that a series of conditions must be met before any true motivation can exist in the workplace. Those needs are not being met by a substantial number of people throughout the country and the world. In order to be happy at a job, one must first have a job. If Herzberg's theory is applied to the macro definition of *work*, we can begin to see the consequences of lack of employment opportunities throughout the globe.

Joblessness is the root cause of all of the global issues that our State and Defense Department attempt to combat on a daily basis. On a global level, the lack of jobs means humanitarian aid, war, terrorism and increased international political and military presence. On a local level, it could mean the bankruptcy of Detroit, the diminishing of property value, civic unrest, or the security of your family. The new hygiene theory defines not just a job but a good job as the number one social value. Before any notions of a higher calling will be present—or as Herzberg would define them, motivating factors—this new world order must exist. In this world, the job acts as a security blanket before we are able to attain higher levels of achievement. Before freedom, patriotism, religion, or even starting a family, we value the job as the provider of the basic needs. This has become a generation-defining problem and distinction. We used to have faith that hard work was enough. Now we are not so sure. This puts a strain on what was once known as the working class and disrupts patterns of marriages and births and will fundamentally change our culture. As author Charles Murray outlines, changes in values can be traced back to an economic problem stemming from lack of good jobs. This is also true for a change in culture. Millennials are putting off marriage and children and seemingly remaining in adolescent states for longer periods of time. The root of the issue, for the most part, is the changing economic factors in modern America. It is economics and not culture that first separates us from the millennials, based on the changing characteristics and needs from work. The young are beginning their careers from a significantly different place than where we were just a few years ago. It may be better or worse depending on the point of view, but it will most certainly require a whole new set of competencies and perspectives.

The engine that propels us forward financially will also propel us forward socially and civically. This is based on very civic mind-set, which is intertwined with economics for the young. It is in our best interest to improve the social mobility in the modern United States because it is historically American. It also happens to align with the values of a new generation of leaders. What then is social mobility in its current context? Social mobility now requires innovation. The access to the possibilities of innovation in the digital world is ironically closing more and more every day as the internet itself is becoming more open. Our educational system, according to Sugata Mitra, dates back to Sir William Curtis proclaiming the virtue of the three *R*s in 1825. Reading, writing, and arithmetic brought us into the twentieth century. That has been the cornerstone the modern western ideal of education for nearly two centuries. Not understanding the digital world and its implications today is the new form of illiteracy. Just about everyone has the ability to read. Almost no one needs to learn how to write, and almost everybody has the ability to do basic math. These skills came from the "bureaucratic machine" that built the west, according to Mitra. These skills are what Daniel Pink called in *A Whole New Mind* "left brain skills." These are exactly the types of functions that the automation of computers seeks today. The nonlinear "right brain," so absent from progress in the past, will be the key to innovation. The past thirty years have brought us MBAs to save the day. These revolutionary masters of business administration proved effective. They were the saviors of capitalism for a generation. Productivity and profits have never been higher. The next evolution in efficiency will be outsourcing these traditionally left-brain thinkers or retraining then for the twenty-first century.

In 2012, Charles Murray published *Coming Apart*, in which he compared statistics in the hypothetical towns of Fishtown and Belmont. Fishtown was the representative of a working-class town with, at most, a high school diploma. Belmont was the representative of an imaginary town where residents had a college education. The results found that as compared to the overall economy, Belmont stayed surprisingly consistent with most socioeconomic issues. Fishtown, however, is where Murray believes that we are coming apart. Fishtown was the sector that was first hit by the possibilities of the new globalization brought on by more liberal trade policies. Outsourcing and automating have decimated the communities inside of Fishtown. In 1960, 90 percent of Belmont households had work as opposed to 81 percent of Fishtown. By 2010, the gap had widened to 87 percent in Belmont and 53 percent in Fishtown. Under these conditions, it is nearly impossible to produce the right type of values, habits, education, experience, and opportunities that are becoming of most value in the new era. To further illustrate the point, Jeffrey Selingo, *College Unbound* author, cited that if your parents earn $90,000 per year or greater, you have a one-in-two chance of earning a bachelor's degree. If your parents earn less than $35,000 per year, however, that stat explodes to a one-in-seventeen chance. We are destined to see the inequality rise in the near future. Meanwhile, cheap technologies are rising with more universal access. We have had the ability to democratize the Internet. Everyone has a free and equal voice to participate and create. Ironically, this freedom has led to less or worse jobs. At best, it leads to more information, cheaper entertainment, and eventually a creative destruction, as found in the music or camera industries. The pace changes, but the pattern remains: one iteration dies to be replaced by another version, updated by technology. To keep up, we need education, opportunity, and self-motivation. We need to replace the vicious cycles with virtuous cycles.

Salon writer Larry Schwartz presented a list of inequality facts with which we must come to terms. He says that wages as a percentage of the economy are at a historic low, even as compared to the gilded age of the 1890s. Children born into poverty today are half as likely to escape poverty as they were in 1946. Wages of the top 1 percent rose ten times as much as the bottom 90 percent. Fifty percent of all investment in the United States rests with the wealthiest 1 percent. This is one hundred times more than the bottom 50 percent combined. Median wealth for those under thirty-five years of age has dropped by 68 percent since 1984. Economist Joseph Stigletz has said, "A bus with 85 of the world's richest has as much wealth as the bottom 50% of humans—3 billion people." Thomas Picketty, in *Capital in the 21ˢᵗ Century*, has said that the modern version of capitalism has evolved in a global economy where the rate of return of capital is higher than economic growth. Picketty says that the period from the end of World War II, which is seen as the golden age of the American economy, was an aberration of centralized control through Keynesian redistribution. Economic equality was controlled through progressive taxation. So the natural trajectory for unfettered capitalism, according to Picketty, is inequality.

Stephen Covey, the best-selling author of *The Seven Habits of Highly Effective People*, has written *Leader in Me*, which attempts to apply his time-tested leadership skills to children as young as four or five. Covey says that in order for a leader to manifest, even at a young age, a child's basic needs must be met. The hierarchy is physical, which include basic safety, health, nutrition, and hygiene. Children also require social-emotional acceptance through respect, love, and friendship. Next, they need mental exercises that stimulate them both intellectually and creatively. Lastly, there must be spiritual hope to grow to another level of being. A connection must exist that prove their unique contributions and meaning. Most children get these requirements in their homes and are the basic building blocks for character. Unfortunately, a great number of children are missing key pieces of the ingredients that allow for personal growth to ever occur. Without these tenets found within, it is not possible to elevate to the levels of accountability, responsibility, or vision for the possibilities of the future. These traits are the precursor to what Daniel Goleman identified in 1995 as emotional intelligence, which allows connection with other people and has been found to be a better predictor of success than even intelligence itself.

Anderson Cooper is a bright, talented, and hardworking journalist who got his start by proving his value by taking both financial and physical risks by covering violence as a freelance journalist in some scary parts of the world. According to Cooper, he was not given a stipend from his wealthy family, and his Ivy League degree did not matter in the war-torn corners of the earth. There was no guarantee of success or safety when Cooper entered hostile territories on his own accord using forged documents. A greater display or fortitude is rare. Undoubtedly, his success has been hard earned and devoid of any nepotism of his lineage of the Vanderbilt family, who were once considered American royalty. The authors of *Scarcity* would attribute Cooper's success to the individual, but a certain amount of attribution should go to what they called slack. He was raised with the basic needs met, which helped him display character. He did not have to contend with social, time, or financial scarcity. The cognitive bandwidth required for excellence was never taxed with the noise that the underpinnings of scarcity can bring. A large population of the United States and an even larger proportion of the world have the capacity to do great things, but they live in the dense fog of inequality. A physiological tunnel vision forms that reaches only for the next basic need in a modern world, which requires 360 degrees of perspective. Leadership, as a synonym for the practical wisdom of humanity and a gateway to happiness and success, must be accessible to all who choose to seek it. By way of individual character does the rest of society prosper.

CHAPTER 3

ANTHROPOLOGY AND GENERATIONAL CHANGE

The modern world caused humans to become removed from the patterns of the earth. We see our lives as a very linear segment from point A to point B. Time is the representation of linear thinking. We have assigned years as benchmarks. This has been most recently represented in the year 2012 during the culmination of the Mayan Pictun, which is equivalent to eight thousand years of life on earth. The end of the world was presumed by many when a symbolic renewal was intended by the calendar originators. The "circle of life" is a very literal symbol representing the rebirth of the earth through the turning of the seasons. Humans, it is said, are creatures of habit. The modern human clings to monotony due to its relative safeness. The ancients feared the opposite. They feared the cessation of change. Their proximity to the rhythms of nature led them to understand the natural cycles, which evade the modern human. We derive meaning from what we know. We do not understand that what we know is greatly in context of when we were born. Not only in terms of linear history but in terms of our generation. We are linked to generations, past and future, in more ways than we know. Nearly every great ancient civilization offered a representation of the cyclical nature of life. From ancient India to Ancient North America, the symbol of the circle represented not just the changing of the four seasons but also the changing of the seasons of life. By the time the temple to Athena was built, it was inscribed with the phrase "All human things are a cycle." In conjunction with the understanding of the circle as a representation of an infinite loop we have incorporated these ancient pagan understandings and have used them as symbols for Christmas wreaths and wedding bands. The circle is the world's simplest and most powerful representation of continuity.

The ouroboros originally appeared in ancient Egypt in sixteenth century BC. Throughout the ancient world various incarnations of the circular snake or dragon eating its own tail and replenishing life in a never-ending sequence is a common theme. The Hindu tradition also uses the ouroboros symbolism in Kundalini or "coiled like a snake." This can be traced back to Kirtimukha from the religious texts Skanda Purana. In this myth, a dragon eats his own body beginning with the tail. The Chinese portrayed the dragon eating its own tail as early as 1,200 BC and had also found its way to ancient Japan. In Mayan culture, the feathered serpent, Quetzalcoatl, could be commonly found devouring itself tail first. Christianity took root in Western culture and the Middle Ages drowned out the pagan symbolism and ideas connected with the ideas of the ourobori across the world. As the Middle Ages unfolded very little in the realm of science, philosophy and art existed outside the influence of the church. The cross, while it predates Christianity, is another universal symbol of the ancients used in cultures as disparate as the Native American Dakotas to represent the four winds. It is also said to have referred to the four corners of the world or to have represented the feminine and the masculine with each bar of the cross. The circle and the cross were universal symbols across cultures and throughout the ancient world.

When Christianity adopted the symbol, it took a much different form and interpretation. The symbol of the cross now represented the Father, Son, and the Holy Spirit. It was also a powerful remembrance to the fashion which Jesus died on the crucifix at the hands of a very barbaric Roman culture. The cross was a symbol that order was coming to the ancient world, and a new definition of advancement was in order. It was a new beginning for the world.

The clocks were reset. It was now a linear world, although progress would be slow for some time. The western world of the Middle Ages stomped out the cyclical ideas of the ouroboros. The idea of a cyclical world did not mesh with a culture, led by the church, in a common direction. The symbols of old had died. Divine Providence of a God-centered world guided the way forward. As the Renaissance and the Reformation spread across Europe, new ideas about alchemy began to disseminate, and old ideas began to be revived. Because science was lost for a thousand years, alchemists took a mystical and spiritual approach to what would be the sciences of the future. In its most simple form, it was the transmutation of a common substance into one of value. It was the grandfather of chemistry. Many of these alchemists took to Hermitism, which claims that God had given ancient cultures one true theology, represented only by the sum of all ancient cultures. The symbol of the alchemists many times was the return of the ouroboros. For centuries, the alchemists used this symbol until the emergence of modern science. It was closely related to the Eastern term *yoga* as a transformation.

The symbol of the ouroboros is a powerful one. It is essentially a way of looking at the modern world, which had been erased by western culture. No one dared speak of the rhythms of the natural world, which had been known for thousands of years until the late nineteenth-century philosopher Friedrich Nietzsche. Nietzsche questioned what he called the delusions of never-ending progress. In his opinion, the linear view trap, which we had fallen into over two millennia did not make sense—as it had not seemed that humanity was making much cultural progress at all. Furthermore, no one would want never-ending progress in one direction because it was boring, predictable, and against the nature of humankind. Nietzsche called himself the first immoralist. To Nietzsche, there was an eternal recurrence, in which we were avoiding and ignoring in the name of evolution. The only infinite being that Christians could conceive was that of God. There was a beginning, Adam and Eve, a middle period of life on earth, and an end with the rapture. Morals were absolute through time and space, which were handed down from God. St. Augustine set the tone for early Christian theology by stating "Only

God is infinite," and the pagan symbols of the old world did not fit the new western world view. The notions of patterns in society were not only passé but they were also forbidden. Therefore, we slowly began to see the climb of progress of human history. We were all only going in one direction. Nothing could be learned from history. Why then, Nietzsche would ask, can we never make accurate predictions about the future if we keep injecting the same civic virtues into great societies?

The infinity sign, sometimes called the lemniscate, is a common symbol found even in early mathematical curriculum of the present. It is an ancient symbol, but it may surprise many that it was not used in mathematics until the seventeenth century by John Wallis. Medieval culture was not prepared to deal with the possibility of the infinite. It was not open for discussion. Not until the Renaissance could mathematicians begin thinking beyond traditional finite math. The figure eight of the infinity symbol is again another variation of the infinite and the union of two opposites. The story of earth as told in the Bible is nothing if not finite. Therefore, one day it will end. No one in the early church shaped modern Christianity more than St. Augustine. He was a bright philosophic mind who shaped thought of AD fourth century and many generations following. He claimed that only God could know infiniteness. One thousand years later, St. Thomas of Aquinas reaffirmed this concept by claiming that all things were finite and that any challenge to this notion was against God's will, not to mention inconceivable to humans. It was the opinion of the church that the notion of infinity is not only offensive to God but also futile and uninspiring to mankind. No good could come of it. The lemniscate was left to appear in the pagan realm of the tarot card the Magician, with the symbol just above his head.

This understanding of linear time is so deeply embedded in western culture that we never question the impact that a drastic and long-ago change in direction has made. Everything we do is in the name of progress and a means to an end, so much so that we set benchmarks for our lives to mark our progress. We never question the possibility that fundamental values and priorities may change from generation to generation. We especially never take a moment to see the patterns that have been repeated throughout history. Learning about history has become a memorization exercise in times and places. The cause and effect is never challenged. We have heard the caution that those who do not learn about history are doomed to repeat it, but it never occurs to us that that might actually be a literal warning. Do we ever really take time to look to the past to predict the future? We used to. Our greatest minds from the past two centuries believed in these mysterious cycles. Winston Churchill once said, "The farther backwards you look, the farther forward you are likely to see." Similarly, Mark Twain quoted, "In America, nothing is older than calling everything new." I am not suggesting that we examine any pagan idolatries or notions of reincarnation, but I am asking that we examine the quiet rhythms of the past that many have already identified. The great challenge in education and beyond in the twenty-first century will be to question the norms that had have stalled progress in our twentieth-century models. The core question for progress, as it has been in every era, is "What can I do differently, and why?"

The answer is as old as the ouroboros itself, and many western thinkers began to carve out these patterns from ancient culture. As history unfolded, that pattern emerged endlessly. Although the circle represents chaos because no beginning or end ever surfaces, many sought to understand the patterns at hand. While sifting through the data, it was found that American patterns were many times the pre-emanate archetype of the ouroboros. To truly examine it, we must first break it down into manageable sections and understand its patterns. Luckily, the ancients have already done most of the work for us. The modern-day social scientists and historians have attempted the difficult process of quantification. The ancients viewed cycles in one of two ways. Some preferred to articulate the cycles in the form of a pendulum, which symbiotically exists with the opposite force that it instills. This is the idea of the yin and the yang in ancient Chinese philosophy. The yin represents the passive and benign nature versus the aggression of the yang. Evil cannot be defined unless we can first comprehend goodness. In the Bible, this is the incarnation of the yin of God versus the yang representation of Satan. The night leads to day just as the day leads to night. Understanding the dualism of life brings us closer to the truth. F. Scott Fitzgerald said, "The test of a first-rate intelligence is the ability to hold two opposed ideas in the mind at the same time, and still retain the ability to function." These forces contributed to a philosophical understanding of the still unseen forces in our world. The sophistication of the ancients is still impressive even when compared to modern scientific findings.

The idea of four is more nuanced yet just as represented in ancient culture. Like the four seasons that differentiate weather patterns, the two extremes of winter and summer call for two transition periods. The four stages of life begin at birth and early life and end at old age and death, but we would be missing two seasons. A battle exists every spring and fall between the heat of summer and the cold of winter. The spring of new life leads to the summer of youth. Middle age is the fall of our years, followed by the eventual decay of winter. However, the entire cycle was dissected; it was comprised of what the ancient Etruscans first defined as a saeculum. This came to be known as roughly the length of the human life span. The saeculum was important because it was one full completion. It was a way to make sense out of a confusing world. It was a demarcation in an age of never-ending cycles. It marked the end of the four hills of the Native American culture and the four ashramas of the Hindu tradition. Heraclitus could be said to be the first major Greek philosopher. He believed that everything was in a constant state of tension by the unity of opposites called the flux doctrine. To many who followed his ideas, they seemed contradictory. He believed that not only was transformation a part of life, but it was the core idea behind life. Four centuries later, in the second century BC, Polybius introduced the four patterns of government from kings to aristocracy and democracy to anarchy in the second century BC, which proved to be the first cohesive social theory of power in the social sciences. Soon, the preeminent paradigm in Hellenic culture was an understanding of the two pairs of opposites. Fire is hot and air is cold while the earth is dry and water wet. One cannot exist without the other. From here, we are able to discern the eight components of the lemniscate, the four components of the ouroboros, or the two components of the yin-yang. Everything has its complement.

So the saeculum is one complete turn. It is the completion of the pattern. Not by chance, this equals one human life. In most accounts, the pattern of an average human life can be defined in four periods; one of birth, growth, decline, and decay. We spend the majority of the first half being shaped by others who came before us and the other half shaping others who succeed us. If we were to inject the Newtonian idea that for every action there is an equal and opposite reaction, we could then conclude that there is a self-sufficient nature to the universe. In other words, things are because of what they were, and things will be because of what they are. The saeculum suggests that the patterns of the past contribute to the future and that these patterns may very well happen again. The medieval Middle Eastern philosopher Ibn Khaldun spoke of the four stages of an empire. As western culture progressed, we were taught the four temperaments, the four worldviews, and the four personalities. Nineteenth-century historian Giuseppe Ferrari studied the four-part patterns of revolution, which led to Eduard Wechssler studying the four bases of perception. Not until the twentieth century did we really begin to understand what psychologist Carl Jung would call the four basic psychological functions called reason, feeling, sensation, and intuition. These archetypes of individuation draw, in large part, to the theory of generations, which latter twentieth-century social scientists began to identify. Jung argued that the "shadow" of one personality over the course of a lifetime contributed to the identity of the next. That is how we begin to identify generational characteristics.

So a true understanding of the cyclical nature of the human condition began to advance in the twentieth century, led by historian Arthur M. Schlesinger Jr. He claimed, "A true cycle . . . is self-generating. It cannot be determined, short of catastrophe, by external events. Wars, depressions, inflations, may heighten or complicate moods, but the cycle itself rolls on, self-contained, self-sufficient and autonomous . . . The roots of this cyclical self-sufficiency lie deep in the natural life of humanity. There is a cyclical pattern in organic nature—in the tides, in the seasons, in night and day, in the systole and diastole of the human heart." Even as we humans began to see ourselves as more of a central part of the earth in modern times, Schlesinger argues that our small role here cannot change the patterns of destiny. American sociologist Quincy Wright studied the historical patterns of war, and British historian Arnold Toynbee published a comprehensive and exhaustive study of the rise and fall of human civilization in 1961. Suddenly, it seemed that the intuition of the ancients was far more progressive than the modern world would have guessed. By the 1990s, William Straus and Neil Howe, in their book *Generations: A History of America's Future 1584 to 2069*, had teamed to compile a completely new perspective of recurring generational archetypes dating back to the founding of America. Not surprisingly, they used a saeculum, or one human life span, as the definition of one complete turning of the generational cycle, and then they labeled these four generations over the course of their life's work.

Carl Jung brought us the term *collective unconscious*. He believed in the duality of the struggle between our conscious and unconscious is what it truly means to be an individual. We can try all our lives to change that of which we are conscious, but the shadows of the past shape our identity more than we know. He developed the Jungian archetype, stating, "All the most powerful ideas in history go back to archetypes, this is particularly true of religious ideas, but the central concepts of science, philosophy, and ethics are no exception to this rule. In their present form they are variants of archetypal ideas created by consciously applying and adapting these ideas to reality. For it is the function of consciousness, not only to recognize and assimilate the external world through the gateway of the senses, but to translate into visible reality the world within us." Of course, he outlined four major archetypes of unconscious understanding, consisting of the self, the shadow, the anima, and the persona. So, beginning with the understanding of archetypes, the saeculum, and the seasons, Strauss and Howe were able to label each generation within the saeculum. Each comes with their unique collective unconscious bred from the circumstances that shaped their ancestors. According to Strauss and Howe, the first generation is the prophet archetype, born during a period known as a high. The second generation is the nomad, born during an awakening. The hero archetype is born during the unraveling, and the artist is born during a crisis period. Each generation is born roughly twenty years apart, and the cycle is completed in roughly eighty years, or about the length of a human life.

So does this theory of a rhythmic history of America really exist? The most profound proof can be found by simply tracing the "fourth turning," or the crisis period, in recent American history. We can start during the American Revolution Crisis period in 1776 and follow that a lifetime later and we arrive at the American Civil War. One lifetime later finds us battling the dual crisis of the Great Depression and World War II. Strauss and Howe teamed up for another book in 1997 titled *The Fourth Turning*, where they prophesized another catastrophic event in American history. According to their projected timeline, this event occurred somewhere around 2005 that would lead to the next great crisis period. Their arbitrary date happened to lie halfway between the dual crisis of September 11, 2001, and the Great Recession beginning in 2008. The goal of their work is to not be soothsayers to the ills of tomorrow but to begin to see the very practical and very rhythmic movements in our history. There is nothing metaphysical about realizing that we live in self-contained cycles brought about by those that have come before us. We will, in turn, very predictably react in a certain manner, and the cycle will continue. Strauss and Howe did outline five plausible scenarios that may act as a catalyst to the most recent crisis. Four out of five are very close to current reality, with the possible exception of states laying claim to federal tax monies. Here are some predictions that are eerily familiar.

"A global terrorist group blows up an aircraft . . . The United States and its allies launch a preemptive strike . . . Congress declares war and authorizes unlimited house-to-house searches (think Patriot Act). Opponents charge that the president concocted the emergency for political purposes. Foreign capital flees the US."

Or "An impasse over the federal budget reaches a stalemate. The president and Congress both refuse to back down, triggering a near-total government shutdown . . . Congress refuses to raise the debt ceiling. Default looms. Wall Street panics." (Think Standard and Poor's lowering the US credit rating from AAA status in 2011.)

Strauss and Howe could foresee these scenarios not because they could predict the future but because they understood the personality and the attitudes of those that would be in power throughout the following decade. They were in tune with the patterns in American life. Each of the four archetypes that they espouse have a very real set of traits and characteristics that follow each generation inherently. We are essentially all born somewhere in a reoccurring tide. Thomas Wolf said, regarding the generation to which you are born, "You're a part of it. Whether you want to be or not." Your generation is as defining as the family to which you were born. Should you have come of age in the 1940s during the aftermath of World War II, you most likely would have had the viewpoint of shared sacrifice and seen the merit of inclusion and conformity. Should you have come of age in the early 1980s under the same circumstances, you would have most likely seen the value of individuality as the zeitgeist, or spirit of the time. Generational patterns in America are composed of two groups of opposites, simplified and outlined best in the 2012 book by Roy H. Williams and Michael R. Drew, *Pendulum*. Williams and Drew agree that one full turn of the cycle does indeed last approximately eighty years, but they view the saeculum through the lens of the constant yin-yang struggle of *me* versus *we* in society. The zenith of the *we* was during the 1940s as Strauss and Howe also described. The zenith of the *me* movement was the 1980s. Society is on a constant forty-year cycle, returning to complete the cycle every eighty years.

Just after World War I, William Butler Yeats penned these words:

Turning and turning in the widening gyre
The falcon cannot hear the falconer
Things fall apart; the centre cannot hold;
Mere anarchy is loosed upon the world,
The blood-dimmed tide is loosed, and everywhere
The ceremony of innocence is drowned.
The best lack all conviction, while the worst
Are full of passionate intensity.

Yeats was commenting on the widening gyre of human progress, always completing a cycle yet always moving forward, possibly in vain and with no recollection of its beginning. The anthropologist would imagine these cycles as nothing more than groups of people with shared experiences. According to Strauss and Howe, there are four key characteristics of generations that exist in American culture. The first is the adaptive generation, followed by the idealist, reactive, and civic. Generation Y, or what has come to be known as the millennial generation, has most in common with the GI generation of World War II. They are the most recent generation to fully reach adulthood. They see the value in connection and collaboration. Their method of resolving situations is most likely one of consensus. Strauss and Howe would call the key characteristic of this generation civic. This is at the other end of the spectrum as baby boomers, who are the eternal ideologues that reject compromise. Boomers were the original "me" generation of modern America. They were born roughly from 1945–1964 and have proven to dramatically change the landscape of the modern world. Strauss and Howe would call them the idealist generation. The second pair of opposites within the saeculum is what Strauss and Howe would call the reactive generation archetype of Generation X and the adaptive "silent generation" born from the 1920s through the 1940s. Generation X succeeded the baby boomers and is known by their retreat from society. Born roughly between the years 1964–1978, they are the reclusive loners due to the fact that a lull in attention was paid to children in society during their youth. The birth of the next adaptive generation is nearly complete today. Very little is known about the millennial's predecessors, Generation Z, as they are sometimes called, because of the lack of any longitudinal studies available due to their youth. According to theory, their key characteristic will be that of adaptation, taking their cue from the civic-minded Generation Y. They will be the next silent generation, although they will be destined for great things. One thing is for certain, they are growing up in an environment that is nothing if not protective of children. This key characteristic immediately differentiates them from Gen X.

Understanding generational differences has always been a key component of American culture. They comprise a roughly twenty-year period, which broadly encapsulates the mood and values of an entire group of people. We just never thought to view them as cyclical because we very rarely view anything as cyclical. All the while, we still fear the linear curve of perpetuity. The social ethic of the 1950s has become something that we viewed as an eternal normal. Sociologists of that period imagined the great ascension of culture from beyond that point. Everything was orderly, the suburbs were symmetrical, children were seen and not heard, and all indications pointed to a social discipline the likes the world had never seen. No one saw the baby boomers coming. No one foresaw a split so fundamental from the values of the time. It was a stark indication that one full saeculum prior that Nietzsche might have been on to something. The pattern was changing, and the new generation was recoiling from the conformist social bliss that they were sold in their youth. The boomers recognized deep problems in the social fabrics of society and could not be kept quiet. It was during this time that the Civil Rights Act was passed, and Vietnam caused many to stake out sides. Jim Morrison said, "Each generation wants new symbols, new people, new names. They want to divorce themselves from their predecessors." A counterculture had been brewing for some time. The pendulum was shifting. No one had remembered what Tacitus had said over two thousand years prior, "Morals alternate, as do the seasons."

Perhaps Tacitus's use of the word *morals* could be more appropriately worded as *values*. Boomers have never been short on those. They reaped the rewards of prosperity and growth began by their parents. Their strong beliefs and hard work led to them to hold most leadership roles in the United States today. Just look around at leaders from corporate board rooms to the upper levels of the US government. They began life with ideological litmus tests such as civil rights and Vietnam War protests. The lasting effects of their ideology have led to the increased partisan problems and less cooperation in government. They were the first to kill the social capital, which took a half century to build. Their insistence on a static leadership style has caused organizations to respond more slowly to change. Let's examine how our modern generations unfolded. Williams and Drew would say that the pendulum began to turn toward individualism in the 1960s. Strauss and Howe could call it an awakening period, one of the many throughout the history of the United States. This would be in contrast to the crisis period, to which we have been immersed in as of late. It is said that the old guard gives the orders and the young shape the culture during the crisis periods. Awakening movements, like the one we saw in the 1960s, shifted real power to the youth. In the vacuum, the senior generation is left to tend to the institutions. This crisis period finds the youth with the skills but without the power. We find ourselves in an inverse period of the 1960s in America. Archetypes exist because they are reoccurring. Once a distant generation has passed beyond the ability of any generation to remember, the generation is solidified in myth, the way many of the GI generation are viewed today. Pretty soon, every individual who shaped that time in American history will be gone. Very few remember what it was like to live at that time or why exactly they held the values which they did. We do, however, still remember the 1950s with a nostalgic fondness. It was a time of baby boomer births and relatively secure and stable family life. The highway system and the suburbs were built. Public education and public works were still strong. Landon Jones coined the term *baby boomer*. He expressed, "What others thought were privileges, Boomers thought were rights." They came of age in the biggest economic boom the world had ever seen. The outer world in which they grew up seemed ideal. All their worldly needs were being met. Why then did they rebel? It was because they were frustrated with the parameters of what they believed to be a conformist and stuffy society, which never indulged in its own self-interest. They saw the hidden chains of a society with distinctly different values. They fought against the notion of the government restricting rights of citizens and sending the youth to a war that was not well understood. They were also a generation indifferent to nuance and were not afraid to speak their mind. The generation in between was called the silent generation for a reason. They showed up, followed the rules, and did not make a disturbance. They were the demographic behind the silent majority highlighted by Richard Nixon. The logic went, because the majority of Americans were not in the street protesting the Vietnam War, it must be popular. Silence caused the boomers to rebel.

While the boomers were the original *me* generation out of rebellion, Generation X was the *me* generation out of necessity. Gen Xers withdrew due to being the first generation in American history that sent both parents to work. They locked the doors upon returning home from school alone and retreated into isolation. Their identity is closely linked with the 1970s, one that John Updike referred to as "a slum of a decade." Individuality was excelling at an unprecedented speed. The social ethic that inspired the idea of 1950s America was long since gone. The attentiveness to youth, as shown to the baby boomers, was denied to Generation X. Almost nothing of arts and entertainment of the 1970s was directed at the youth. They grew up tending quietly to their own needs. Millennials are the fourth generation since the civic-minded GI generation. They have a reputation for being coddled, immature, unsociable, and lazy, many times at the insistence of the boomers themselves. While much of that may be true, the same generation who complained about it is the same generation who raised them. The baby boomers will soon begin to retire, and this group, which will enter the workforce in greater numbers than even the baby boomers, will need to fill leadership vacancies. Their tendencies will involve a leadership model foreign to many that came before them through the magic of technology; this generation has the power to lead in counterintuitive ways never possible before.

Birth cohorts make easy classification. Keep in mind that birth dates are not necessarily indicators of generational belonging. In 1776, the civic-minded spirit rose up against the British oppression in unison. Eighty years later, the next civic generation defeated the evils of slavery, and eighty years after that, the civic-minded GI generation overcame the Great Depression and defeated fascism around the world. Now, another eighty years beyond the Depression, we find ourselves at another crossroads. This time, there may not be one clear threat to overcome but a series of obstacles to tackle that require the civic spirit. We have overcome 9/11 and the Great Recession, but we must be diligent in our optimism for the future. The zeitgeist of the American spirit must come together to achieve our personal, professional, and societal goals for the new millennium. This is an instinctual embrace of the modern natural world for the millennial, but it is a threat to everyone else alive. So we look to Generation Y as the leaders of a new civic generation. This is manifested in their need to belong and connect on social networks. They want to belong to organizations that serve the greater good. They reject the need to retreat in isolation like their predecessors or judge values like their parents. They *are* very educated and involved and *not* overtly cynical or particularly rebellious. The 2010s will be known as the decade of social media, for the most part due to the insistence on connection by the millennials. Collaboration by this generation was predetermined long before the technology was available. They were born to be the connectors. They are not an updated version of their parents as we continually expect. They are a distinct generation, perfectly suited for their time in history. It is by no accident that this is their moment.

They have already brought great contrast to the patterns that we saw just fifteen years ago. In 2000, Robert D. Putnam published *Bowling Alone,* a woeful manuscript that documented the downfall of what he called social capital. He told of the political, civic, and religious institutions, which had been so carefully mended for years and were in complete decay at the turn of the last century. The boomers and the Gen Xers simply were not joiners. Grassroots organizations were outsourced to professionals. The pressures of time, money, and the company of modern technology made the value of social networks of the past obsolete. Putnam called for new structures and policies (public and private) to facilitate renewed civic engagement. Much like the way Dr. Benjamin Spock called for the need of a new era of idealistic children in the 1960s, both remedies were enacted. Millennials built the infrastructure for the greatest social capitalist movement ever created; the social network, and the boomers made good on their prescription for narcissism and idealism. Born beginning in the late 1990s, many have already identified today's youth as

Generation Z. Assuming the existence of generational cyclical theory, the generation that they will most resemble is the silent generation. This group is submissive to authority, hardworking, and loyal. They belong and identify to a group mentality and strive for consensus building. The theory claims that this adaptive generation is the first turning of the eighty-year cycle. They call this period the high, as in high conformity to norms, risk management, and institutional obligations. Their life will be defined as basking in the glory in the incredible technologies and economies that the millennials will create. They will quietly and easily adapt to the starkly different world of the future. They are the first generation to be coined digital natives.

Following this model, the yet unnamed Generation Z successors will be the "prophet" archetype of an awakening period. They will eventually break the conformity of their elders, and we will see the rebellion of the 1960s again around the 2040s. This generation will be closely aligned to what we know as the baby boomers. The rise of individualism will increase into the 2060s, where society once again becomes a cartoon of itself, much like the early and mid-1980s. Coming of age in the 2060s will be an alienating experience. Strauss and Howe classify them as the nomad of history. We can identify them as closely related to Generation X. Not until the 2080s will the following generation reach adulthood. They are what we today call the millennials today and the greatest generation before that. They are pragmatic and civic minded and have usually undergone a traumatic cultural experience due to the unraveling of their predecessors. They are once again the saviors. Of course, the theory has been examined to a mixed review of scientists and scholars over the past two decades. Finding the Rosetta stone of culture certainly has implications of which we could not even begin to imagine. The entire subject of cyclical theory, be it from fashion to philosophy, will always have its detractors. What this theory adds is that birth cohorts do not necessarily make a generation. The young tend to force change, but the zeitgeist is truly defined by the groups involved. Williams and Drew call them life cohorts. They claim that the whole of what drives society evolves into this prevailing worldview. We know it is not always up to the young to change society; a majority has to buy in to the prevailing cause as well. Birth cohorts make easy classification, but real generations are a constantly evolving creatures with certain societal tensions forever struggling. The weight of the pull differs, depending on the position of the pendulum. Certain perspectives on the great dualities of life may have already been determined based on the times in which you live, but yet we are all individuals.

Imagine the ruckus of the Roaring '20s. Women dared cut their hair into a bob and spend their evenings dancing in speakeasies to jazz music. Prohibition begot a seamy and violent underworld of illegal alcohol sales. The 1920s began amid a reportedly corrupt Warren G. Harding administration, which deferred to big business concerns, specifically big oil before it was officially accepted in Washington culture. Enter "Silent Cal" Calvin Coolidge, who extolled the virtues of light regulation, a small federal government, and tax cuts for the rich. He was the original perpetrator of supply side economics at the presidential level. Coolidge and the plutocratic administration believed wealth will always trickle down, should we first take care of the concerns of the rich. Nearly sixty years later, his disciple Ronald Reagan would remove a picture of Thomas Jefferson in the White House and replace it with Calvin Coolidge himself. Coolidge, however, was successful in his mission. The rich got richer. The market was bullish, and real money was to be made. Meanwhile, the earnings of the backbone of America at the time, industrialists and farmers stagnated. While the stock market was in full swing, the middle class, as we know it today, had not yet been built. The stock market was an instrument of the investor class. The market rode the tide of the Coolidge Prosperity. With the rollback of any sense of regulation at the New York Stock Exchange, overinvestment led to the illusion of a much larger economy than what actually existed. Because of the prosperity of the stock market, banks began to accept stock as collateral for loans. Just months after Coolidge left office, the ride had ended. The stock market crashed in October 1929, and the Great Depression immediately followed.

Herbert Hoover had already been elected. He had won riding the tide of two consecutive Republican Presidents who had sold an illusion of prosperity. By the next election, Franklin Delano

Roosevelt set the tone for a mostly big government era, which would last for decades. By the 1950s, the American economy was the envy of the world. Many of the early boomers entered the workforce in the 1960s when the economy was still at its peak. That generation benefited from the progressive aspects of big government investment in education, infrastructure, and innovation, which fueled a middle class of citizens unprecedented in human history. By the 1980s, that same generation, who will be the last generation to collect a pension on a wide scale, began to see the merit in keeping their hard-earned money. They had forgotten their path to prosperity. So it should not be with much wonder how those born in those early years of the 1980s during the Reagan Revolution feel disenfranchised. While those who complain about the millennial entitlement syndrome invest their lump sum pensions and collect their Social Security benefits, in which they will receive much more then they originally invested. They are secure in their new Medicare plan and lament Obamacare for the young. Economically, the young are doing historically very poorly. Wages are low, and student debt is high. The young are competing against a job pool that is extremely educated, talented, and global. They do not have the luxury of a job pool where the middle class is not a matter of working harder to succeed. Seventy-nine years after the Black Friday crash of 1929, the worst crash since that day occurred in 2008. Is it coincidence that this is one full saeculum, that this is one full human life span? Seventy-nine years is just enough time for someone to forget the lessons of the past.

CHAPTER 4

BIOLOGY AND PROGRESS

World history is an evolution of ingenuity, a self-contained inevitability of further productivity. Cycles and patterns are everywhere in everything we do. The story of earth, however, is very linear. Billions of years ago, conditions became present for a carbon-based life to exist on earth. Because of the earth's position in the solar system and the sun's position in the galaxy, earth had been given the gift of the "goldilocks effect" of ideal geospatial location. Moderate conditions on earth were ripe for life. Two hundred fifty thousand years ago, man tamed fire. Fifty thousand years ago, we developed the power of language and the expression of art. For the next forty thousand years, we lived identically as hunter-gatherers roaming the earth. This practice proved unsustainable as the earth warmed. Agriculture gave us permanence. A system of writing developed, which helped communicate our new distinct cultures. After tens of thousands of years, the human story was finally developing. Twentieth-century German philosopher Carl Jaspers coined the term *Axial Age* for the period between 800–200 BCE. He meant for this term to be quite literally the foundation of all political, philosophical, and religious systems as we know them today. It was the time of Lao Tsu and Confucius in the East. It was the age of Buddha and the Upanishads in India. The idea of Zarathustra emerged in Persia to represent the eternal struggle of good versus evil. The Palestinian prophets of Elijah, Isaiah, and Jeremiah laid the foundation of Judaism, Christianity, and eventually, Islam. Philosophical foundations were being built concurrently around the world. The manifestation in the west was the idea of freedom, democracy, and truth. The great poets and thinkers of ancient Greece, including Plato, Socrates, and Homer, were changing the consciousness. Something serendipitous was happening at the far corners of the world in uniformity.

Determinist philosophy would have us believe that this was no accident. According to Belgian cell biologist and Nobel Prize winner Christian de Duve, "Those who claim that life is a highly improbable event, possibly unique, have not looked closely at the chemical realities underlying the origin of life." According to de Duve, this means that the mind of the human being was inevitable from the beginning of creation. Stanford University professor Ian Morris has been quoted as saying, "The agency of individuals actually matters less than historians tend to assume." This "big history" argument discounts the traditional thought that history is just a collection of biographies. In fact, de Duve and Morris would argue that individuals are the least likely to shape history. The approximate arc of history is due largely to biology and geography. When we think of the traditional tale of linear history, we think about the benchmarks that have led us to the present day. Moving forward on the historical timeline from the Axial Age, we would encounter the students of the Greeks, the Romans, promulgating their mighty empire. The Gregorian calendar, as we now know it, was retroactively adopted around AD 800. The rise of Christianity as the preeminent force of Western thought lasted until the seventeenth century. The long period of the Middle Ages logged very few benchmarks that we associate with our modern culture. The printing press in the fifteenth century was one of the very few documentable demarcations of progress, which bridged the Middle Ages with the Enlightenment via the Renaissance. Not until the time of Francis Bacon with the birth of empiricism and the scientific method would the world fundamentally change. The Enlightenment made it acceptable to disassociate progress from the divine. Science gave us the Industrial Revolution.

In his book *Why the West Rules-For Now*, Ian Morris depicts the very slow anthropologic graph of human history represented by what he calls social development. He defines this by "a group's ability to master its physical and intellectual environment to get things done." In Morris's opinion, social development was painfully slow throughout almost all of human history. Prior to the Enlightenment, most humans would not have noticed any particular progress in their life for hundreds or perhaps thousands of years. Not until well into the Industrial Revolution and into the twentieth century does the spike of social development begin. In other words, we as people have just recently began to progress at any measurable speed. Technology, it turns out, is the arbiter of the tale of human history, and biology is its blueprint. As *Wired Magazine* cofounder Kevin Kelly chronicles in his book *What Technology Wants*, the story of human progress is simply one of technology. This technology is, quite literally, a biological evolutionary process, which begins from the creation of the earth as de Duve suggests. Every invention requires its predecessor invention to be created. There could be no combustible engine without the steam engine. We laud the great inventors as geniuses, which they rightly are, but for every great idea there is a precursor. Sir Isaac Newton said, "If I have been able to see further than others, it is because I have stood on the shoulders of giants." Even the great Newton, who pioneered mechanics during the Enlightenment, would have been assuredly replaced in his field had he been born a few years later. It is by no accident that the great ideas of the Axial Age developed when and how they did. If the mediums were not the Buddha or Plato, they would have been someone else with very compatible ideas.

Kelly talks about the convergent forces in nature that complement the understanding of our greatest evolutionary biologists. Animals evolved in disparate global locations in very similar patterns. The reason was always adaptation for their characteristics to serve a purpose based on their needs. Chameleons changed color just as humans required less hair and smaller teeth with the discovery of fire. There is a cosmic order, which must be met for any type of evolution. The hierarchy suggests that humans must tame fire before to write poetry. Homer could not have come along .eenth century because someone would have served in ace in western culture. His ideas were destined whether he riginal purveyor or not. This is what Morris means by the rela.. ınimportance of any one individual in history. This theory dissolves in the twentieth century, where one person may have access to nuclear weapons. That coincided with the great inflection point in human history.

Morris claims that the only real transformation that humans have ever seen began with the perfection of the steam engine by James Watts. Watts may be the hero in this narrative, but as Kelly describes, most great ideas occurred nearly simultaneously, many times in different parts of the world throughout history. The steam engine may be the most important invention of all time because it spurred the Industrial Revolution and exponential social development. Columbia University sociologists William Ogburn and Dorothy Thomas in their studies have attributed four individuals "exclusive" ownership of the invention of the steamboat. Many other contemporaries observed the sun spots at the time of Galileo. Alfred Russel Wallace simultaneously developed ideas about natural selection and evolution at the time of Charles Darwin. The same narrative occurred regarding the discovery of photography, medicines, and even the telephone. The convergence of technology was destined by a time and place. Technology, it turns out, was the conduit of the human experience.

This "big history" perspective offends a lot of historians and academics who not only believe that this perspective undermines their specialization but also negates the freewill of humanity. Determinism only works from the big-picture perspective. Freewill and determinism are not mutually exclusive when viewed through this lens. Determinism suggests that certain ideas and events occur on a sliding scale. Inevitable are the building blocks that lead to certain demarcations of progress. In Kelly's opinion, if we were to "rewind the tape" of the history on earth and replay it, many of the details would change because of freewill, but because the effects of man have been very negligible prior to the last two hundred years, history would wind up at a very similar position. Technology would be approximately where it is now, and technology is the true driver of real and lasting change on earth.

Technology is a system bigger than any one human. For reasons as disparate as colonialism, better raw materials, individualism, and the adoption of capitalism and finance, progress in the developed western world skyrocketed in the twentieth century. The twentieth century in the United States would eventually become synonymous with the rise of the worldwide automobile industry, yet the extrapolation of previous transportation methods would never have predicted this outcome. The horse, the beast of burden of western lore, was suddenly replaced by the automobile. Disruptive innovation has consistently been the story of life on earth. As Peter H. Diamandis and Steven Kotler explain in their book *Abundance*, "If I pluck all the oranges from the lower branches, I am effectively out of accessible fruit. From my limited perspective, oranges are now scarce. But once someone invents a piece of technology called a ladder, I've suddenly got new reach. Problem solved. Technology is a resource liberating mechanism. It can make the once scarce now abundant."

The twentieth century in America was a collision of fortuitous time and place. It was a large isolated land, mostly free from the atrocities and occupations of the world wars on its soil. It attracted the brightest minds from across the world eager to thrive in science, art, and education. It constantly was expanding and building. The educational opportunities were the preeminent of the world. When Apollo 11 landed on the moon in 1969, little did anyone know that historical and unfettered growth of decades was slowing. The third wave of economics was beginning, according to futurologist Alvin Toffler. The agrarian society was slow and arduous and lasted tens of thousands of years. The Industrial Age, not yet two hundred years old, was winding down. We had entered the post-industrial world. Intel cofounder Gordon Moore introduced a theory in 1965, which was eerily accurate and has been used as a metaphor for exponential progress in the post-industrialized world. Moore hypothesized that the transistors on a circuit would double every two years. This theory turned law is still a staple of the tech industry today and is predicted to continue for some time.

In other words, according to Diamandis and Kotler, "Over the past 150,000 years, *Homo Sapiens* evolved in a world that was 'local and linear,' but today's environment is 'global and exponential.'" When the inflection point occurred, which Morris documented just prior to the twentieth century, it never stopped. Google executive chairman Eric Schmidt estimates that the human race is producing as much information in a matter of days as we did from the beginning of time until 2003. In his book *The New Digital Age*, Schmidt says, "By 2025, the majority of the world's population will, in one generation, have gone from having virtually no access to unfiltered information to accessing all of the world's information through a device that fits in the palm of their hand." Even as the Industrial Revolution raged on in the nineteenth century, many American settlers were self-sufficient, entrepreneurial, or a combination of both. Today, most are neither.

Scientific management changed the trajectory of work in the world and especially in the United States. The first decades of the twentieth century coincided with the birth of the automobile and a new division of labor that perfected standardization and specialization. The loose configuration of the working world applied science to productivity. It was determined that "switch tasking" was inefficient, so the tedious repetition of the factory was the new normal. The engineers and the laborers multiplied, and the artisans dwindled. By the midcentury, William H. Whyte Jr. had penned *The Organization Man*, which sneered at the increasing purveyance of collectivism and corporatism. He examined the monotone aura of the suburbs. He feared the ruin of the liberal arts education for the compliance of the assembly line. He queried even the great Descartes himself for attempting to quantify the human condition. The science and structure of culture offended him. From the same frustration at roughly the same time sprung rock and roll. America was once again changing.

Science became pervasive, but the fields of anthropology, sociology, and psychology were still relatively in their infancy in the late nineteenth century to the early twentieth century. Statistics had existed in theory for thousands of years. During the Enlightenment, it was used to count the stars. In the nineteenth century, it was used to infer populations. By the twentieth century, statistics became a discipline and a main component to the rise of the social sciences. This new form of measurement, with principles being taught around the world, crept out of the physical and life sciences and into the mainstream. Political science and business could gain new insights. Suddenly, statistical significance understood that an event was unlikely to occur due to chance alone. We learned random sampling, normal distributions, mean, median, modes, sampling errors, design of experiments—essentially all the components that may infer cause and effect and correlation, as well as our confidence in that assessment. The controlled and random began to give us insights that the pre twentieth century never could. Productivity was extrapolated in new ways. These principles let Margaret Meade extract science about what it was like to come of age in Samoa in the 1920s, it informed the ad men of 1950s Madison Avenue and allowed Reagan to overcome the largest deficit in presidential history in 1979. Twentieth-century progress was about studying the results to find root cause. It was about dismantling the system into small operational units for maximum efficiency. The social sciences gave us understanding of human behavior, which was never before quantified. Assigning numbers to thoughts, actions, and tendencies of humans was a new phenomenon. It was the rise of the marketers, economists, the behaviorists, and of course, scientific managers, who were pervasive to every industry.

It is by no coincidence that the rise in population meant a rise in innovation. Silicon Valley investors live by the understanding that innovation is a numbers game. One thousand new ideas may constitute one hundred good ones. Ten of these may be considered, and finally, two or three actually implemented. More people lead to more ideas, which lead to more innovation. Our history of immigration in the United States stands to this fact. We sometimes forget that we are a nation of immigrants. This may be the issue that we are the least self-aware of as a nation. The world sees us as the melting pot of the rest of the world, and all too often, we see ourselves as nativists with a common culture. This mixture of ideas throughout history has helped propel us through our toughest times. The immigrant values of hard work, strong social ethics, and personal freedoms has propelled us through centuries, showcasing the greatest experiment in democracy the world had ever seen.

More and diverse has led to specialization without meaning or context. In 1963, Bernard K. Forscher of the Mayo Clinic published an article in *Science Magazine* titled "Chaos in the Brickyard." He spoke of the trend of the dissection of knowledge into such small and useless "bricks" or facts that when it came time to apply those bricks, or to build a metaphorical house, it would come crashing down. We used to focus on constructing grand buildings, but somehow, we became consumed with the bricks. Knowing the intricacies of the bricks did us no good as our end goal was always to build with them. Understanding the bricks was the quest of the twentieth century. We injected quantification into the essence of every problem. Experts controlled the realm, so we had to keep specializing to progress. Social scientists and, especially, historians began to dig deeper into quantitative meaning. Edmund Burke has been quoted as saying, "Those who do not understand history are doomed to repeat it." Twentieth-century novelist Kurt Vonnegut said, "We're doomed to repeat it no matter what. That's what it is to be alive."

In the 2006 movie *Little Miss Sunshine*, Steve Carrell played brooding uncle Frank Ginsberg, who happened to be the foremost authority and scholar on Marcel Proust, the early twentieth-century French novelist. One hundred years prior, Carrell's character may have been a famous historian or critic. He may have been an expert on writers, novelists, or even French literature. Modern-day Frank was not even an expert in Victorian culture at large but of Proust, who wrote one, albeit very large and multi-volume, work. The life and times of Proust may very well be interesting, and Frank's ability to teach and deconstruct his work may be at the very heart of critical thinking and cultural awareness in which academia can offer. Tragically and comically, however, Frank has dedicated his life to Proust, only to have his lover stolen by his rival Proust scholar. Dr.

Forscher would ask Frank to stop and look for application, if not for himself, for the sake of his students. In other words, if the works of Proust justify the investment of a lifetime, his accomplishments and ideas should move us forward even today.

History is inextricably woven into the humanities and the social sciences. Every subject asks us to understand the roots of knowledge, especially when those subjects revolve heavily around people. To truly understand Proust, one would have to know what it was like to grow up in France as the Jewish son of a pathologist and the importance of his mother's Catholicism and how it had shaped his life. You would need to know what it was like to live a life in poor health and great wealth and to never have had a job. Maybe Frank would argue that one of these very general characteristics define the real Marcel Proust. Perhaps his nemesis and competitor, the second foremost authority on Proust, would argue that another characteristic was pivotal to gaining insight to the real man. It was a *system* that formed the ideas of Marcel Proust. It was a unique life, with unique circumstances in a unique place. Do two very nuanced and hypothetical accounts of a fairly obscure long-form novelist who died in Paris a hundred years ago matter to world history? His masterpiece *In Search of Lost Time* was 4,215 pages long yet will not be mentioned in most western civilization textbooks. Art moves the person; the communication of art moves the culture. Even the historian is subject to bias. Two historians reviewing the exact same documents of Christopher Columbus may illustrate two very different people. Walt Whitman once wrote, "Do I contradict myself, very well then I contradict myself" (I am large, I contain multitudes). History is a lens as biased as the purveyor of the original happening. History as a discipline is a method to understand the complex realities of another time and place. The history of transportation is an interesting story. The application of the history of transportation measures significance.

History can be told in many ways. We can examine the history of religion, morals, architecture or fashion. The *Economist* editor Tom Standage tells the history of beverage in his book *A History of the World in 6 Glasses*. Through the prism of drink, the history of the world can be told. Beer was once important because it added the all-important calorie and was more likely to kill deadly bacteria than water alone. The availability of coffee and tea served the same purpose yet injected caffeine into society. The coffeehouses of the Enlightenment are credited with the reinstatement of political, philosophical, and scientific conversations unseen since the great gatherings of the Greek Agoras. If water is essential to life, understanding how we have cleaned, mutated, and added to our beverages over thousands of years is interesting and provocative. The sixth glass is Coca-Cola, symbolizing the complexity of the modern beverage and the very idea of branding itself. Yet despite the eloquence of Standage's argument, glasses of liquid do not accurately represent history nor do they point us in a direction ahead.

The idea of big history is an interdisciplinary attempt to inject truth and significance into the history of the universe. Scientists tell us that the world existed long before humans. Replication is the essential history of life as we know it. Evolution occurs when life communicates a need. This was the beginning of information technology. Stardust at the beginning of time wanted to be heard and replicated. A system developed slowly for those possibilities. The biological system that evolved more than any other was modern man. Paleolithic people scratched the walls of caves. Thousands of years later, objects turned into symbols and grunts turned into letters until alphabets were formed. The purpose of language was as biological as evolution. Man wanted to communicate and could only use the body and the voice as the transmitter. The same coding and the decoding principles were used for life to replicate for billions of years. Big history understands man's historical unimportance and present dominance. In this case, all history is biology.

For progress to succeed requires documentation, communication, and replication. Even in ancient Greece, documentation occurred mostly in the mind. Socrates felt that writing was a shortcut to true knowledge. Contemplative understanding was the key to knowledge, yet oral traditions have a tendency to evolve in their own right. The ancient world of Greece found ways to communicate quickly over long distances. As historian James Gleick points out in his book *The Information: A History, A Theory, A Flood* as early as twelfth century BC, fire was used to signal messages across mountain-tops. The carrier pigeon was the quickest and most efficient form of communication for thousands of years. *The Talking Drums of Africa* documented in the 1949 book by John Harrington told of the many miles that the sound of a drum can travel, which can be relayed from village to village. The skill of the drummer could actually replicate the human voice and essentially speak the language.

If technology ultimately leads to progress, information informs technology, and information spreads only through communication. In 1790s France, Claude Chappe designed the first telecommunication system, known today as a semaphore system. These were a system of towers, which relayed messages based on the codes of the position of the regulator on top. A half a century later, Morse code allowed the transmission of messages electronically via a telegraph in seconds. Another half of a century later, the world had ten million telephone users. Suddenly, the world was connected. The Industrial Revolution finally allowed mankind to do what it never could before, replicate exponentially. Lifespans and populations skyrocketed. Productivity levels were unforeseen. The new availability of communication had finally let information replicate. The world had finally changed. We had become modernized.

That period of modernization began during the first ideas of the Industrial Revolution. It would take a hundred more to organize and develop these ideas, products, and processes into measurable productivity. That is the inflection point of which Morris speaks. We were making shoes, cars, and radios. We were building skyscrapers, bridges, and highways. The twentieth century, the only century in the history of mankind to ever achieve exponential progress, was owned by America. Alexis de Tocqueville, perhaps the most astute outside observer of American life, certainly before 1900, published the final edition of *Democracy in America* in 1840. He saw the American people as a radical balance of individual freedom seekers with an understanding that only through the virtues of collectivism may tyranny be fought. The aristocracy and inequality woven into the fabric of old-world Europe did not motivate the rich or the poor. In America, your station in life could be determined by your work ethic.

Hard work is in our collective unconscious as a nation. We spent close to seventy hours a week working in the early nineteenth century. This dropped to the low sixties by the Civil War. During the 1920s, because of factors including better working conditions, less child labor, labor union rights, and overtime pay, the average work week dropped to forty-eight hours. By the end of World War II, we had settled at a forty-hour work week, which is still considered the norm today. The engine of economics is productivity. Technology had made it possible to complete more work in less time. No nation had ever been as productive or as profitable as the United States in the twentieth century. We ended the Gilded Age of the late nineteenth century and began making progressive reforms. Thirteen-year-olds no longer worked side by side with grown men in factories. The high school graduation rate in 1900 was 6 percent. It peaked at 85 percent one hundred years later. We put the kids in school and brought the (mostly) men to work.

By midcentury, the world wars were behind us, and the progress of the Industrial Revolution was still rising. Labor union rights had been introduced, social safety nets in place, and market subsidization for farming. State and federal sponsorship of education and government infrastructure projects were expanding. The highest tax bracket was 90 percent under Eisenhower, a Republican president. Jobs were abundant, low-skilled, and relatively high-paid. The 1950s are remembered nostalgically as the golden age of capitalism, when in fact, it was the closest to socialism that we have ever gotten. It worked because of the collectivist mind-set of the postwar years. In the 1960s, we built the "great society" to combat the racial injustices that the 1950s never examined. Medicare and Medicaid were introduced as an entitlement to reduce poverty based on economic models that the rising tide of the American GDP would last indefinitely. By the 1970s the term *stagflation* had entered the American lexicon, and the 1960s model quickly became obsolete.

The fruits of the Industrial Revolution were drying up. America was modernized. Unemployment began to grow, the economy began to slow, and inflation was rising. We had arrived with no immediate direction forward. The 1960s began with John F. Kennedy proclaiming that we would land on the moon before the end of the decade. Apollo 11 landed on the surface one month before hundreds of thousands of people flooded to a small town in upstate New York for the Woodstock music festival in the summer of 1969. Just months later, Futurist Alvin Toffler published a bestselling book titled *Future Shock*, which was the first to prepare Americans for the coming post-industrialist society. He warned that the entire economy would change. It was inevitable that mass production would kill jobs and create a disposable mind-set. We had just organized our society during the last and most productive years of the Industrial Revolution. The change prophesized from our rock and roll gods was coming true.

Thomas Hobbes once wrote that throughout most of history, men live on gross experience alone. He said, "Life was nasty, brutish, and short . . . There was no method: that is to say, no sowing or planting of knowledge by itself apart from the weeds and common plants of error and conjecture." We had finally organized our innovation in such a way that we took all that hardship for granted. In *People of Plenty*, David Potter wrote, "Affluence has shaped the American character." Since the time of de Tocqueville, we believed that the future will be better than the past. It was the American birthright to believe that the value of hard work will suffice, and it did for two hundred years. It was not until the 1980s that we understood that our entitlements, for now and the future, would not evolve under the current structure. The Reagan Revolution fundamentally changed our view of the world.

Deregulation changed the way we think about finance. The trickery that we attributed to the 2008 crash was still in its infancy. Former Labor secretary Robert Reich exclaimed, "In the 1970s, finance was a servant to the American economy." By the 1980s, it had become its master. Neoliberalism opened up trade and began to deteriorate the American manufacturing sphere. Americans began to demand cheap goods only possible by importation. Taxes were lowered to spur the economy. The United States began to cut entitlements and run up deficits. America had become a risk-adverse mature enterprise. Investment in the future had subsided. The idea of government as a partner had changed to government as pest.

Materialism and individualism had faded the postwar social ethic. Scientific management was applied from the absent manufacturing floor to the entire company. This wave of innovation was efficiency, wherever it would lead. It was the age of buyouts, mergers, and takeovers. The rise of the MBA was the savior for the American economy and the scapegoat for the labor force.

Capitalism lifted us out of poverty. Carefully cultivating the gardens of capitalism formed the middle class. The experiment in democracy in the United States and the life cycle of the Industrial Revolution introduced the phenomenon of middle-class origin. In all the organizational methods of finance throughout history, only through this cross section of freedom and economic manipulation did we build the very artificial idea of the middle class. French economist Thomas Piketty released his book *Capital* in 2014 arguing that the present configuration of capitalism is destined to lead to more inequality and less social mobility. His main contention was that the rate of return on wealth is greater than the growth of the economy. He fears that the feudalism which Americans had escaped in favor of the meritocracy, which de Tocqueville witnessed nearly two hundred years ago may creep permanently into our culture. There is an intuitive understanding by the young that political power is not within reach for them. In other generations, it would have manifested in revolution or cynicism. The virtue of the future was to keep the focus on what can be controlled, which is the development and education of our future population and workforce.

The founding father of modern-day economics, Adam Smith, knew that specialization of skills would lead to less well-rounded workers, but it was the price for progress in the meantime. For most of the twentieth century, we asked workers to do one thing well in return for a paycheck. The considerably more leisure time could be spent in other pursuits. The mundane factory jobs of the mid-century, including overtime, may have paid over $100,000 in today's dollars, including overtime. The mundane work of today, which may include stocking shelves in retail, may pay less than $20,000 annually. Were we wrong to artificially inflate the value of the factory worker, or are we drastically underpaying the fast food and service economy workers of the present? Generally, neither have the skills to drive productivity, yet we have romanticized the former. From that barometer, we have formed our idea of entitlement. Not just from what the government owes us but from what a job owes us. Unfortunately, the structure of the middle class, bred of mediocrity by a century of the division of labor, is our only source of reference.

Democratic President Bill Clinton, with the help of a Republican Congress, momentarily sent our deficits into surplus. The Internet kept productivity rising into the 1990s. The dotcom bust, and the terrorist attacks on 9/11 reinstituted a malaise not seen since the 1970s. The country was broke and fighting wars on two fronts. Meanwhile, at home, we built a large new government agency called Homeland Security; we instituted new entitlements for pre-scription drugs called Medicare part D, all the while lowering taxes. Deregulation, borrowing, and financial trickery were used to main-tain the illusion that nothing had changed. Consumerism was lauded as patriotism. We were piling up debt and losing control. Economist Thomas Friedman has called this decade the Terrible Twos. By 2008, the economy collapsed due to hollow mortgage-backed securities. The system was out of control.

To recover from the Great Recession that followed required large and controversial federal bailouts. Unemployment rose, and world financial confidence in the United States fell. The recession was government malfeasance and inability to lead the American peo-ple to a more prudent reality. It was a rational economic outcome of policy neglect for over a decade. President Barrack Obama inherited the worst financial situation in eight decades. The deck was stacked against him for two reasons. First, the enormous debt, which was quickly accumulated over the beginning of his presidency, would be immediately attributed to him, and secondly, the economy that he would try to restore to good standing had been artificial for a decade, if not possibly four. When a recession hits, the jobs that are killed never come back. The 2000s were a fiscal Indian summer based on a lie. Instead of contemplating financial trickeries to reclaim past glories, what was needed was a clear path forward.

Innovation has always been the avenue to progress and the accelerator to productivity at large. Although we mistake innovation as an idea that strikes us out of individualism and isolation, history has taught us that it is a lot closer to a team sport. The philosophy of western thought was created in the center of the Greek city-state, the agora, through the transfer of ideas. Many of those ideas were lost when the great Library of Alexandria was burned in AD 391. They were revived in the coffeehouses of the Enlightenment, eventually propelling the Industrial Revolution forward. The telephone was as instantaneous and as ubiquitous of a communication method that we had until well into the 1990s. Around that time, the telephone line doubled as an analog connection to a new invention in the lexicon called the Internet. Soon the telephone companies perfected a digital signal frequency to share the copper spectrum of the telephone line. Internet speeds increased, and Internet access was suddenly a staple at home and at work. Wireless technologies and smartphone advances gave us portable access, anywhere and always.

In less than a decade, we had restructured the way that humans had communicated for a hundred years. Social media made us rethink the way we view networks. Connection to people and ideas was easier than ever. This mass rearrangement of communication is still in its infancy. We are in the same position as Claude Chappe, Samuel Morse, or Alexander Graham Bell at the dawn of their inventions. Most of the world still remembers a time before the digital revolution. Soon many more of us on earth will not. We will remember, however, the next scientific breakthrough, which follows a very strict set of laws innate in the universe. We, as humans, are just along for the ride. We are simply the executors of the will of our biologic nature. The permutations of the possibilities of human progress are ever expanding. In 2009, Google CEO Eric Schmidt met state department representative Jared Cohen in Baghdad. Schmidt was there, researching the opportunities for technology in the new Iraq. They found a land decimated by war. Food, water, and electricity remained scarce, yet Schmidt and Cohen were surprised to see the ubiquity of cellphone usage by the population. Sadam Hussein had outlawed this technology years earlier. The exponential progress of the digital world was hidden to the Iraqi people. Schmidt had remarked that instead of spending close to a trillion dollars on regime change, "What we should have done is laid down fiber optic cable and built out a wireless infrastructure to empower the Iraqi citizens." Communication, collaboration, and new opportunities for the distribution of ideas and technologies are the most powerful force in the world.

In 1894, there was a crisis from New York City to Sydney, Australia. Tens of thousands of horses traversed the cities on any one single day. The horseshoes on the cobblestones would have been loud, the fresh manure would have been piled up, and the dry manure would have turned to dust and blown through the air. Dead horses lay for days in the street. Accidents were commonplace with high mortality rates. The systematic effect of providing for such a large number of large animals decimated farming practices. Populations were growing also. No one predicted the rise of the automobile. Over four thousand cars were sold in the United States in 1900 and eighty times that amount in 1912. Henry Ford democratized the availability of the automobile by the scientific advancements of manufacturing. The disruptive technology of the automobile changed the world. New York City of the 1920s would have been significantly cleaner, healthier, and safer than New York City of the 1890s, resulting from a technology that did not exist a short time prior.

That is the history of innovation. That has been the power of human capability time and time again. The beginning of the twenty-first century has arrived at a similar turning point. Prior to the year 2000, just a small fraction of the world's information had been digitized. After roughly the year 2000, almost all of it has. As Eric Schmidt surmised, we now create as much information in two days as we did from the dawn of civilization to the year 2003. That same amount of data will soon be collected in matter of hours and, eventually, minutes. As of yet we are still in the infancy of the potential of all that information. The perfection of the steam engine in 1775 may have been the most important invention of the Industrial Revolution, but the eventual ramifications of that power would not be known for decades. Yet here we are, just two decades removed from delivering digital potential to people's homes and just one decade out from delivering digital connection to people's fingertips.

Complete digital connection has already changed the world. The great infrastructure project of communication began on March 10, 1876, when Alexander Graham Bell made the first phone call, instructing "Mr. Watson, come here, I want to see you." The evolution of our communication systems mirrored the progress of technology in general throughout history, the inflection point coming near the beginning of the twentieth century with the invention and distribution of the telephone line system. Transcontinental to Transatlantic, vacuum tube to coax to T1 to fiber optic were the delivery methods as telephones themselves went from candlestick to rotary to cordless. All these modest improvements were added to the communications infrastructure throughout the twentieth century, but its functionality remained essentially the same. Services were provided in an analog fashion through a switch at a central office. Its next phase will be software defined, instantaneous, and automatic.

Totalitarian regimes like Iraq under Sadam Hussein, the Soviet Union under Joseph Stalin, and North Korea under Kim Jong Il are the very opposite of global. What they have in common is a very centralized organization of control. Technology and communication undermined their power. The Internet is the most decentralized invention ever created. What the modern world has known for some time is that too much centralization can be dangerous. As Steven Johnson recounts in *Future Perfect*, Paris was, of course, the center of French culture and government in the mid-nineteenth century. Anywhere in France, literally, all roads led to Paris. The rail system was like a spoke of straight lines jettisoning from the center of Paris. This design was known as Legrand's Star to allow easy access into the city from anywhere. When the Franco–Prussian War began, one fell swoop of track removal isolated the French troops. Meanwhile the decentralized rail system of Germany proved highly favorable and more agile for troop movement that led to victory.

DSL and, quickly, VDSL delivered to residences changed the amount of information that customers were consuming digitally. The proliferation of cellphone usage and the data required by these devices shortly followed. The analog network of the telephone lines is akin to the German rail system of the time. Trunk lines connect the various central offices where the switch assigns them to their local loop. Greater investment in IP infrastructure via fiber optics lines and wireless technologies are allowing the evolution of distribution from the fragile Legrand Star model with one center to the decentralized version of the central office and now to a fully distributed network identical to the Internet itself. Imagine the changes as a group of Legrand Stars connected by a main trunk compared to a lattice model of communication where all directions are possible. The metaphor of the evolution of the telephone line closely follows the same trajectory of technology since the beginning of the twentieth century. The demise of spoke and hub networking will mirror the road to bankruptcy, as described by Hemingway, "gradually and then suddenly."

These new possibilities are what Thomas Friedman identified in his 2005 work *The World is Flat*, which defined globalization in the modern world. He describes "work flow software" as being important in the coming reality of machine to machine communication. As more and more products are made to connect to the Internet and more people are uploading more data, more storage space and faster speeds will be required by the data providers. In less than a decade, the Internet has transformed from a passive form of entertainment and learning to a collaborative and interactive medium. Social media has raised participation and increased communication speeds exponentially. We now have the ability to create, connect, and target broadcasts to all our connections online. Our identities are increasingly tied to our digital consumption and ability to share.

We have always relied on disruptive technologies to change economies. In many ways, Mexico is a very cosmopolitan and civilized country. In other ways, the infrastructure is reminiscent of developing country standards. Jalisco, Mexico, is a vibrant state where one could also visit the tourist destination of Puerto Vallarta or the iconic industrial town of Tequila. It is also the home of Guadalajara, the second largest metropolitan area in the country with over four million people. It is about the size and climate of San Diego, California. On any one day, you will see trucks traversing the streets selling twenty-liter water bottles to people's homes. The water on tap is not safe to drink, nor for cooking. Most kitchens are equipped with a stand for the water, much like you would see in a water cooler at the office. Mexico, in fact, drinks more bottled water per capita than any other in the world. When it rains, the streets become nearly impassable as the drainage systems cannot handle a heavy downpour. This is the reality of the infrastructure of emerging markets.

The major US cities mostly solved these problems many years ago. Now there are opportunities for these markets to attack these problems anew with the rise of digital technologies. Bangladesh, one of the poorest countries in the world, had added $650 million to their GDP even by 2006 with the emergence of the cellphone. Peter Diamandis and Steven Kotler explain in their book *Abundance* how everything from energy, healthcare, education, and freedom will become more abundant, specifically to the developing world that still live in relative poverty. Scarcity was at the core of economics for most of history. The exponential nature of digital technologies makes scarcity increasingly obsolete. As Diamandis and Kotler say, "Goods and services once reserved for the wealthy few are now available to anyone equipped with a cell phone." The world is truly flat, connected, and increasingly available to all. Technology has brought a new optimism to the possibilities of progress. The trajectory of history is one that understands that progress is linear as a function of technology. Technology gives opportunity to the individual; however, the individual must be ready to take a stand for technology in the name of progress.

CHAPTER 5

ECONOMICS AND ABUNDANCE

The American spirit has always been an egalitarian dream infused with the notion of rugged individualism. The same year that Adam Smith published *The Wealth of* Nations, America declared its independence. Three years prior, a revolt in Boston Harbor destroyed an entire shipment of tea from the British East India Company, which had established an unrecognizable organization called an international corporation. The large shipments from the powerful company were dwarfing the supply from American companies. At this time, the understanding of economics was still tangible and local. Society was still developed around the idea that what was grown and what was produced was not tied to a complex system of global finance and trade. The artisan and the farmer could acquire the most abundant resource in the new world, the land, and work hard to provide for a family. Small business was the only business. Over the next century, the progress of the Industrial Revolution changed the way Americans viewed the next iteration of capitalism. By the gilded age of the late nineteenth century, the labor movement surfaced, sometimes violently, to combat child labor, long work days, and unsafe work environments. In 1906, Upton Sinclair published *The Jungle,* which documented the plight of the modern immigrant factory worker, as well as the unsanitary conditions that existed. Many saw it as an indictment of a new and different version of capitalism. The noble farmer, artisan, and small businessman were now drawn into the factory life to make a living. Five years later, Fredrick Winslow Taylor published *The Principles of Scientific Management.* The new distribution of labor, now fully industrial, called for a new understanding of finances and efficiency. Small business was inevitably becoming big business.

The entrepreneurial spirit ingrained in the ethos of the American Dream wavered. The independence of the vast American landscapes of Jefferson's visions now required mass production. The moral superiority of self-sufficiency in the wilderness became dependency of low-wage jobs in urban areas. The founding fathers' fear of America being introduced to the urbanism of the old world was coming true. Horatio Alger wrote a series of books in the late nineteenth century specifically targeted to young men. Alger's characters relentlessly propagated the belief that through hard work alone opportunities will arise to lift the character out of poverty and into the comfort and security of the higher class. By the Great Depression, the Horatio Alger legacy had been relegated to myth. Truth in one economy was propaganda in another. Following the unregulated Roaring Twenties and the stock market crash of 1929, economics was again reexamined. Economist John Maynard Keynes wrote *The General Theory of Employment, Interest, and Money* in 1936. The "invisible hand" of Smith's classical economics was failing, he claimed. The perfect equilibrium dogma of unfettered capitalism had become inefficient for progress. The new complicated realities of macroeconomics required public sector intervention. So began the midcentury's private and public relationship of putting America back to work. Franklin Delano Roosevelt had already issued the first New Deal and the second New Deal, no doubt propelled by the new Keynesian idea of economics, fractured the country into the very modern idea of Liberal versus Conservative by the end of the 1930s.

The middle of the twentieth century in America found Detroit as the beacon of the western world. It was the center of art and commerce by offering middle-class jobs in abundance. The American economy was propelled by the headquarters of the automobile industry. General Motors was the world's largest employer. Adjusted in today's dollars, the average worker earned $35 per hour. Around this time, economist Friedrich Hayek wrote *The Road to Serfdom*, where he argued for the continuity of liberal conviction similar to the Boston Tea Party. Hayek sought to reclaim the idea of classic economics, which was lost after the Great Depression in the United States. It was in direct contradiction of Keynesian economics, which dispelled the notion that equilibrium was only possibly by government control and focus on demand. The state of affairs, which required freedom against the burden of the multinational conglomerate in the late eighteenth century was seeing a rebirth. This time, however, the illiberal institution was our own government, which was hindering the perfect and efficient machine of classical economics. Eventually, the method that propelled the United States out of the Great Depression was subjugating individual freedom. By 1960, Hayek had penned the reasoning why he did not consider himself a Conservative even though he had been the key intellectual against the Keynes Liberal ethic, which dominated economic policy for forty years.

Hayek's ideas were original, but they were not American until Milton Friedman wrote *Neoliberalism and its Prospects* in 1951. In conjunction with the demand side, economics failing to bring the prosperity it once had in what came to be a post-industrial economy of the 1970s, a period of stagnation and inflation set in. Stagflation, as it was called, was resistant to Keynesian economics, which at one time had been responsible for the most robust economy ever seen. In response to fascism and communism, decades of describing demand side economics as serfdom, and in reaction to a faltering economy, both the political right and left began to accept the messages of the neoliberal economists. Federal Reserve chairman Paul Volker ended the long adherence to demand by raising interest rates peaking at 20 percent by 1981. Manufacturing output and income were immediately and substantially reduced, but unemployment rose above 11 percent. Inflation had finally been tamed, however, the long-standing idea that being employed was more important than higher interest had met its philosophical challenger. The neoliberal rhetoric of a new version of individual freedom did, in fact, spawn a wave of democracy around the world. Debt, however, would be its global consequence. A host of neoliberal policy, now championed by the right and the left under Ronald Reagan, would set the economic tone for the next three decades.

The discipline of economics itself was quite literally built from the philosophical discipline of ethics. Aristotle contemplated the tension of public versus private ownership, and Thomas Aquinas in the thirteenth century sought the ethics of economics as "fair pricing." By the sixteenth century, French philosopher Jean Bodin became concerned with the economics of inflation. David Hume discussed economics in 1739 in *A Treatise of Human Nature*, stating "Where riches are engrossed by a few, these must contribute largely to the supply of public necessities." Adam Smith himself, a moral philosopher, spawned the understanding of modern economics, which outlined the constructs of the Industrial Revolution and the neoliberal resurgence. Aristotle had begun the idea of the natural law of economics by stating that self-interest is the primary human motivator. In perhaps his famous line from his most famous work, *The Wealth of Nations*, Smith says, "It is not the benevolence of the butcher, the brewer, or the baker, that we expect our dinner, but from their regard to their own interest. We address ourselves, not to their humanity but to their self-love." Self-interest itself was the major motivator for the shared interest of strong economics.

Midcentury America, amid decades of demand-side Keynesian ideas, mutual support to rise from the economic disaster of the Great Depression, the tragedy of a world war, and a collectivist nature that still strived for shared progress was losing momentum to an individualistic world. Novelist Ayn Rand espoused the idea of "objectivism" or rational self-interest, economically quantified through the prism of neoliberal laissez-faire capitalism. Rand's philosophies marked a turning point into a new cultural era. She had established that the modern world, which saw a grand narrative and an economic model to follow, was in its final stages. Heroism, to Rand, was no longer clinging to an artificial role at the behest of society but seeking what is best for the individual. There was no better messenger of individual achievement as a noble endeavor than Rand. While the economists like Hayek and Friedman were busy updating models to fit a new economy, Rand was arguing the new ethics of identity, which would shape culture at large based on economics. She used Aristotle's rational self-interest as a universal truth. She believed that once humanity came to see the objective understanding of the subjective nature of mankind, economics, which had always organized around scarcity, would fundamentally change it. Decades of economic policy, which acquiesced to the public's demand, was turned back to the favor of the suppliers. According to the neoliberals, focusing on demand was a disruption to the machinery of laissez-faire capitalism as well an infringement on the freedom for those who wanted to offer goods and services on the free market.

Classical economics operated under the assumption of Say's Law, based on the early nineteenth century economist Jean-Baptiste Say, who said, "Supply creates its own demand." The middle third of the United States economic policy in the twentieth century rejected that notion. By the 1980s a reorganized economy began a return to the prescription of Say's law. This time, removing the barriers to the producers of supply, as was the argument for classical liberal economic freedom for centuries, was not the only purpose. Economists began to espouse the idea of "trickle-down economics," whereby lowering barriers to suppliers in terms of trade, taxes, and regulation would provide better demand in terms of lower pricing, taxes, and more jobs to those who were not the suppliers of the economy. The narrative had transformed from neoliberalism as a freedom for the supply-side of the economy to a freedom on the demand-side of the economy. Lower prices equaled lower taxes and lower wages. John F. Kennedy had cut taxes drastically, which raised government revenue substantially. Twenty years later, Ronald Reagan also lowered rates to less than a third of the top marginal rates, which Kennedy had inherited. This too had caused a surplus of government revenue due to the ability of increased spending now capable. The neoliberal ideology had assumed that further tax decreases would do the same. Reagan had room to drastically lower taxes, but instead of shrinking the deficit as projected, he had tripled it by the end of his term.

For the most part, our system of economics has been an ideological cycle that constantly searches for equilibrium in drastically different circumstances. There has been an oscillation over the last eighty years, which had rejected classical economics in the name of Keynesian economics, then neoclassical economics in the place of Keynesian. The values of the next generation will reflect on the contrasting history of our last two ideologies to determine the next iteration of economic policy under their leadership. The logical conclusion would be a neo-Keynesian model in the vein of the Bernie Sanders model of a new "New Deal." As is always necessary when understanding values that will be attributed to the next generation, we must consult history to find clues to the future. On the surface, the Father of Classical Economics, Adam Smith, would tend to be at odds with a neo-Keynesian economy. The strand that connects Smith, Keynes, and the next generation, according to William Dugger, is the optimism of economic abundance. It is true that the reason capitalism works is based on freedom of choice of a finite amount of goods and services. Scarcity from all the needs and wants of the individual can never be alleviated, but it has done a tremendous job curtailing absolute scarcity since the nineteenth century. Because today's youth do not succumb to ideological litmus tests, politics and economics may finally consult pragmatism rather than dogmatism for the first time in decades to find equilibrium.

They will see that the world is alleviating absolute scarcity in the name of relative scarcity. There will be more humane models that bridge the extreme scarcity of the few in the name of extreme abundance of the many, while simultaneously rejecting the artificial equality of socialism, which demands universal averageness. Even 240 years ago, Smith believed in the potential of an economy of abundance through the repetition of specialization and the promise of innovation. Economist Thomas Malthus was a pessimist who modeled population and resources. David Ricardo imagined that a "subsistence state" would stop human progress. Specialization and innovation was a finite resource once the population hit a certain point. Neoclassical economists feared the loss of freedom due to government intervention. In his first inaugural address, Ronald Reagan proclaimed, "Government is not the solution to our problem; government is the problem." Thirty-five years later, the economic bogeyman has been less the government and more economic policy, which has given greater control to business. Still, our youngest generations would not, as a whole, display such declarative statements without examining the solutions. They seek to stake out their own realm, which is pragmatism at its core. It is the optimism always assumed by abundance economists who believe that the allocation of resources should not be based on ideologies but possibilities. Technology has finally made it possible for relative abundance to become a reality.

An abundance mind-set seeks to create the environment for the individual to meet his or her full potential for the better of the individual and the whole. With this philosophy, it must be assumed that economic win/lose scenarios can be replaced and reorganized in the name of win/win possibilities. This includes organizations with new models of information sharing and cooperation where there used to be competition. Nearly one hundred years ago, in a much simpler time, economist Thorstein Veblen said, "Why do we, now and again, have hard times and unemployment in the midst of excellent resources, high efficiency, and plenty of unmet wants?" Since that time, we have developed many more wants, much higher efficiency, and an array of new resources, many of which can be organized, virtually online. In fact, economist Paul Sweezy, in 1966, labeled the Veblenian Nightmare as the human desire for always more abundance. In 1971, psychologist Philip Brickman called it the Hedonic Treadmill. It is a sound belief that because of the exponential nature of the relationship that technology has on standards of living, it leads to a never-ending evolution of wants. The next generation of leaders will not have access to the financial maneuvering that allowed wealth creation through commoditization, privatization, and the one-time capability of the opening of true market globalization. However, efficiency and productivity will have much more complicated formulas that involve not a redistribution of wealth, which is the greatest fear of neoclassical economists, but a redistribution of the capabilities to create wealth, void of ideology or politics.

Keynes spoke of demand deficiency, which has returned as an issue. Nick Hanauer, a self-described plutocrat says, "Inequality is essential for a high functioning capitalist democracy." Yet Hanauer has described the same fear as Keynes is his TED talk that calls for a practical rather than an ideological argument against inequality, which has been drastically rising in the United States since 1980. He has come to the same conclusion that economists such as Joseph Stigletz and Robert Reich have in recent years, which is that the years of trickle-down economics have been great at creating wealth but poor at injecting money back into the economy. Economist Umair Haque answers the question "Why No One Will Implement the Best Solution to Economic Stagnation." He says that the ideology of the classic economist as a rational and eternal model has been so ingrained in our psyche that even common sense approaches to increase middle-class wages, and spending is politically unfeasible. The abundance mind-set has already given us the capabilities of more business opportunity, better education, less crime, less pollution, and better human resources. Denial of abundance contributes to the vicious cycles of inequality manifested through poverty, lack of education, access to health care and nutrition, and negative role models. Sociologist C. Wright Mills identified systematic inequality as a pathological problem as far back as 1943. It remains a line in the sand as to who enters the middle class. Today that lack of access has an effect on the entire economy.

It was apparent that the twentieth century would be the American century. A nation needed to be built. The technology, resources, and the spirit of growth and entrepreneurship met the call. We spent decades building America. For the lightbulb, we built the power grid. For the telephone, we built a communications infrastructure. Advanced systems were constructed to provide water to a house and then just as easily take it away. The invention of the combustible engine replaced the remaining need for horsepower. The history of transportation had suddenly been altered, so we built the roads and bridges. By the mid-twentieth century, we had advanced to connecting it all by the interstate. The growth that took place during the Industrial Revolution was exponential. Steam had allowed man to travel the world by boat or train. It helped the Wild West become tamed, and allowed Mark Twain to sail the Atlantic Ocean fifty-one times. By the beginning of the twentieth century, the rudimentary outlines of our modern conveniences were in place, all that the twentieth century required was for us to build it. In September 1901, Teddy Roosevelt took office after the assassination of William McKinley. He was the young nation's youngest president to that date. His zeal and enthusiasm prophesized a century of progress of which the world had never seen. The midcentury found a new and growing class invented by the explosion of all this productivity. America invented the modern middle class. As long as new and large forms of innovation kept materializing the engine of growth would continue. Once the linear understanding of technological progress was cemented into a way of life, no one imagined that it would ever slow. The stagnation of the 1970s seemed to be just a momentary setback to the trajectory of the American way. By the 1980s, we traded debt to maintain a facade of an era of productivity, which we no longer enjoyed. By the 2000s, we had exhausted the ways to create financial value out of thin air, and we entered the Great Recession in 2008. By August of 2011, Standard and Poor's financial services, one of the "Big Three" credit rating institutions in the world, lowered the United States's rating to AA status. It had been the benchmark of AAA status since 1941. For the better part of forty years, our government and our people have been living as if the once again slow progress of technology was still bringing the same amount of wealth to the country with the same distribution.

For years and decades after the stagflation of the early 1970s, our organizations still provided secure jobs with healthy pensions for retirees. Big government could sustain the waste, entitlements, and bureaucracy that the largest economy in the history of the world provided in the decades after World War II. Once the entitlements of big government have been introduced, they are extremely difficult to eliminate. Americans are an optimistic people. We always believe that the next great economy is just on the horizon. As the words of Tyler Cowen in his book *The Great Stagnation* suggest, "We have been living off of low hanging fruit for at least 300 years . . . Yet during the last forty years that low-hanging fruit started disappearing and we started pretending it was still there." We have stripped the cupboards bare of the Industrial Age. Manufacturing for functionality can surely be done somewhere cheaper and on a larger scale. There was an inverse relationship between innovation and efficiency. The 1970s, 1980s, and 1990s saw an explosion in quality initiatives. Executives with Masters of Business Administration degrees (MBAs) rose up the ranks and invested in the efficiency of operations. Decades prior, in the age of growth, there was little need or time to focus on these measures. As long as the core competency for most organizations was innovation, the strategy of efficiency was counterproductive or moot at best. Once all the fruit had been removed from the trees, as Cowen's analogy suggests, leaders began to cling to what value they could control. Most of the time, that included increased quality and efficiency measures at the expense of innovation and development.

What has remained is the United States as leader of the World's Gross Domestic Product (GDP). Output has been the cornerstone of our economy since anyone alive can remember. Offering services, making things, selling things, and recording the sale has made for a simple mathematical model to record the growth of the economy. This was our perception of the measurement of economics in the twentieth century. It could be that everything we believe about modern economics, which began with Smith and was amended by Keynes, was true within the time capsule of the Industrial Age and is still evolving. Economics lives on, but the definition of wealth, currency, and value has finally begun to change. The discipline of economics, after all, is based on human rational behavior. It makes an assumption that a person, when theoretically offered the same product by the same two people at the same time, will always choose the lowest price. Economics are inevitably linked to the GDP. Economics, however, as we have learned in recent years from social scientist/economics crossovers such as Stephen Dubner and Steven Levitt of *Freakonomics* fame and Dan Arielly of *Predictably Irrational*, can be both freaky and irrational. Every day, we get further away from our comfort zone of the safe arithmetic of the Industrial Age and the scarcity that makes us feel safe and assign meaning and priority to our lives. The digital age does not know scarcity; it only knows abundance, yet our models were developed under the auspicious circumstances of scarcity. The price of much of what we do now is absolutely free, although we may pay in privacy. That is the fundamental change in the next evolution of economics.

In the old-world economy, we would have had to drop a quarter in the slot to be able to access Facebook. It may have been that many of us would drop in coins to access Facebook, but it is not a requirement. The reality is that we are making a choice to access a free service and spend our time there *rather* than spend our money buying and listening to music or going to the movies. Economics are still involved in the modern economy, but the idea of traditional economics has been altered. The quantitative values that we, as a society, still cling to are fading. The things that we hold dear and where we choose to spend our time are no longer reflected in the GDP; they are reflected in the algorithms of our Big Data companies. As Erik Brynjolfsson and Andrew McAfee say in their book *The Second Machine Age*, "The great irony of this information age is that, in many ways, we actually know less about the sources of value in the economy than we did fifty years ago." Stocks and bonds originated at the dawn of the seventeenth century. William Petty soon began to count economies by inventing the easily quantifiable GDP. The idea of land ownership made these ideas more complicated. Today we have to quantify data and experience through irrational power laws such as Chris Anderson's *Long Tail*, which suggests that the sum of everything previously unavailable is greater than the sum of everything that has always been available. In other words, the traditional retail shelves had no space for the eclectic, but the virtual shelf of the Internet is infinite. Value has been dispersed to the previously unquantifiable. Soon, even manufacturing, outsourced and offshored for lower cost, may be insourced to the individual via software and 3-D printing in our own homes.

A generation ago, we still clung to the stalwarts of the old guard. Anheuser-Busch, Southwestern Bell, Kodak, and Chrysler were companies where we went to seek opportunity. The beer and car company giants are no longer American-owned, Kodak lost its edge, and the phone companies have reemerged with an IP-based infrastructure. Google, Cisco, Amazon, and Facebook have become the companies that Americans now identify with as the future. The problem is that they employ very few at a very high skill level. The local and national economies have migrated to an international supply chain of globalism. The factory job still employs widely, just in other more developing parts of the world at lower wages. Throughout the last century, we were programmed to believe that the natural evolution of capitalism would produce to an ever-widening pool of middle-class workers. We based our entire way of life on this idea, even though modern economics is a very recent phenomenon and has absolutely no link to the scientific method. The brand of capitalism, which flourished in the twentieth century in the United States, was magical. The relative protectionism and our manufacturing might propelled us. Our output matched only our consumption. By the twenty-first century, forces of globalization and technology had altered the course of history as we knew it. The writing on the wall, it seems, was invisible ink, legible only to the younger generations, who, curiously, were the only ones to see the contrast.

New evolutions of the same system began lifting new economies. Cheaper prices meant well-paying jobs, which supported families, now done in other countries. Recessions had happened before throughout the century, but living wages were becoming insufficient even with education and full-time employment. Naturally, the all-powerful tide of capitalism would return to provide the jobs we needed. In the last couple of decades before the turn of the last century, we came to realize that real wealth would only be derived from the investor class, or the absolute outliers in sports, business, and entertainment, and middle-class jobs were depleting. Americans are historically optimistic. We always believe that we will make more money next year in real wages, although that very rarely happens anymore. No one believed in 1984 that the net worth for those thirty-five and younger would be four times less now than it was at that time. Futurist Marina Gorbis sees two worlds in the making. They lie on what can be called an incumbent curve and the nascent curve. Every fashion, political, or generational cycle begins in its infancy with a nascent curve. These are the rumblings of disruption that threaten the status quo. The incumbent curve is where the power influencers of the present live. Millennials have almost entirely reached adulthood to realize that they cannot compete in the incumbent world. They do not have the knowledge, experience, or social, or financial capital to make changes by playing by the old rules. The deck is stacked against them. The promise of capitalism shining on those that follow the rules is diminishing. So the youth have sparked the birth of the nascent micro-economies, which will change the world. They are the green economy, the social economy, the sharing economy, the idea economy, to name a few. The entire twentieth century was about the means to drive the price of production toward zero while driving efficiency into our economies of scale. This holds true in our smallest factories to our largest hotels. Corporatism can be virtuous if done responsibly, but we do need to understand its limited history and the cultural permeation that it extols. We forgot that there was ever any other way. Organizing in mass to affect change drives polarization. Where the boomers kicked the door down, the millennial generation surrounds the room.

Of course, the young are going to be different. Because they have forty-seven times less net worth than those thirty or forty years older, they will have a natural tendency to relinquish the quest for the ownership society. Physical possessions will become less valuable. Social connections matter less when we have more money. We can pay for a bevy of services which may be traded as favors in various networks. If money is an abundant commodity, we may pay for a personal trainer, a housekeeper, and a personal chef. In the connected economy, a landscaper may trade the service of mowing the lawn for a weekly personal training session. Financial transactions will eventually be just one factor of our ability to pay our debts. The US dollar and all currency is man-made and not infallible. Local currencies have been used for decades around the United States. Bitcoin is a virtual currency, which works as open-source software on the Internet. While much skepticism exists surrounding this type of commodity and its place in the modern economy, all that is truly required, just like any monetary system in the world, is an agreement on its value.

Salt, pelts, cattle, and plants are just some of the many currencies, which have been used throughout the years. Why are we steadfast in the permanence of the present system? The idea of economics is changing more quickly than we can actually define it. Technology has expanded the capabilities of distribution beyond the comprehension of traditional methodologists.

Throughout the past decade, many articles and books were written about how the youth need to "fit in" to the system. There is a narrative which suggests that the 18–35 demographic is at once entitled yet acquiescent to the powers that be. Their subversion is not protesting in the streets. Their subversion is pragmatic conformity through patience. Due to economic realities, their power is only a function of time. Value will be created in very innovative and creative ways. They are the experts of the future, and they will shape it in their image. Economists measure progress in terms of productivity. Value as an employee lies in the extent to which one is productive. Great gains in productivity are largely factors of innovation. The job escalator since roughly the end of World War II was high, wide, and orderly. Employees knew their place by age, tenure, education, and ability to cooperate. They got on at an early age and rode it to the top. At retirement, they gently stepped off to free up one of the many positions along the way. A small token of appreciation was given at retirement, and they were thanked for their years of service to the company. A pension annuity or lump sum was offered to get them off the payroll. The promise of social security benefits as well as 401k plan and personal investments still offer a promising outlook to those currently retiring.

The problem with today's generation is that the well has dried up and that escalator is shorter and skinnier. Large companies have become more efficient. The number of workers required to run a company has diminished. Dips in the market have caused employees reaching retirement age to prolong the rat race. Droves of highly educated entry-level workers are parked at the escalator entry waiting for their turn to ascend. In the new virtual world, getting an actual foot in the door may be that much more difficult. The lifespan of companies is becoming shorter, and the market has become hyper-competitive. The money to invest in pensions for worker loyalty is nonexistent. So the modern-entry level worker has almost no hope of a pension entering a competitive labor market and dubious hopes of social security benefits upon retirement. Just at the time where personal savings has become more crucial than any time in generations, the dream of a middle-class life is becoming more difficult to accomplish. From the factory worker to the union worker to the postal worker to the white-collar worker, wages have been in decline for some time. Globalization and automation have changed the way we view a career. The chronological benchmarks to the good life are in disarray. Breaking through the crowd and getting on the escalator is still an option; it is just a lot different of a ride.

The loss of the pension is a financial incentive to diminish loyalty to a company that had previously conjured gratitude. William Whyte's "organization man" of the 1950s and the social ethic to which it subscribed, has become Daniel Pink's "free agent" or Reid Hoffman's "startup of you." Even within the confines of an organization in the present day, we are first loyal to ourselves, because financially, the organization cannot be loyal to you in the current marketplace. The top-tier organizations will recognize this sooner than later. It will be imperative to keep the finest workers through other forms of loyalty incentives. Once we hit a wall in our careers or the escalator becomes jammed, we now jump ship for new horizons rather than focusing on pension as the guiding light. A change in organizations in our midthirties to a slightly higher-paying job could potentially mean hundreds of thousands of dollars more in our 401k. That could mean a huge difference in our retirement prospects. We no longer have the time and the patience to wait it out. The pace of business is much faster, our skills have to be that much sharper, and our education has to be that much more effective. The organization still offers opportunity, but it must also offer reasons for loyalty, especially to those who have the most transferable skills. It would be a mistake to assume that we stuck with companies out of loyalty rather than self-interest in the past.

Economics, then, has become more than a formulaic freshman college course or a political budgetary argument. Amarta Sen, the

1998 Nobel Prize winner in economics, is an abundance economist who prescribes new methods of the availability of abundance in terms of development and abundance around the world. In his 1999 book *Development as Freedom,* he said, "Just because we can produce is not the question." The capability of production allowing "conspicuous consumption" has been an idea since Veblen published *Theory of the Leisure Class* in 1899. Overproducing began being perfected when sales forces merged with marketing and public relations, which introduced psychology to advertising in the years to follow. Around this time, the precursor to Sen, economist John Hobson, began speaking of maldistribution in economies while outlining the very real possibilities of relative abundance. Americans consume over $33,000 worth of stuff every year per capita and have the world's largest GDP, but this number is still less than Norway, United Arab Emirates, and Switzerland, which spends over $40,000 in US dollars. Compare this with Egypt ($2,088), Iran ($2,714), or Bangladesh ($541), and Ethiopia an amazing $292 dollars spent over the course of a year. The very conservative Heritage Foundation ranks countries with the freest economy. The United States still makes the top ten nearly every year. Some of the greatest fortunes in human history have been amassed recently, thanks to technology. Mark Zuckerberg created a platform where people can communicate for free. Now he is worth more than the GDP of Bolivia (that's all ten million people). So a great dualism in tech culture symbolizes the economic culture at large. Great economic opportunity is available to the talented and hardworking more than ever, yet simultaneously, these technological advances make it more difficult to compete financially and less necessary. Finally, the efficiency capabilities of the abundance economists have the potential to enact the freedom ideals of classical economists.

CHAPTER 6

POLITICAL SCIENCE AND ACCOUNTABILITY

American politics has long confounded the world. Alexis de Tocqueville observed American democracy firsthand and told the world of the exceptional understanding of a new world order. America was free of the aristocratic remnants of feudalistic Europe. De Tocqueville declared that it was true; there was an exceptional quality about America. This concept of American exceptionalism was revisited by American sociologist Seymour Martin Lipset in his 1963 book *The First New Nation*. America was truly exceptional, not in the modern jingoistic and ethnocentric sense of rabid and mindless patriotism but because of an experiment in freedom and democracy that unified a land in the new world, under a culture of its own doing. Thirteen colonies revolted against the mighty British Empire, solidifying the values of "life, liberty, and the pursuit of happiness" for centuries. Lipset argued that liberalism was the defining value of American politics from its inception. The United States was nothing if not progressive in defining the value of humanity. When slavery affected our national identity, we ended it; when the Gilded Age introduced an understanding of the danger of monopoly, we regulated it. The notion of "freedom of contract" initiatives of the late nineteenth century, which drove down wages for immigrants and children and demanded long hours, were banished in the name of progress. The labor movement arrived to outline the rules that many of us take for granted today. By the 1950s, 35 percent of Americans belonged to a labor union. Now that number is down to 6 percent. Beginning with the New Deal under Franklin Delano Roosevelt in the 1930s, government spending to promote work was a popular measure. Even into the 1950s, there was still a lot of work to be done under government initiatives.

Today, Liberalism and Conservatism argue over the role and resources of government. The division, according to moral psychologist Jonathan Haidt, is a fundamental distinction in morals. The precursor to modern political division was not argued under the context of democracy but of kingdoms. In ancient China, Confucius may have made some of the first arguments toward historical conservatism. He believed in the "morality of the elite" as superior men. Their benevolence and character would trickle down to the masses as an example of how to live. The reciprocity of goodness lies in protecting the elite status quo as a means to uplift the population. Plato had fear of "the common man" and instead called for "philosopher kings" in *The Republic*. By the seventeenth century, Thomas Hobbes had recovered the philosophic mantle of political conservatism through his work *Leviathan*, which argues the inherently pessimistic view that a strong state is necessary to protect the individual from the violence of mankind's nature. "The divine right of kings," which granted absolute worldly control to an elite class, he claimed, was a necessity of government. The "democraticals," as he called them, who sought to overthrow the status quo of monarchy, were dangerous and immoral. Meanwhile, the British colonies in the new world had begun formulating progressive ideas in contrary to the long-held state of political affairs of the old world.

Ben Franklin said, "Aristocrats are conservative and unproductive." The new moralities lie in the capability of freedom and entrepreneurship outside the reach of the authoritarian monarchies. Jean Jacques Rousseau, who may be considered the first modern Liberal in its political context, wrote *The Social Contract* in 1762, which rejected the notions of Hobbes ideal of handing over freedom to Leviathan at the expense of protection. The ultimate morality, in tune with the Enlightenment, was individual freedom. The pessimism of Hobbes was being replaced by the optimism of Rousseau. The American Revolution was based on the moral foundations of mankind awakening to their self-evident natural rights. This new identity, classified as American, disrupted centuries of the conservative social order of politics. Social hierarchy was distributed from a class-based system based on lineage and status to one based on meritocracy and democracy. A sovereign nation was formed in a faraway place, based on theoretical concepts that did not seem consequential or even possible just decades prior.

The revolutionary tide spread to the old world in a decade via the French Revolution. The "Third Estate," which consisted of 97 percent of French citizens, had glimpsed the democratic ideals now possible in the New World. Edmund Burke declared Rousseau to be almost completely responsible for stoking the fires of rebellion against the status quo, which led to the bloody revolution. If Rousseau had become the quintessential modern Liberal, Burke would become the hallmark of modern Conservative thought. Burke's moral philosophy consisted of defining natural rights not within theoretical constructs of human potential, but the belief that upholding tradition is the true practice of adhering to natural laws. Burke defended the Leviathan representation of the French Crown against the violent terrorists of the revolution. So at that moment, the intellectual basis for all Conservatism thereafter was formed. Goodness and morality lie in what is. Existence of circumstance itself requires nearly constant counterrevolution. In his book *The Reactionary Mind,* Corey Robin argues that the core tenet of Conservatism has nothing to do with social values, small government, state's rights, or personal responsibility, those are just the ramifications of an ideology that first seeks to preserve existing power structures.

Haidt's Moral Foundations Theory identifies that Conservatives determine morality in terms of eternal models of sanctity, namely God, authority, which is usually based on past models, and a higher loyalty to their in-group. Liberals mostly reject these notions and tend to base their morality on caring, fairness, and liberty. According to Haidt, in his research, caring, which denotes empathy and compassion, is the least important morality to Conservatives and the most important to Liberals. Haidt calls his research of moral foundations the "decoder ring" for all political issues throughout history. Using Haidt's methods of moral prioritization, political polarization begins to be understood. To Burke, the French Revolution was among the most immoral endeavors in human history. Burke preferred Britain's Glorious Revolution of 1688, which he said had been "to preserve our ancient, indisputable laws and liberties and that ancient constitution of government which is our only security for law and liberty." Thomas Paine penned *The Rights of Man* in 1791 one year after *Burke's Reflections on the Revolution in France*. Paine attempted to remind Burke of the dying idea of the Divine Right of Kings. Thomas Jefferson only said, "The Revolution in France does not astonish me as much as the Revolution in Mr. Burke." Political warfare had begun its modern context.

American political theorist Russell Kirk has called Conservatism a system of ideas which "has sustained man . . . in their resistance against radical theories and social transformation ever since the beginning of the French Revolution." Michael Oakeshott says Conservatism is "a man who is acutely aware of having something to lose which he has learned to care for." John Maynard Keynes asked "What makes a person more conservative—knowing nothing but the present, or nothing but the past?" Burke believed that there was never any greater evil than the French Revolution. Robin defines *liberalism* as the long march against perceived "superiors" in society, which included the church, state, and business. The battles won in the name of liberalism were slavery, labor rights, women's suffrage, and equal rights. Conservatism in any era has consistently been the demarche against progress as a reactionary fear of the disruption of the status quo. The nineteenth-century Conservative creed demands obeisance to the current system of hierarchical order because a natural order assembled the hierarchy in the first place. The current lens of which we view the two factions of modern political thought is simply that Liberals seek equality while Conservatives seek freedom. Historically, the narrative suggests that Liberals were the ones seeking freedom while the Conservatives were the ones seeking equality, mostly by protecting the status quo of inequality.

The first political battles in the new United States concerned the organization of government to give control to the few or the many by concentrating power through the federal government in the favor of Hamiltonian federalism or offer more state's rights in favor of Jefferson's populism. Over the next 150 years, the liberal ethic of enlightenment and progress against plutocracy and aristocracy were continually defended regardless of political affiliation. Andrew Jackson took on the "Master Bank"; Lincoln suggested Wall Street speculation of Union defeats should be shot. Teddy Roosevelt despised the aristocracy leftover from the Gilded Age, and Franklin Delano Roosevelt enacted the "New Deal," which put the understanding of Conservative and Liberal into modern context. Thanks to the adoption of Keynesian economics used to pull the United States from the doldrums of the Great Depression, government spending became much more ideological. Prior to this period, cultural values of Liberal versus Conservative philosophy concerned grand ideas. Just decades prior saw children earning a substantial amount of household income. In just thirty years during the turn of the twentieth century, over 150,000 railroad workers were killed on the job. Long hours, lack of education, and poor working conditions caused government intervention in the name of human progress.

In 1955, Louis Hartz wrote *The Liberal Tradition in America*, which he explained that the great progress in America consisted because of an historical aversion to ideology. According to Hartz, the United States, unlike Europe, did not have a feudal and hierarchical past; therefore, a liberal consensus for the possibility of progress had always been the overarching ethic. Conservatism in the United States could not exist as a dominant belief system because we never allowed ourselves to become entrenched in an elitist power structure. So the wins of the liberal ethic incorporated economics throughout the 1930s, 1940s, and 1950s. The symbol of 1950s leadership, Dwight D. Eisenhower, was a moderate Republican in a Liberal era. Into the 1960s, Lyndon Johnson built "the Great Society" aimed at wiping out poverty altogether. The poverty rate of 40 percent dropped to 10 percent by 1970. New resentment was swelling, however. The radio priest Father Tom Coughlin spoke to forty million Americans about the "forgotten man" in the 1930s, Senator Joseph McCarthy stoked reactionary fear of communists in the 1950s. By the late 1960s, President Richard Nixon had seized the term *silent majority*, as the large group of reactionary, angry, and counterrevolutionary citizens who had felt that they had gained power in recent decades, and portions of the population were trying to take it away. Today, Donald Trump has filled that classic Conservative void.

Economically, the previously winning ideas of Keynesian economics were causing record stagnation and inflation in the 1970s. The culture wars of the 1960s left a shell of the preexisting social structure of the 1950s. The postmodern period, in full bloom, was defined as the questioning of the capabilities of the liberal ethic since the Enlightenment. Common culture, power structures, shared interests, and shared goals were diminishing. The Baby Boomer Generation was hitting adulthood, fully divorced from the collective social ethic from which they were born into two decades prior. The very definition of progress was questioned. Liberals were running out of causes for freedom. Their individuality and distrust for government through the Vietnam and Watergate years made personal identity and individualism the ethos against the former lifelong security promised by business and government through pension and healthcare. The political ideas of neoliberalism were the prescription for the fading North Star of liberalism. Economists such as Friedrich Hayek and Milton Friedman had convinced a neoliberal sector of the population that existing power structures were preventing the next evolution of human progress.

Ronald Reagan and Margaret Thatcher were elected as Conservatives carrying the neoliberal torch. This optimism for the future was a clean break from traditional Conservative dogma of defending existing power structures. According to Steve Fraser in *The Age of Acquiescence,* this new personal freedom through lower taxes, creating commodities that were previously outside of the market's reach, outsourcing, and deregulation was creating a new "ownership society." The Homestead Act of 1892 tied people to their homes, which made them less likely to strike. Fraser believes that this new era of personal responsibility and ownership created circumstances whereby adherence and acquiescence to business and government was the byproduct of these newfound freedoms. The grand ideas of neoliberalism would drastically transform society. Quickly, the new power structures had become conservative dogma. Conservative intellectual thought reorganized to create obedience and protection of the new system. Conservatism had found its modern mojo, thanks to reaching toward the Lockean liberal tradition to which we all agreed since the American Revolution.

After decades of Democrats and Republicans turning left, both parties agreed that a rebalancing was in order. By the early 1990s, a new generation of baby boom leaders who were raised on individualism and ideology began filling leadership voids. Old political friendships across party lines in Washington were soon seen as traitorous. Great tides of partisan media and networks began framing and dividing the messages. Jonathan Haidt has developed a giant visual that represents bipartisanship from both parties as purple dots throughout the decades of the twentieth century. The greatest swaths of dots on the issues throughout the decades indicate the centrism represented through the vast middle ground coded as purple. By the time the baby boomers assumed power in the 1990s, the pragmatic middle ground was purposefully breaking down. As the years passed, the purple dots diminished as the middle ground on issues no longer existed. By the turn of the millennium and beyond, the political parties had set up a near-perfect disunion on nearly every issue, represented as clearly red or blue on the diagram. Louis Hartz had theorized that American success was the result of the lack of ideology in 1955. Inevitably, it could be concurred that a generation leading by ideology was its main reason for failure a half century later.

The New Deal and the production efforts of World War II lifted the United States out of the Great Depression. So much so that President Eisenhower warned of the false hopes of the military industrial complex. The great victory in war must not be misinterpreted as a model for the economy going forward. Not only is it unsustainable but it is also dangerous for military and industrial leaders to acquire power beyond the realm of what was necessary in peace time. This sentiment was even more poignant coming from the supreme commander of Allied Forces during World War II. Eisenhower oversaw a time of relative peace, and instead of defense, he chose to take aim at the American infrastructure. America is recognizable today by the Federal Aid Highway Act of 1956, which he signed. The government effectively put America to work. Union membership was at an all-time high in 1954. We, as a society, rode this wave of growth to the largest economy the world had ever seen. We were living proof that capitalism, with a partnership for growth with the government, could create a stable middle class with real purchasing power. The ideals of capitalism and democracy were complete. America was truly "the Shining City on the Hill" of which President Reagan would speak. In September of 1962 at Rice University, President John Kennedy declared, "We choose to go to the moon in this decade and do the other things, not because they are easy, but because they are hard." Seven years later, that prophecy was realized. The leadership and vision of the American government could still steer innovation and make discovery. The United States sent a man to walk on the moon. We still believed in government, and we were still optimistic about the future.

Five years later, Watergate damaged that perception. Inflation had begun, oil prices were high, and the Carter administration had been labeled a time of malaise. Decline, when viewed through the prism of politics, called for something completely different. The cure was Ronald Reagan. He was the leader of a new generation of Conservatives who sought to undo a century of progress gone wrong by issuing the ideology of neoliberal progress. The big ideas that were partnered by government in the past were obsolete in the new America. This was complete with privatization, deregulation, and free trade. It was the beginning of the inevitable. Globalization would change the structure of the United States. In 1981, the same year, Ronald Reagan took office, GE Chairman Jack Welch championed a little-known principle called shareholder value maximization. Shareholder profit skyrocketed and marked the end of the golden era of labor. The New Deal had to be dismantled and the ownership society built to compete in the new world. The problem is that the people who began the ownership society passed off the sacrifice that comes with it to the next generation. This monumental shift in the way we think about government as a nuisance coincided with the birth of the millennial generation.

It is ironic that just as Reagan exclaimed that as a government, "We are coddling our people," we began coddling our young, as the narrative suggests. They would be the first to reap the true effects of a lifetime of taking responsibility for themselves. Reagan's policies cut taxes initially and gave us access to cheaper goods and middle-class access to modern finance. The cost was a new era of excessive debt, lower wages, and decreased opportunities. From 1980 to 2004, number of people covered by pensions went from 60 percent to 11 percent. In this same period, 17 percent of employees were responsible for their 401k plans, which rose to 61 percent by 2004. In 1979, 69 percent of employers provided healthcare for their employees. In roughly the same time frame from 1979–2012, productivity of the average worker rose by 85 percent after inflation, while wages only increased 6 percent, and the manufacturing sector actually saw wages drop by over 20 percent. As Fraser says in *The Age of Acquiescence,* "A newly hired auto worker now brings home what his grandfather did in 1948." Policies begun in that era fundamentally changed a complete generation born during that time. A culture of personal responsibility was created, but the parties tasked with the highest burden of responsibility were just being born.

Reagan found that given the option of conservatism that Americans would take it. Who would not like to have larger stock dividends, lower taxes, and cheaper goods? Ideologically, this cure for the stagflation and fear of a new post-industrialist economy was the remedy from a risk-averse peanut farmer turned President Jimmy Carter. The precedence of a high standard of living that always got higher was the reality of the early Reagan years. A new theory formed that deficits do not matter, so we began to borrow from China and against our children's future. Reagan's predecessor, Vice-President George H. W. Bush, would call for prudence, only to be lampooned on *Saturday Night Live* by comedian Dana Carvey. It was funny at the time, but looking back, much less so. The problem with the idea of personal responsibility in the United States over the last several generations is that it has been just that—an idea. The second third of the last century brought in a decidedly Liberal economic view of the world. The GI Generation, so popular and heroic in American mystique, was collectivist by today's standard. They believed in personal responsibility because they lived it. They also believed in the power of government. They lived in a time when America was wealthy but still immature. If America was on the life cycle of a modern American company, it would still have been in the high-risk and high-reward stage. It would have been long before the risk management analysts entered and killed the entrepreneurial spirit and sacrificed the future.

Through the years, industries died, new generations were born, and the trusted government became a pariah. As America grew, so did its government, and so did dissatisfaction levels. In fact, an entire political party surfaced that thrived on making American government not function properly. Between the very real pressures and realities of a bloated government that needed to prepare for the future and a new culture that treated the institution with disdain, a generation was born. The majority of millennials were born in the heart of the Reagan Revolution. All the adults were cemented into their time and place. Many of their pensions still intact, their education from years prior had been dirt cheap, their social safety net still guaranteed. The grown-ups were overseeing the resurgence of personal responsibility. The first step was, of course, privatization. Anything that the government could do the free market could do cheaper and more efficiently. This would come to a class of people who would socialize the risk and privatize the reward. Taxes plummeted, and free trade was liberalized. The adults were still riding high from thirty years of the best economy in the history of the world. The world was changing, however, as the Pandora's box of globalization had opened the world. This restructuring of the economy brought in big gains. Lots of people did really well. Even the average blue-collar worker was certifiably stock market savvy. The hiccup in the economy in the early 1980s was a small roadblock in the indestructible power of American progress.

No one paid for these things but everything has a price. The idea of Ricardian Equivalence, which was developed two hundred years prior by economist David Ricardo, assumes that the short-term impact of lower taxes will inevitably require burden of repayment in the long-term. We enjoyed a stimulus to the economy with lower taxes, but the equilibrium that supply-side economics promised the federal coffer never materialized. Instead, we just had lower taxes but less money to invest. Of course, the middle-aged orchestrators never sacrificed. Our great organizations never blinked. Economies of scale allowed Wal-Mart to perfect the global supply chain. Now small-town shoppers could buy just about anything they wanted at one store for rock-bottom prices. We paid with small business owners' life savings and minimum wage jobs. If it were not Wal-Mart, it would have been a very similar company. The trajectory was inevitable. So those kids from the 1980s grew up remembering no different than a government they couldn't trust and a free market that had no allegiance to the middle-class American worker as we once believed it did. Some saw their parents escape with entitlements of a bygone era. They retired from Fortune 500 companies with healthy pensions, a 401k, personal savings, stocks, bonds, and the promise of the Social Security system and Medicare for their health. Others saw their parents lose the job that the pension promised, only to search for that security in a world that no longer offered it. The grown-ups had delivered on their promise. They wanted a world of more personal responsibility. They just didn't mean it for themselves.

The size of government is really not the question for the future as much as the role of government. The wealth in this country has never been as lopsided against the young as it is now. A war has been waged against a generation. It is the dirty secret that America has been keeping for thirty years. The average person over sixty-five has forty-five times the wealth the average person under 35. Inevitably, and preferably, this will always be many times higher, but those numbers are many times the historical mean. The Great Recession in 2008 came at a time when many in the millennial generation were just about to launch a career. This, of course, derailed millions of pursuits, as recessions are wont to do. A blow just as great for their future struck in January of 2010. In Citizens United Vs. Federal Election Committee, the Supreme Court ruled that it was unconstitutional to restrict expenditures for elections. Essentially, it became easier for a voice to be heard if it had more money. Historically, the young tend to have a poor voter turnout. The current generation is no different. Even in the age of indifference, distraction, and dysfunction, they still have voting levels on par with the baby boomers at the height of the Vietnam War. One critique of the Citizens United ruling is the fear that the poor will have even less of a voice in the future. Increasingly, the poor are equating with the young. Unfortunately, politicians are not concerned with a demographic who does not show up at the polls and doesn't have any money.

By and large, political decisions are what got millennials here in the first place. Many companies will cite studies that point toward understanding the behaviors of the modern youth. There are two critical errors here that span the spectrum of misconceptions of an entire generation. One is that economic factors are being credited with social ones. For instance, it is widely believed that millennial aged children return to live at home after college because they have such a close bond with their mother and father and just cannot grow up. It may be true that they have better and closer relationships with their parents, but much more likely is that they don't have a job or are potentially underemployed. This same concept can be applied across the "prolonged adolescence" argument from entering a viable career to getting married. They learned personal responsibility much earlier in their lives and understood the need for stability before life-altering decisions could be made. Secondly, because many have never truly tried to understand their perspective, we have developed a false sense of cause and effect. For instance, millennials enter our companies and demand meaningful and important roles immediately. Naturally, the immediate reaction is that this person is childish and requires instant gratification. They are immature and do not understand how the world really works. Clearly, the cause is from a lifetime of entitlement. Let's examine another perspective. Most of the people at the company have been grandfathered into a pension. Their goal is to stay on board until retirement. They want to be a good worker, occasionally great and very occasionally brilliant. Most importantly, they just want to know that it will all end well.

Meanwhile, the millennial has no pension. They have no incentive to remain with the company. Their pay is their pay. Their pension, in essence, has become their ability to acquire skills and move on. They are not trying to undermine coworker experience. They are not trying to shine a light on deficiencies; they are simply trying to acquire the capital to make it to their next job. The reciprocal loyalty of the pension is an undervalued and silent attachment to an organization, which allows for an entire generation of freedom. It allows for more personal responsibility, just as they were always promised. The organization pays for this trade off by offering other incentives to a generation with different priorities. It could be casual dress, working at home, more flexibility, or more comfortable workspaces and activities. So the cause has nothing to do with entitlement. It is, in fact, quite the opposite. The cause of their urgency is they are not entitled, by and large. The free market system has been good to the investor class over the three decades since they were born. As Thomas Piketty highlights in his book *Capital in the 21ˢ Century*, the rate of return on capital exceeds the rate of economic growth in the west. This is partially to blame for increased income equality in recent decades. We believe that education is the great equalizer. We believe that if you find your talent and work hard enough, the opportunities will arise. These tenets we must continue to believe if we are to survive. But we must also acknowledge that someone who came before us under different rules and different circumstances and then rigs the game was not looking out for the future. It is no longer uncommon to pay over $100,000 for college, and we have well surpassed the $1-trillion-dollar mark for student loan debt.

Not only did we politically finance the future by spending all the money, borrowing the rest, and making sure our entitlements were intact but we also began gouging them on education. The only commodity on the consumer price index to rise higher than healthcare in the past thirty years is education. Education was once considered a near human right that advanced society as a whole as aggressively as it advanced the individual. The price of education was raised because the market could handle it. Education was once a gateway to the middle class. Now it is simply a prerequisite. We must now finance our future to bet that we can take advantage of our accredited certification. The biggest insult is that the government is now complicit in making money off it. Government-backed student loans are an asset on the balance sheet. The chickens came home to roost. A very large and educated generation who could have substantially more buying power has started their lives in debt. By now, we should understand that for every action, we will assuredly get a reaction. It has finally become a pressing issue to the economy that a generation, the marketer's dream demographic of 18–35 has less disposable income than in the past. The houses, cars, and vacations are foregone. On the heels of a recession, workers who survived feel pressure to be more productive and older workers tend to remain. Companies can stretch out the unpaid internships a little longer, and wages can remain stagnant for another year. For the first time in their lives, their problem has become our problem.

William Small and George Wythe were teachers. What else do these two have in common besides the fact that practically no one has ever heard of them? They were central figures in the education and formation of young minds at William and Mary College. No doubt, their most successful student was a young man named Thomas Jefferson. The synthesis of disciplines that is a liberal arts education inspired a revolution through critical thinking about the nature of mankind. Mr. Small and Mr. Wythe, two absolute side notes in the pages of history, helped form the context of the greatest document ever written, the Declaration of Independence. Jefferson believed in an educated populace. As governor of Virginia, he proposed a free education for all. To Mr. Wythe, he once wrote, "I think by far the most important bill in our whole code is that for the diffusion of knowledge among the people. No other sure foundation can be devised for the preservation of freedom, and happiness . . . preach, my dear Sir, a crusade against ignorance; establish & improve the law for educating the common people." Jefferson was so proud of the education system in America that he once wrote to St. John de Crevecoeur, famous essayist of revolutionary America through his series of essays, *Letters from an American Farmer*, observing proudly, "Ours are the only farmers who can read Homer." Three years was the time required to have a sufficient public education according to Jefferson. The rigor of education, however, was the ability to contemplate new and compelling thoughts. Farmers had just overthrown the most powerful military in the world based on an ancient theory of democracy. To sustain it, a pensive population must consider education for all a public good and a requirement for good citizenship. One hundred years later, most states required a formal education through the age of fourteen. As the twentieth century progressed, the teenager went to high school. The idea of adolescence happened abruptly in American culture. To meet the needs of new industries and technologies, we stayed in school.

In 1960, the state of California offered the Master Plan, a promise to educate everyone who sought a postsecondary education. By the end of the decade, Governor Ronald Reagan likened free education in California to socialism. The tide was turning on the role of public education in American society. By 1982, the public good of education was a private commodity for a California state school, to the tune of $441 per year. The reasons for going to college, which included self-confidence, learning and sharing ideas, contributing to society, seeking diversity and independence, and of course, simply an educated electorate, was facing the increasing free market pressures of the shareholder value maximization zeitgeist. Going to college was the ticket to making more money. Because this formula was suddenly uncovered to the masses on the free market, prices began to rise drastically. The Chivas Regal argument was introduced to America in 1988. This argument said, of course, college should be expensive because it was a luxury. If it was the ticket to a better life, then it had been drastically underpricing itself for the past three hundred years. Like a sales strategy of the finest liquor, elite colleges would not lower prices to compete because there was no financial incentive. The proof of return of investment throughout the course of a lifetime left little room for argument. In terms of return on investment (ROI) in lifetime wages, college was delivering.

In June 2001, Erik Larson wrote an article for *Time Magazine* titled "Why College Costs Too Much." He described the $3,790 he paid at an Ivy League school in 1976 through a summer job, help from parents, and a loan. At the time of his article, he was astounded at the $21,130 that the University of Pennsylvania charged at the time. According to the 2013–2014 US Department of Education survey, the cost at Penn was over $40,000 and over $60,000 including room and board and supplies. The scary part was that there were thirteen more expensive colleges just in the state of Pennsylvania that year! Education has spiraled out of control to the tune of a 1,200 percent increase in costs in the last thirty years. This has taken an effect on who is going to college. Between 1992 and 2004, low-income enrollment dropped 14 percent, middle income dropped 6 percent, and upper income increased by 18 percent. According to Thomas Frank, two-thirds of students have student loan debt an average of $24,000. The paradox that the young face is that they must take on crippling debt for the opportunity of the middle class. When politicians such as Bernie Sanders suggest that, just as we have always done, which was invest more in education at every new iteration of economic eras, the reaction is immediate attacks on the character of a generation rather than a revisit of the entitlements that were entrenched in citizenship in the past.

Some form of higher education is a necessity in the modern world. Jobs that sought a high school diploma a generation ago now demand college degrees. The market understands this and maximizes that potential. There have been endless articles written about the reason for spikes in college educations. Some may say unnecessary facilities, overpaid faculty, too much educational customization, or bureaucratic administrations. These are just symptoms of the fever. We have outpriced college for a large population or simply caused seekers to pursue other interests. A college degree used to allow you to compete and get ahead; now it just keeps you from falling behind, while driving you into debt. The public value of an education has been completely monetized and privatized. Frank Bruni of the *New York Times* wrote, "Dear Millennials, We're Sorry." Spending in this country is greatly focused on the past generations. Social Security,

Medicare, and Medicaid accounted for 6.7 percent of GDP in 1990 and is now well over 10 percent. As he quotes former Nebraska governor and Senator Bob Kerrey, "If we're trying to figure out how to advance the next generation's future, we need to be spending more on the next generation, and we're spending it on yesterday's generation." This trend will only continue as the baby boomers surpass middle age by the tens of millions.

Many of the young are focused on sustainability and the long-term effects of climate change. Any hope of the government leading the way to a new economy of renewable energy is futile in the current environment. Those in government have made it absolutely clear that the future is not what it once was. We have to cling to what we have today and cling to a more balanced budget. The days of the role of government spurring innovation and collaborating on big ideas are picked apart and politicized by well-funded anti-government machines. The civic pride in Kennedy's statement "Ask not what your country can do for you, ask what you can do for your country" is all but gone. Older generations can point to the spirit being lost by the apathy of youth. The entitlement and selfishness of the past thirty years has caused the country to be sent into economic and cultural remission. The truth is the spirit of government was killed before they were born. We never put our money where our mouth was to finance the possibilities of our last generation. We complain that their education levels are not on par with the rest of the world. The scientific grants have dried up, and the Pell Grants are fewer. As Thomas Friedman has said, "Medicare is fighting against the Pell Grant opportunities, and the War on Terror resources are fighting against the Research and Development and infrastructure investments."

We are now spending our money on past generations when we used to spend it on future generations, even though Generation Y is every bit the size of the great Baby Boomer Generation. By the time the ambassadors of the Reagan Revolution in both the public and the private sector retired, they had climbed the ladder and pulled it up with them. They never had to feel the effects of privatization, except for the initial surplus to those at the right place at the right time.

We call the next generation entitled even though we spend the least on them and expect the same civic pride of the 1960s. A window in time opened for a generation to be low-skilled, highly paid, poorly educated, benefit-rich, and every reason to be debt-free yet chastise youth who have the exact opposite life experiences. Any mention of the government battling climate change is seen as waste, even though this translates to innovation and forward thinking. We are now in the midst of a generation that will not be better off than their parents. That means the true American dream is lost. We have become paralyzed by fear of losing. An overwhelming majority of Americans do not want to climb the economic ladder but simply not fall backward. We now believe that winning is defined only as not losing and that the status quo is acceptable. Cutting the budget is the safest way forward for our country. We believe the government should be run like a business. Meanwhile, the best modern business strategies for growth include constant innovation.

The innovation and excitement that government once espoused are gone. The youth will innovate and take civic pride while they are doing it; it will just be beyond the realm of the government. Beyond the military industrial complex, at his farewell address, Eisenhower also warned to "avoid the impulse to live only for today, plundering for our own ease and convenience the precious resources of tomorrow." No two issues are more poignant in the half century since they were uttered. The reactionary compulsion of a strong military out of fear is understandable. The latter warning speaks to the investment of youth and our obligations to prolong their resources. Today, General Eisenhower, Republican president, Supreme Commander of the Allied Forces in World War II, D-Day tactician, and champion of the garrison state of a strong military would be seen as weak and out of touch. Ironically, by even acknowledging that this possibility may exist in the future, it made him appear weaker in retrospect. His signing of the Federal Aid Highway Act would be wasteful or, worse, "communistic." Policy of this scale would be to the left on any president that the Democratic Party would or could run in the present environment. Our views about the government have changed. Today, propositions about great government achievements would not be seen as a noble partnership but a great overreach of power. We have gotten government out of the way for millennials. Personal responsibility, of which we claim they have none, is their only option.

Conservatism, the contention and ideology of putting the brakes on progress, has found a winner in the modern power structures. Niall Ferguson, in *The Great Degeneration,* reminds us that Adam Smith talked about the dangers of the stationary state, where the population forgets about investment in the future because they assume the comforts of the present will remain indefinitely. No access to the political arena has yet been given to the largest generation in American history. Corey Robin has said, "Conservatism is about power besieged and power protected" since its ideological birth. Politics, as an ideology, is of no use to the millennial generation. Their liberal ethic of storied American tradition is pragmatic progress, which is at odds with the ideological generation still in charge. The near perfect separation of Liberal and Conservative policy between parties has united only on conservatism against the requirements of the future of the young. The vast new realities for success in the world are beyond the cognitive constructs and interest of today's leaders. Max Planck's assertion that "a new scientific truth does not triumph by convincing its opponents and making them see the light, but rather because its opponents eventually die, and a new generation grows up that is familiar with it" has never been more reticent. Conservatism then is the risk management strategy by a mature enterprise in the "stationary state." Progress, in the name of generational change, is soon on the horizon. Whether the mantle be carried by the political right or the political left may be in question, but it will assuredly come at the return of the long-standing liberal ethic.

CHAPTER 7

TECHNOLOGY AND SPEED

The myth of Prometheus may be the first metaphor for what technology wrought of humanity. Prometheus was said to have stolen fire from the gods to bring to the mortals. His punishment from Zeus was to be bound eternally as a large bird ate his organs. The moral of the story is that there is always a price to pay by gaining access to technology, which had previously been solely the realm of the gods. The same story was told in 1818 by Mary Shelley in a novel called *Frankenstein* and subtitled as *The Modern Prometheus*. What technology ultimately searches for is the one commodity that cannot be purchased—time—yet it may sharply disrupt previous patterns. Technology visionary Kevin Kelly's 1994 book *Out of Control* had a theme that "as we shape technology it shapes us." Technology writer Nicholas Carr sees man as *Homo faber*, or "man the tool maker." Similarly, he says that as man makes the tools to alter the environment, which is quite literally technology, the tools will inevitably alter us. The Prometheus myth is at the heart of humanity's connection with the technologies that lead to progress. Mythologist Joseph Campbell considered Prometheus a Christ-like figure of the ancient world. He was bound to a rock and subjected to torture while humanity was enriched by his bestowal. As history unfurled, so did the understanding of the double-edged sword of progress, quantified as technology.

Mary Shelley published *Frankenstein* in the same decade in which a group of English textile workers, known as Luddites, began destroying the job-killing machinery, which was at once advancing society and destroying their livelihood. The American folk hero John Henry tried to keep a steel-driving pace with the steam-powered hammer, only to win and die of exhaustion. Today, being a Luddite is synonymous with the opposition to technological change. Now, the machines that John Henry would race or that the Luddites would destroy are mostly computational rather than industrial. On March 22, 1876, the *New York Times* declared the telephone to be an economic disaster. It predicted that the churches and concert halls would empty due to this new invention. As trains started to go faster, people feared that this newfound speed would make their bones fall apart. The Great Horse Manure Crisis occurred in 1894. The thousands of horses in our largest cities around the world were causing health issues for its people. The manure would spread through the muddy streets during rain, and the dry residue would be windblown throughout the cities. No one anywhere in the world could find a permanent solution to this problem. The horse had been the staple of power and transportation throughout the world since its domestication. Out of this need the automobile was born. At this time, every industry in the world still relied on the horse. Henry Ford's lawyer was said to have been told by the president of the Michigan Savings Bank, "The horse is here to stay, but the automobile is only a novelty—a fad."

No one knew the extent of the disruption which lay ahead. The invention of the automobile fundamentally changed the way people lived. The Luddites of the time evolved from fearing the way that horses would react to machines to the way humans would react to machines, to the even scarier proposition of the way that machines would react to humans. Through Prometheus and via Shelley, the sentiment of modern science fiction was born. As technology was embraced as the tangible item that could benchmark linear progress, fiction began to contemplate the ramifications of the Promethean fire. The anxiety over the fire was that it was irreversible. Values can change over time and space depending on circumstances, but the combinational power of innovation, represented by technology, is an evolutionary progression. Just because we may choose to disregard the capabilities of the digital world does not mean that it does not exist. Gordon Moore, Intel founder, predicted in the 1960s that computing power would double every 18–24 months for the foreseeable future. That trend is still alive today. In *The Second Machine Age*, authors Erik Brynjolfsson and Andrew McAfee describe what they refer to as the second half of the chessboard. In an age of exponential progress, which follows the Moore model of duplication, the first half of the chessboard may take a while to conquer; however, the second half is nearly immediate. This is similar to the old algebraic equation that says it will take twenty days for a collection of lily pads to cover a pond. Assuming the growth of lily pads is exponential, on what day will the pond be half full? The answer is, of course, on the nineteenth day. The entire second half of the chessboard gets filled in one day.

World War II passed, and nuclear power had been displayed on earth. Computer scientists of the postwar years traded the vacuum tubes for the much more efficient transistor. Moore's exact prediction was that the amount of transistors that could fit on one circuit would be able to double for decades. Luddite fear would escalate from the big powerful machines whose might would steal jobs from the man and the horse to the increasingly intelligent structure of our machines. Essentially, Luddite fear transformed from the manual slowly to the cognitive. In the Industrial Age, value was added by the size of our creations. In the Digital Age, value lies in what cannot be seen. Miniaturization is now what marks progress. Intellectual property is the new real estate, information is the new raw material, and software is the new manufactured good. Economically, no one is quite sure how to value these vague and dynamic terms. Facebook has assets of over $6 billion yet is valued at well over $100 billion. These are the great organizations being built today, yet most of the world functions in the structure of the vacuum tube. Our reality is an exponential world on the cusp of the second half of the chessboard subjugated to the structure retrofitted from a bygone time.

Technology, which has marked progress for eternity, has never been more pivotal in daily existence. Information and connection, which defined western culture via radio and television for a century, has given way to a personal computer that fits into our pockets, complete in only a decade. The idea of broadcasting in the modern world to share objective realities collided with the subjectivity of the postmodern world. What better way to define individuality than our own narrow cast device which will draw the exact filtered information that we seek? The Promethean bargain asserts that we can outsource the rigor of thought to a network that reaffirms our already solidified convictions. The automation of our thoughts free up our focus to other matters that require productivity and efficiency. Cognitive neuroscientist Maryanne Wolf, author of *Proust and the Squid*, says that reading is not an innate brain function of humanity. It took nearly two thousand years for mankind to really understand how to decipher depictions of letters on a page and connect them as words to form meaningful sentences. Now we expect children to read in the first two thousand days of their existence. Nicholas Carr says that maps and clocks changed our cosmology of space and time. The mass written word propagated by the printing press over half a millennium ago changed the way humanity dealt with consciousness. If the focus of reading, which trained the brain to contemplate a deeper level of stimuli, ceases, we are left with our natural brain functions of shallowness. We do not challenge our brain to push the bounds of its neuroplasticity.

In his follow-up book, *The Glass Cage*, Carr fears what he refers to as "the autopilot of the human condition." He recounts the difficulties of the Igloolik hunters of the Arctic Circle, who have survived on intuition for four thousand years. With the introduction of GPS devices in recent years, their wayfinding skills, which required the sharp intuition learned only through long periods of intense focus and immersion with their surroundings, has diminished. In a land with very little physical markers, technology obviously seems to be the key for safety and efficiency through the deadly terrain. The newfound reliance on technology, it turns out, had the opposite effect. As the Igloolik outsourced their senses to the new lifesaving devices, their wayfinding senses eroded. Injuries and death climbed. This is the metaphor that Carr believes is indicative of the human condition in the Internet age. The human attention span has severely diminished, and it has been mostly caused by the Internet. Wolf would say that the natural tendency of the brain is much more in tune with the distractive nature of the Internet itself. The success of the Internet is that it has aligned itself to prey to the natural inclinations of our brain. So the book and the Internet are at a juxtaposition in the modern world. Books, as they always have, allow for progress in thoughts and ideas as a form of technology. The Internet is structured in a way that suffices in the preexisting pathways in our brain. Books gave us long periods of immersion where we could transfer ideas into our long-term memory. The Internet is delivered via a suite of applications that inundate our senses, keeping the brain happy by living in the immediate gratification zone of our short-term memory.

Our smartest scientists are converging in areas of technology surrounding data. Science, technology, engineering, and mathematics (or STEM) industries represent the greatest growth in terms of skills and professions according to most, including the United States Department of labor. The goal of all programmers is to eliminate complexity and deliver content in simplistic terms to the individual. Essentially, they immerse themselves in complexity to communicate simplistically. For those of us who simply rely on these outputs without introducing mental rigor do a disservice to the neuroplasticity in our brains. Technology makes it easier for us to excel, but if that excellence comes at a detriment to what Carr calls the intellectual ethic of the individual, it lessens our ability to deal with the complexity in our lives. Despite an unprecedented loss of rigor due to the requirements of a multitasking world, many studies say the human brain is performing better than ever. The Flynn Effect of higher expectations claims IQ has risen by as much as an average of fifteen points in the last seventy-five years. The Promethean message is that as we get smarter, we outsource our deep thinking to the platforms and media that have previously reinforced our worldview. The duality of technology affects the internal world as much as the external. Paradoxically, wisdom is lost in the name of intelligence.

There has always been a mystical quality of the collection of information. In the third century BC, Ptolemy began summoning all books coming through Egypt to be stored at the Great Library of Alexandria. One thousand years later, King Ashurbanipal seized all the books in Sumeria for his personal collection. In the early twentieth century, Paul Otlet continued the ancient quest of information collection. He imagined what he would call an electric telescope for people to see his collection from afar. Otlet believed that a central repository of knowledge would open the world, eliminate war, and cause humanity to evolve with deeper connection. In 1941, the author Jorge Luis Borges imagined a physical Internet of information. He called his work the *Library of Babel*, where every permutation of every book ever written was stored. Because every truth and every falsehood was stored side by side, the readers were left with essentially no information whatsoever. The Roman philosopher Seneca has been quoted as saying, "What is the point of having countless books and libraries whose titles the owner could scarcely read in an entire lifetime?" The ability for humanity to digest and comprehend an increasingly abundant amount of information has been a fear for thousands of years. In the Borges world of 1941, that possibility was mythological and ethereal; in today's world, it is already taken for granted. We have all of the information at our fingertips. Our inability to review and organize the massive data of the new world leaves us in despair like the librarians in Borges's imaginary library.

It is said that we are on the precipice of the greatest infrastructure project ever built. Every utility that we can imagine has been implemented in the western world. Delivering the Internet via a network of wireless, fiber optics, and copper is mostly complete. What is called the Internet of Things (IOT) will be the next great change in our lives. As we have the ability and the demand with more and constant flow of information, we will begin to incorporate various household items which we never imagined to our personal networks. To optimally translate and synthesize these measurements will demand software. Efficiency and productivity will again hit new heights as costs begin to be driven down. We mapped the land, we mapped the sea, and we mapped the human genome. The next map will be the usage of every product in our lives through the Internet. The amount of data transmission and storage will continue to grow. The digital world is still in its infancy. The birth of digital technology and quantum mechanics both occurred in the twentieth century. Analog signals copied a wave in its true form and were the source of nearly all information transfer throughout the twentieth century. As we converted to digital technology, we found ways to code these signals with 1s and 0s and then decode them upon arrival. Digital proved to be the preferred method to scale our information, but it also gave us the ability to compress. Scientists have been consumed with the subatomic for a century. The twentieth century gave us the great physicists Niels Bohr, Albert Einstein, Richard Feynman, and Stephen Hawking. These are considered the greatest minds of the century particularly because they dealt with the theoretical aspects of physics in which Feynman himself has admitted that "no one truly understands."

Albert Einstein was once informed by one of his students that he had given the same test the previous year. Einstein is said to have remarked, "It is but the answers are different." That is the nature of quantum mechanics. Similarly, Niels Bohr said, "The opposite of fact is a falsehood, but the opposite of one profound truth may very well be another profound truth." Lev Grossman introduced the world to quantum computing in his February 2014 cover story for *Time* magazine. Even though we accept and respect our great physicists, we are reluctant to embrace the ambiguity of the quantum state. It is counterintuitive to everything we know about classical physics, best understood as the laws of motion first introduced by Newton. When this theory is introduced into computing, the 1 and the 0 of classical computing enter a quantum state of 4-bit possibilities (because each 1 and 0 can either be a 1 or a 0). This potentiality makes even today's supercomputers resemble analog technology by comparison. From this starting point, we inject the idea of Big Data, in which the change in human consciousness surrounding the idea is as important as the science behind it.

Big Data could not have existed until we were saturated with digital information. Google CEO Eric Schmidt has been quoted as saying, "Every 2 days we create as much information as we did from the dawn of civilization to the year 2003." Alvin Toffler feared the "future shock" of information overload prior to the digital revolution in 1970. The way that we organize and interpret information is changing all the time. It is called Big Data because there is a lot of it, and there is a lot more to come. For every new device, switch, tool, appliance, or toy that we begin to connect to the Internet will create that much larger of a network. All these new data points collect information, which can be stored. With modern technology, we can actually count, measure, and make predictions about entire populations where we could only infer based on samples in twentieth-century statistics. A scientist using the scientific method in any subject would gather what was considered to be a representative sample of the entire population. It is the role of the scientist to set up a hypothesis to be proven or disproven. The very specific testing procedures produce quantifiable results, which can be interpreted by the tester. The power and control lie completely in the accuracy of the data input, the correct interpretation and veracity of the tester, and the ability for the tester to replicate the experiment. All of this requires human intervention with manageable data and a finite number of testing possibilities.

One thousand years ago, William the Conqueror issued a land assessment of the British Isles called the Domesday Book. It was an attempt at true measurement of a population, as well as their life and death, much like the modern census. It was an exhaustive and expensive endeavor, which would not be replicated for hundreds of years. In seventeenth-century London, one could find death by just about every simply treated malady in modern life. John Graunt began to tabulate this information and, hence, became one of the world's first demographers to use a method of modern statistics. As we inched toward the twentieth century, new fields of the social sciences emerged out of the traditions of demography. The sociologists, anthropologists, and psychologists were using the sampling method of demography pioneers like Graunt. More information and more specialization allowed scientists to dig deeper into the intricacies of human behavior. Eventually, the reasoning did not matter to the laymen, and the multitude of avenues of learning became more difficult to put into the context of the human experience. It seemed the more we knew, the less things made sense. The human mind is the greatest computer ever built . . . so far. Even the abilities of the human mind filter, sort, infer, forget, and prejudge. For the specific role of data sorting, the power of the human mind has been usurped. Big Data is not just using an ever larger sampling of data. It is effectively handing over the controls of the experiments to the computers themselves. The data scientist becomes the interpreter of the end results rather than the driver of the test data. This allows for unlimited permutations of data working in mysterious combinations that the human mind would not consider nor have the time to test. Small data, or statistics, can help us determine causation. In the Big Data world, causation must give way to correlation. The human mind and its need to know and control must finally cede to a greater understanding of objective reality. The technology is finally here.

The algorithms of the probability of Big Data do not claim to be clairvoyant. It is not a magical formula to predict the future, but the end result may assign a percentage to an event occurrence based on a configuration of data points beyond the realm of human understanding. The human brain instinctively asks why, and when we don't get an acceptable answer, it leaves us frustrated. Big Data scientists currently work behind the scenes in industries that do not care why, such as marketing and advertising. As humans, we have not even begun to cede our decision-making processes to artificial intelligence. Very soon, the networking of various items in our life will link to Big Data software of our own, which will help us with our own decisions. Based on current weather patterns, the amount of tread of your tires, the traffic conditions on your street, and your current health and alertness based on your health monitoring device, what if your personal dashboard warned of an 80 percent chance of getting into an accident on your way to work? The development of these types of software and the administration and management of these types of projects will surely create very new economic conditions and demand high-tech skills across every industry. Technological knowledge is no longer just a prerequisite for jobs surrounding information technology; it is the fundamental building block in education as important as basic reading and math of the twentieth century. Network science, programming, and statistical understanding will transcend industries. Information is becoming more abundant as technology is increasingly more inexpensive. This means project life cycles will continue to decrease, and software updates and replacements will be continuous. This will require agility beyond the traditional bureaucratic structure of our organizations. The volume, velocity, and variety of Big Data will transform the way we make business intelligence decisions in the very near future.

The ability to unlock, organize, manipulate, and apply data is the next great efficiency surplus. The *define, measure,* and *analyze* steps of Six Sigma initiatives may have taken months to implement in the 1990s through countless hours of organization. Decision-making for implementation and control can go from months to minutes with instantaneous and accurate data taken from the population rather than the sample. *Root cause,* the ultimate goal of Six Sigma analysis, will be less important. We will be able to assign probability and apply them to potential models of the future. Data will increasingly drive our decisions, but it will be up to the data scientist gatekeepers to collect and distribute information accurately and ethically. We will essentially turn our organizations from twentieth-century manufacturing companies like GM to twenty-first-century data companies like Google. The Internet is the mechanism to allow the volume, variety, and velocity to rise exponentially. Simultaneously, we are changing culturally, politically, economically, and generationally. The Big History perspective of certain historians such as Ian Morris claim that any significant social development outside of the norm of previous patterns of human history only began just over a century ago. The conveniences of the modern world of indoor plumbing, electricity, and cable TV were all dreamt and perfected in the analog world. Just twenty years ago, a small portion of all information on earth had been digitized. Now only a small portion has not. Moore's law of doubling technological capabilities every 18–24 months has also led to affordability for nearly everyone. For decades, digital technology was only accessible to scientists in labs with very little practical applications. Computer scientists spent the majority of the middle of the twentieth century developing the framework and protocols of computing. In 1943, even Thomas Watson, chairman of IBM, famously said, "I think there is a world market for maybe five computers."

By the late 1960s, engineers at IBM still could not foresee the practical applications of the microchip. Ken Olson, president and founder of Digital Equipment Corporation, quipped in 1977, "There is no reason anyone would want a computer in their home." By 1993, not only did the personal computer enter homes but 1 percent also began to use their analog telecommunication network to access a new phenomenon called the World Wide Web. Within a few years, new technologies allowed the telecom companies to begin to provide digital access to these networks. By the year 2000, we had increased our digital information transferring by fifty times in just seven years. Just sixteen years beyond Y2K (the year 2000), analog technology has become a relic. We now have a generation of young adults, digital natives as they are sometimes called, with no memory of a time without 24/7 information access. The inflection point that occurred near the beginning of the twentieth century, which exponentially increased productivity in all forms, seems less drastic when provided the context of the last twenty years. Drastic change in short periods of time warranted a new discipline in the twentieth century known as futurology. These futurists, as they were called, applied the science in "science fiction" from fields as disparate as neuroscience, robotics, computer science, demography, as well as the social sciences. In 1967, the first issue of *The Futurist* magazine billed as forecasts, trends, and ideas about the future. Three years later, Alvin Toffler became the first futurist to historically encapsulate the psychological trauma of the new post-industrial world. His best seller *Future Shock* explained the ramifications of "too much change in too short a period of time." He warned of information overload even in the analog world.

So the great repository of human knowledge, the mythical idea of the electric telescope, whereby all information would be available to everyone, has come true. The capabilities of data mining our entire lives depict our digital footprints as reality. The trail we leave allows us to use all the previously useless secondary data, which had never been collected in the past. This new data can be injected into algorithms for insights that were previously beyond the comprehension of the human brain. The census required a decade to count the specifics of an entire population. Big Data counts the entire population instantly without having to make inferences about representative sampling. The results, however, are counterintuitive to the cognitive processing of the human brain. Machine intelligence and machine learning will truly be the second half of the chessboard. Swedish philosopher and economic PHD Nick Bostrom in *Superintelligence* says, "As soon as a machine surpasses human intelligence—they can make machines even more intelligent that human could . . . leading to an intelligence explosion." According to predictive models that machines are already giving us, there is a 50 percent chance that this could happen by the year 2040. As Pedro Domingos explains in *The Master Algorithm*, as machines continue to collect more and more information, they collect more and more complex algorithms. Traditional programming was a man-made algorithm designed to solve an equation. Machines have redesigned science itself whereas probability replaces proof in some cases by a biologic urge of technology to search for the more complex.

Domingos says that in the case of machine learning, the ultimate goal is what he refers to as the Master Algorithm. This is a unified theory of machine learning whereby algorithms combine in such exponential complexity that the last algorithm essentially mirrors reality. It is the String Theory of physics combined with the alchemy of the mystical Philosopher's Stone, believed to turn base metals into precious metals, which was considered to be the Magnum Opus, or great work, of the Middle Ages. In the 1990s, computer scientist Ray Kurzweil renamed Moore's Law to the Law of Accelerating Returns. He began to discuss the real possibility of the science fiction concept called singularity, which is essentially the state of supreme machine learning absent human intervention. Alan Turing's Imitation Game Test, which attempted to distinguish machine intelligence from human intelligence in the 1950s, will be a reality by 2029, according to Kurzweil. In the 2020s, we will map the human brain like we have mapped the human gene. By 2030, computer power will equal the total of all human intelligence on earth. According to his Law of Accelerating Returns, by the year 2045, computer intelligence will be 1 billion times more powerful than all of human intelligence combined today. Technology, as a result of human manipulation, has been able to spur progress through science. Economist Joseph Schumpeter said, "Capitalism is the framework . . . but technology has created our world." He is best known, perhaps, for the term *creative destruction*, which saw combinational technologies as the root of all innovation and hence technology. We are at the precipice of an era where capabilities of the exponential are going to be the sole domain of the machine. As *The Nature of Technology* author Brian Arthur contends, technology was very recently just the process of the means of production. It is now becoming a chemistry to spur progress. Art, which was always left to be solely the realm of the human, will give way to what Kurzweil calls the Age of the Spiritual Machine. Because of the inherent combinations collected in machine learning, they can play jazz, compose original symphonies, drive cars, and understand language.

Prosperity is essentially the exponential increase in exchange as measured by productivity. In *The Rational Optimist*, Matt Ridley asked, "How long you would have to work to read a book in the dark for an hour?" In 1800, the cost to light the page by tallow candle would have been six hours' worth of work. In 1880. by kerosene would require the equivalent of fifteen minutes of work. By the incandescent bulb of the 1950s, the time was lowered to just eight seconds, and today, it would be the equivalent of just a half second of work with a compact fluorescent light. Increased specialization brought on by technological advances throughout the world may have drastically reduced costs. This drastic increase in productivity inevitably leads to higher levels of competition. Doctorate of computer science and researcher John Seely Brown says that the speed and competition brought on by these realities will require a complete renewal in skill sets every five years. Two generations ago, one skill set would be able to propel and individual throughout their entire thirty-year career. In today's world of fast-paced technology, the average person may require six unique skill sets throughout their life just to remain in the same industry. The metaphor for our capabilities is a treadmill that continuously increases in speed. Pretty soon we are running where we used to be walking just to keep the same pace. Bostrom says, "History inevitably produces growth modes more rapid than its predecessor." Rates of growth, productivity, and technological capacity all fall on the same curve when it comes to technology, which is exponential increase.

The technologies of specialization have allowed the average person to afford items, which in previous times would have only been accessible to the super rich or perhaps not at all. This is why some technologists such as Kurzweil claim that what has come to be known as the digital divide of those who have the education and skills to work with digital technologies and those that do not is relative. The fast-paced speed of technology means that throwaway items of today may have been worth millions in the world of just a few years ago. The cell phone in our pocket is quite literally more advanced than the rocket science which sent mankind to the moon a half century ago. Artificial intelligence pioneer Jaron Lanier fears the divide in a form of Luddite anxiety. The sharp increase in productivity since the Industrial Revolution always brought with it the fear that the work of machines would replace the work of humans. Much of the blue-collar work has been replaced by machines or is now considered low-skilled jobs, which drives down wages. White- collar work, often seen as a Luddite haven, has been subjected to the efficiency squeeze of recent decades. Creative work, the last refuge of humanity against machines, is no longer safe from robotic capabilities.

Father and son researchers Daniel and Richard Susskind talk about the transfer from the "brick-based society" to the "information-based society." In their book *The Future of Professions*, they compare the old and new gatekeepers in industries from teaching and management to architecture, law, and healthcare. Khan Academy is a virtual teaching resource with ten million members. More people visit Web MD every year than go to the doctor. The *Huffington*

Post has displaced the *New York Times*, and EBay handles 60 million legal disputes without lawyers. We can use Legal Zoom for our attorneys, Turbo Tax for our accountants, and Second Life has virtual worship and counseling services. The creative destruction as told by Schumpeter has always led to a new organization of work with new and usually higher level skills to compete in the proceeding work environment. The pessimists, as related by Luddite anxiety, have always reacted as if jobs were being lost forever, which they were. Humanity, however, has never seen the likes of the capabilities of the machines on the horizon.

On January 2, 2010, the *Washington Post* reported that between the years 2000–2010 there were zero net jobs created, whereas using models of growth from the past, there should have been a growth of ten million. Tech founder John Jazwiec said in a blog post, "I am in the business of killing jobs." He estimates that he alone is responsible for the loss of one hundred thousand jobs in recent years. He goes on to say that automation, outsourcing, and efficiencies by services and software decrease the requirements for additional workers. Employing fewer workers equals more simplicity and consistency. Once he is able to automate a job, he says, it is gone forever. To compete in this environment, we must be proactive as individuals but also as a society. According to Martin Ford in *Rise of the Robots*, we are no longer doing enough to prepare ourselves for the future. He says, "It should be kept in mind as well, that much of the basic research that enabled progress in the IT sector was funded by American taxpayers. The Defense Advanced Research Projects Agency (DARPA) created and funded the computer network that ultimately evolved into the internet. Moore's Law has come about, in part, because of university led research funded by the National Science Foundation. The Semiconductor Industry Association, the industry Political Action Committee (PAC), actively lobbied for increased federal research dollars. Today's computer technology exists in some measure because millions of middle class taxpayers supported federal funding for basic research in the decades following World War II. We can be reasonably certain that those taxpayers offered their support in the expectation that the fruits of that research would create a more prosperous future for their children and grandchildren. Yet, the trends . . . suggest we are headed towards a very different outcome."

Richard and Daniel Susskind talk of the two futures of the Promethean fire. Of course we must move ahead with the natural trajectory of progress without the reactionary impulse of the Luddite fear, but we must also understand that the disruptions of technology in the near future will become much more complicated issues. Software will soon map all routine tasks in the world. Only the creative tasks that ask for human connection can outperform the capabilities of computers. The University of Phoenix has come up with a list of the ten skills of the future, which mirror many of the world's best futurists. Some of these skills include understanding new media, virtual collaboration, computational thinking, and cognitive load management in the fiercely competitive and fast-paced world. Others include design mind-set, adaptive/creative thinking, and literacy across disciplines, cross-cultural competencies, determining deep meaning, and social/emotional intelligence. Most of these skills have little to nothing to do with technology itself. According to Richard and Daniel Susskind, the six reasons for these skills can all be traced back to technologies. Whatever we do will require participation in the technical world, even if we believe, like Nicholas Carr, that technologies are causing detrimental mental cognition or, like Lanier, that we have not reorganized around the new realities of technological capabilities.

Twentieth-century philosopher Lewis Mumford called technology "an instrument of liberation and one of oppression." It, at once, raised the world out of poverty and simultaneously makes it more difficult to achieve the middle class. Julian Huxley, author of *The Techno-Human Condition*, says that the great anxiety moving forward is that technology is now beyond the level of comprehension of man. Level 1 technology, as explained by Huxley, was the train. It was a sophisticated and complex piece of machinery, but it was also concrete and tangible. The next phase of technology was the system surrounding the trains, which now may include the schedules, the GPS, the infrastructure of the tracks themselves, as well as the entire human component necessary to operate it. Although this is exceptionally more complex and less tangible, it is still within the realm of technology that we can understand. In fact, this might sound like a day in the life of the modern worker. Level 3 technologies, however, are how the entire rail system interacts with other systems, technologies, ecosystems, economies, and value systems around the world. We have always believed that human judgement would be eternally beyond reproach to any information that machinery may give us. Computational thinking, for instance, one of the top skills of the future, will be understanding the advanced outputs of Big Data. We will be able to answer questions we thought could never have even been asked. The metamodern ethic regarding technology will be to continue to search for benefits for the progress of humanity while using the lessons of the past to nourish the potential of future generations.

CHAPTER 8

MATHEMATICS AND GRIDLOCK

Philosophy has been said to straddle the world of science and religion. The philosopher's historical role has been to find new ways to interpret reality and consciousness. Pythagoras used math to define reality, Hume used the human experience, and Descartes relied on reason, while Kant critiqued it. What is good? What is virtuous? What is moral? Eighteenth-century British Utilitarian philosopher Jeremy Bentham would have argued that whatever idea brings advantage to the most people is the most moral. Soren Kierkegaard would say that only the freewill of the individual has the capability of morality. In the late nineteenth century, American Charles Peirce introduced Pragmatism as a type of antiphilosophy that suggests that practical application to our surroundings is just a tool that humans use. It is just a problem-solving method for our time and place with no long-term or universal truth. History is littered with the philosopher shining a light onto the circumstances of his or her surroundings, and unique interpretation is their mark.

Perhaps the greatest metaphor for the goal of philosophy was conceived by Plato in his work *The Republic*. Here he imagines a community of people bound and shown the shadows on the wall of a cave as a fire burns behind them. These shadows are reality as they have come to know it. They have no understanding of the three-dimensional human form nor color or light. In the cave, they are prisoners. One such prisoner escapes and makes his way out of the cave and into the light to see reality in a new form. He has completed the philosophical transformation. Once the prisoner has glimpsed the real world, he feels an obligation to return to the cave to share his authentic experiences. The new sage tells the other prisoners an unbelievable tale of what he has seen. It turns out that those prisoners, adroit only at interpreting the shadows on the wall, still cannot accept the information outside of their shared and surreal experience. The former prison mate turned philosopher is now regarded as an outcast for telling his strange stories.

This is the simple allegory of all philosophers over thousands of years. Plato's venerable teacher Socrates was the original social gadfly. He questioned the norms of society and was, therefore, accused and convicted of corrupting the youth and of impiety. The philosopher's role is to always question, even if it means his demise. Socrates was said to be a congenial man about town with genuine interest as to the disciplines and professions of the citizens of Athens. His method of asking questions, memorialized forever in education as the Socratic Method, more often than not, proved the vulnerability and ignorance of the supposed experts of the day. This process led Socrates to the conclusion that he was the wisest man in Athens. Not because he purported to have any exemplary knowledge but simply for the fact that he was the only one that recognized his own lack of knowledge. Socrates was the first to understand that he knew that he knew nothing, the philosophical foundation of wisdom.

Philosophy has ceased to be an independent discipline. It has melded into every aspect and profession in our lives. We have formed camps and tribes like the Cynics, the Epicureans, the Stoics, and the Skeptics in the ancient world. Our fundamental worldview too often begins not by questioning but by blindly aligning with the values of our favorite personalities, institutions, teams, organizations, media source, and political parties. We are corrupted by the limiting view of the loudest voice in the cave. We seek truth through the lens of our predetermined vantage point. It is the responsibility of the philosopher to disrupt the dogma. The polarization and individuation of present-day culture, represented best by the Internet, allows us to reaffirm our own self-interests in moments of doubt. Traditional philosophy's battle with truth has two historic origins. Plato believed that by reasoning with those in the cave using the natural cognitive functions of thought, man can transcend the limiting passions of emotion. David Hume believed the opposite. To Hume, reason was but the servant of the passions.

According to Hume, we can easily alter our reasoning to coincide with the decisions of our emotions. Emotion is the person in charge, and reason is but the press secretary who justifies the emotion's position. It wasn't until the 1970s that science attempted to tackle the age-old battle. Researchers Daniel Kahneman and Amos Tversky studied human judgement and found that the errors in cognition were the processes that humans were using to think rather than the misinterpretation of reason or the corruption of emotion. The root of human error as it pertains to truth is a lack of statistical intuition. Most of humanity has a very poor understanding of probability and statistics. Mathematical disciplines in education rely heavily on geometric and algebraic roots as it relates to reason. Moral psychologist Jonathan Haidt has studied brain functions in humans which cause them to stake our moral positions. Like Kahneman and Tversky, he says that humans are first intuitionists. Complex factors of intuition based on past experience drive our thoughts first and foremost. So reality is always interpreted as a function of past experience. Therefore, it is much more probabilistic than algebraic, although we assume it is the opposite.

In *Thinking Fast and Slow*, Daniel Kahneman understands the human mind as a heuristic. It is not perfect, but for the large majority of most problems that we face on a day-to-day basis, our intuition, which he calls system 1 thinking, is efficient and mostly error-free. Due to the constraints of time, we tend to reverse-engineer new experiences as old experiences. The infinite availability of sensory experiences in our world requires us to constantly surrender to system 1 thinking, which is an automatic and instinctive human operation. Refining system 1 is an absolute requirement to function in the modern world. The danger, however, is not conceding to the much more thoughtful level of system 2 thinking when appropriate. If system 1 is immediate, subconscious, and stereotypical, System 2 is deep, slow, and intentional. It is also where we tackle the large and complex. System 1 works very well so much of the time and does not require the deep processing required of the statistical mind. Oversimplification indicative of system 1 is always the easiest route, especially when we do not have a good grasp of statistics, which at its depths is the quantification of error itself.

Claude Shannon's Information Theory shook the academic world in 1948. It was, at its core, applied mathematics which announced that a new computer age would be able to quantify information like never before. Immediately, the possibilities of its applications could be seen across disciplines. Although it was a treatise and a prophecy that the role that data would soon play in our lives, it set the stage for perhaps the greatest metaphor for truth in the metamodern world. Nate Silver, who predicted the presidential outcomes in every state in 2012 that same year wrote *The Signal and the Noise*, which referred to the modern communication methods in which Shannon had pioneered. Silver, in statistical terms, understood truth as the signal, and noise as the interference represented by an ever growing flurry of outside influences which curtail our own reasoning. Since Johannes Gutenberg perfected the printing press in the mid-fifteenth century, we have been subjected to increased rates of human knowledge, represented as the signal, but unfortunately, we have been just as susceptible to increased rates of human error represented as noise.

Silver, who may be the most well-known and accurate celebrity statistician, uses an interpretation that is mathematically more in tune with that of Hume. His contemporary and fellow Scotsmen Thomas Bayes introduced a philosophy of statistics, which explained what came to be known as Hume's Fork. The discipline of statistics lies within the cold confines of mathematical probability. Any theoretical notion of probability is subjected to the mean, median, and mode, which leads to Hume's Problem of Induction of assuming that what comes before will likely come again. Silver via Bayes assumes the human element associated with real-world events. All possible outcomes in an equation are not as equally likely as our mathematical models assume. Bayesian Statistics requires the assumption of degrees of belief. Proper interpretation of real-world statistics requires constant updates of the model. System 1 thinking does not automatically recalculate to update the latest puzzle pieces of knowledge because they are rejected as outliers to our preconceived and harmonious notions of reality.

Statistics in the Bayes tradition is much more in line with the constructs of the human condition. Instead of a recipe for the probability of one irrefutable objective conclusion, it assumes that the truth always lies predictably closer to the most recent, subjective, and widely collected prior beliefs. In 1953, Isaiah Berlin wrote an essay deriving from a long tradition of philosophy beginning in Ancient Greece with Archilochus, who is known to have said, "A fox knows many things, but a hedgehog one important thing." Silver is the fox in Berlin's allegory. What makes Silver the preeminent predictor of his time is that he embodies the multidisciplinary polymathic scientific path, which assumes all possible scenarios. He updates his assumptions by following the signal and attempting to eliminate the noise. The hedgehog, however, is the expert in one field, and attempts to conform the rest of the world around that idea. This bluster makes for good television but poor science, leadership, and prediction. Hedgehogs are the embodiment of noise, which obfuscates the virtuous path of the signal.

The little-known discipline of futurology "gets people unstuck from the past," according to Cecily Sommers in *Think Like a Futurist*. She recommends dispersing with ideology to see the true interdisciplinary relationship of facts in our lives. Sommers says, "Prediction is the primary function of the brain and the foundation of intelligence." The best strategy for prediction is to use the tools that the hedgehog would never dare. These include collaboration, advice from diverse parties, cultures, industries, and even government. Like Bayes, the best futurologists weigh evidence based on the various and diverse information systems, not how closely it aligns with our preconceived and solitary subjective system 1 status quo. Futurology transcends disciplines from the probable of all facets of the arts and the sciences, but the methodology remains the same across all disciplines. Futurologists are not pundits on the infotainment news but experts in what Kahneman called the availability heuristic, which is the applied intelligence of turning system 2 thinking into system 1.

Phillip Tetlock has done exhaustive research into the predictions of so-called experts and found that there is much to be desired. This is because most of our experts who rule our sources of information are the loudest voices in the room, which, by definition, may classify them as hedgehogs. The Bayes Theorem mathematically discounts the subjective first-person nature of the individual, which we intuitively use for understanding the future. The true reality of all future events lies outside of the narrow constructs of the single mind. There are no guarantees for the future, but the best futurologists use approximately the same methods as Big Data in the realm of technology, which, until now, have been counterintuitive to the human path of cognition. Through Tetlock's research, he has found seemingly very average people, considered foxes due to their method of data accumulation and accuracy, go unnoticed in most aspects of cultures even though they are our best predictors. Most hedgehogs are superstars who share their predictions of the future and have definite opinions. When their opinions happen to be wrong due to erroneous methods, the masses remain oblivious. We only know them as strong leaders who can sway opinion. Never mind the fact that their disposition itself makes them worse problem solvers. Their application of statistics can be a sleight of hand based on persuasion rather than accuracy. Even though Darrell Huff taught us *How to Lie with Statistics* in 1954, we have failed to realize the cultural significance of being blinded by the masters of certitude.

Updating information as a philosophy is called Pragmatism. Psychologist Carol Dweck would call it a growth mind-set rather than a fixed mind-set. Biologists would call it adaptation, sociologists would call it culture change, and politicians would call it flipping. Mathematically, this is the Bayes method of statistics, which calls into question the signal and the noise of the individual. In any one circumstance, it is possible that truth, as represented by the signal, could arrive at an individual's doorstep, which requires their unique interpretation. It is much more likely that the diverse path taken requires them to reach out beyond their comfort zone. Today's media suggests that truth lies in the reticence of the message. What is broadcast or delivered on a Facebook page may be simplified, framed for personal consumption, and prioritized based on the geographic and demographic distance from the source. These delivery methods automatically assume universal objectivity when we know system 1 thinking overtakes the vast majority of our mental processes. Bayes Theorem is the statistical method that does not pretend that the human mind lives and breathes without an erroneous filtering system.

The best futurologists use what might be called degrees of probability, which give weight to the best articulated situational explanations. To Tetlock's point in his book *Superforecasting*, most experts in prediction are not experts in the topic at hand but, rather, generalists who have the mind-set to consult the expert methods based on the situation. Prediction is a situational methodology derived from contemplative system 2 thinking rather than simply using intelligence and expertise derived of system 1. As the world gets more complex, the traditional experts become less competent to prepare for the path forward, even though they may have a better grasp on the past in their respective field. In 2013, esteemed economist Gregory Mankiw wrote an essay titled "In Defense of the One Percent." He spends most of his twenty-six pages outlining his case to the rest of economic academia. He reports that essentially, those in the higher 1 percent in terms of wealth are simply financial superstars. They have the talent and work ethic for which the normal person can never hope to equal. He concludes that there may be an inherent inequality to their situation, but it has almost nothing to do with money. Mr. Mankiw is an Ivy League–educated Harvard economics professor. If he were to have a professional archenemy, it would be Princeton Professor Paul Krugman. Krugman would argue the opposite point of view. It has everything to do with money, just in a much more nuanced socioeconomic perspective. We have two world renowned men in the same discipline, with the same data, who have come to two very fundamentally different conclusions. How can that be?

If Krugman could get Mankiw to capitulate that money is truly the driving force behind inequality, he would more than likely conclude a system of righting the wrongs of financial inequality may not only be inefficient but also unfair to the 1 percent who have earned their position one way or another. Krugman would do the opposite and advocate for policy—a true "Liberal versus Conservative" perspective. Both men agree on the facts but disagree on how the facts came to be. An endless supply of data can justify almost anything. Mark Twain has been quoted as saying, "There are lies, damned lies, and statistics." Even world-renowned economists are subjected to the prejudices of their own cognitive machinery. Economist Sherwin Rosen first identified *The Economics of Superstars* in 1981. It was apparent even thirty-five years ago that wage polarization would only continue. The economic inevitabilities of the future would call for a smaller percentage of people making an extraordinary amount of money. Krugman would say that policy and tax code have changed to better insulate the rich and allow for an almost impenetrable plutocracy. Mankiw concludes that this has almost nothing to do with a monetary legacy or nepotism but simply good genes. He has very credible citations to justify his opinions, whether you agree with them or not, but he cites a vague Geno economics study and concludes, "IQ, for example, has been widely studied, and it has a large degree of heritability. Smart parents are more likely to have smart children, and their greater intelligence will be reflected, on average, in higher incomes. Of course, IQ is only one dimension of talent, but it is easy to believe that other dimensions, such as self-control, ability to focus, and interpersonal skills, have a degree of genetic heritability as well." This statement makes a lot of suppositions, most notably that any of these characteristics were present in their parents, that these traits can actually be transferred genetically, and that the presence of these traits account for the discrepancy of earnings. Mankiw goes on to state, "My view here is shaped by personal experience. I was raised in a middle-class family, neither of my parents were college graduates. My own children are being raised by parents with both more money and more education. Yet I do not see my children as having significantly better opportunities than I had at their age."

Mr. Mankiw has enough self-awareness to conclude that his perspective is shaped by personal experience, but he is also clearly and overtly using anecdotal evidence to submit to an academic journal. Even world-class economists are not immune to their own perceptions. This trend will only continue as we shift from pooling our resources as a society to solve large problems, like we did in the Great Depression and World War II, to solving a large number of relatively smaller problems. If we cannot trust the economists to find consensus, then surely we can trust the biological and ecological sciences to point the way. Here we will find much more consensus, yet the opinions of Americans are diverting from the scientific findings. We are less and less positive about evolution and global warming. It is much easier to introduce doubt into our lives. We have essentially become more tribal with the proliferation of information sources on the internet and cable news. Instead of watching the "hard news" of the networks, we subscribe to the narrow and skewed perspective of Fox News or MSNBC. We consume the information that already fits our world view and reject what does not as misinformation or bad reporting. This makes it harder and harder to find truth in the world. It also makes us more reactionary and polarized. We view not just politics as political but also the whole spectrum of the news cycle as well as what our family and friends are doing in their personal life. We first see differences and separate them into a politicized compartment in our brain.

If not the social sciences nor the sciences themselves, then surely mathematics is the final frontier of truth. No matter the complexity of math, we can still feel safe knowing that we do not need to rely on ambiguity. The great mathematical minds of the world throughout history have given us many proofs that have been replicated and are now held as mathematical fact. All these proofs have been used as building blocks for the obscure and cutting-edge theorem of modern times. A simple search of unsolved math problems in *Wikipedia* will provide a laundry list of conjectures that the math world has been contemplating since 1975. Mathematics itself, the foundation for science, is now even subjected to the noise of opinion. In the modern industrialized world, we have solved most of the "big" problems of scarcity from the past. This has freed us up to begin to tackle some of the more intricate problems. Nowhere is this more apparent than in the world of mathematics, for which we could always defer to answer the universal truths.

Max Planck initiated the quantum movement in in the late nineteenth century. By 1905, the entire world knew Albert Einstein by his Theory of Relativity, which said space and time are not absolute. The very fact that it took world-class physicists a decade to even acknowledge the validity of the theory illustrates the fundamental shift in the way humanity viewed the mechanics of the world. Isaac Newton, two centuries prior, had written about the mathematical principles that govern the universe. From the time of Newton until the time of Planck, all of science and mathematics was derived through deduction, order, and logic. By 1927, Werner Heisenberg outlined his Uncertainty Principle, which declared that the world was not, in fact, governed exclusively by the laws of classical physics. There was a nonzero chance that particles could pass through barriers even if they did not have the required energy to do so. Sir Arthur Eddington, who assisted in helping translate Einstein's ideas, said that quantum physicists had discovered that "a particle can have position or velocity but not both." He went on to state, "Religion first became possible for a reasonable scientific man about the year 1927," which was a prophecy of the implications of the finding.

The view of scientific unknowns as the "not yet discovered" suddenly had to face the possibility that ultimate discovery of the natural world may be forever unattainable. $E=MC^2$, or the idea of special relativity, where the laws of Newtonian physics break down when incorporating the speed of light said that time and space, the ultimate absolute properties in the universe, may vary depending on perspective. In the early 1930s, the world was still trying to come to terms with a new view of reality, especially one which is notoriously difficult to explain. The Copenhagen Interpretation said that because position and velocity cannot both be measured and because any attempt to measure in quantum mechanics leads to errors, truth now lies more in probability rather than measurable results. In 1935, Erwin Schrodinger, in a thought experiment, which came to be known as Schrodinger's Cat, applied a real-world scenario to scientific understanding at a subatomic level. If states of matter can be reduced to an either/or, as represented by a 1 or a 0, quantum systems have the capacity to define a superposition, whereas the two states actually become an altogether different reality. The hypothetical interpretation of the quantum cat suggests it is sealed in a box with a flask of poison where the chances of it breaking are governed by the uncertain laws of quantum physics. The superposition is a cat that is both alive and dead at the same time. Only the act of observation itself determines the cat's final eventuality. This is an unnatural state of human kind, whereas fate itself is probabilistic, and our own perspectives are inadvertently and infinitely subjective.

If finding causality is the ultimate goal of the scientist and order is the ultimate goal of the human mind, not learning the lessons of quantum mechanics is a recipe for anxiety. Culturally, this lesson in science eventually only amounted to more system 1 errors and more noise. As Kahneman has taught us, the algebra in our head that takes our experiences and computes them as a formula to navigate the present and the future is subjected to faulty variables. Our cognitive machinery must be intentionally cleansed through system 2 thinking, which purposefully monitors the errors in our system 1. It must also use an intuitive form of probability through the vast amount of subjective realities to which each of us succumb in our own system 1 errors. The best predictive method is the collective subjective, carefully attuned to errors and always aware of the uncertain. Nassim Taleb in *The Black Swan* sees the mind as a giant map, which can never be accessed all at once. We fold the map in our minds to access the parts we require at the moment. This is not reality but a dumbed-down version that can fold away the portions of the map which point to uncertainty. Only the entire map itself forms a quantum perspective, which is much more closely aligned with the truth; however, our natural cognition searches to destroy the inevitable inconsistencies.

It is true that the world used to be a simpler place. Certainty propelled us beyond the tyranny of British rule, the evils of slavery, and the horrors of fascism. Certainty still protects our ideals and shapes our identities, but to move forward, we must conclude that usefulness of certainty is dead. As the noise of information increasingly bombards us, the tendency for the negative, as represented by the noise rather than the signal, has become the status quo. This is a by-product of the volatile times in which we live and the fear of the unknown, which comes with change. The layers of perception learned over the years only reinforce our own feelings of righteousness. Certainty without clarity is what led us into the very complicated and disastrous Iraq war, for instance. The sources of our media and information are more diverse. In the past, the facts were reported. In the world of entertainment news, the experts command thought processes. People look for certainty in uncertain times. Zealots stake out extremes as leaders of certainty even as new information arises to contradict our patterns of thought. Older generations are by nature more fearful of change or inherently conservative. Author and humorist Douglas Adams has noted, "Anything invented before your 15th birthday is the order of nature. Anything invented between your 15th and 35th birthday is new and exciting, and you might get a career there. Anything invented after that day, however, is against nature and should be prohibited." Baby boomers, who have effectively earned and inherited positions of power in society across the spectrum, is a generation marked by ideology. Put this all together, and the rise in extremism and polarization can begin to be understood.

In the 1990s the United States Military began using the acronym VUCA to describe the present and future state of the world. This acronym stands for volatility, uncertainty, complexity, and ambiguity. This accurately describes the condition of anxiety found in the twenty-first century. The natural human inclination is to stake out a side, to place blame, and to understand the root cause. A fog of faux clarity erupts where groups and poor leaders raise what futurologist Bob Johansen calls the Threshold of Righteousness. In the absence of ambiguity, humility, or empathy, fundamentalism ensues, and the neurological impulse of certainty begins. Anyone who does not draw these same conclusions without deviation is clearly wrong. Knowing that you know without clarity is opposite the oldest definition of the wisdom in the western world. Socrates lived in a world where information was so limited that oral traditions were sufficient, and the focus on mental processes as intelligence was a virtue. Today information is the most abundant resource in the world, yet we must apply that same rigor that Socrates recommended in a much simpler time.

Unfortunately, this trend will probably continue. Never have we had a group of leaders in a position of power who have developed their values within a cultural era so distinct from the present. Max Planck said, "A new scientific truth does not triumph by convincing its opponents and making them see the light, but rather because . . . a new generation grows up that is familiar with it." The one saving grace is that younger generations are a lot less ideological and more prone to seek solutions. Johansen calls this process constructive depolarization. There are more than two points of view and the art of managing conflict through dialogue will be an important attribute. A good grasp of the social sciences and diversity can make this paradigm shift complete. STEM disciplines are essential in the future, but a well-rounded education in the humanities can provide a basis for understanding. They have the tools to change the trajectory. Technology can bolster awareness across cultures and income brackets. Certainty is simple-minded. Clarity is the ability to see through the complex.

George W. Bush convinced the United States of the virtues of going to war with Iraq. His arguments were not very sound and constantly changing, although the American people saw a very certain man who communicated his certainty very well. Complex situations call for nuance and thoughtfulness. Powerful leadership is not just making the tough decision but making the right decision. To solve the major issues of the world, we need a generation committed to problem solving. What we have now is a generation of leaders committed to polarization and gridlock to give psychological comfort to their system 1 mind. The baby boomers have always stood on principle, even if their principles affected the greater good. This is a foreign concept to the younger generations. Theirs is a culture of openness and communication. They value clarity over certainty. Early in life, boomers waged a full-scale assault both for civil rights and against the Vietnam War. They are an excessively idealistic generation who openly rebelled against a very tame and pragmatic generation. This was certainly very evident in the turmoil of the late 1960s, but how does it apply now? The millennials have waged a war of pragmatic idealism, which is foreign to almost every generation alive. Boomers at once scold them for not taking a stand yet chastise them for seeking the utilitarian methods.

Americans are historically economically Conservative in theory yet operationally much more Liberal in practice. Most simply put, we do not like government spending unless that spending is beneficial to us. We do not understand socially Liberal causes unless we can relate it to a personal narrative in our lives. Millennials are apolitical not because they do not care but because they are more pragmatic than we give them credit. They simply pursue their ideals in a manner that makes sense. They are issue-driven and consensus-building. In the eyes of many, they are fighting unfairly and must be discredited. They have no representation in Congress, which means no national voice to speak for them. They seek power in other manners. They are not cynical, so they do not see politics as a waste of time; they just choose to redirect their resources to avenues that offer them the greatest benefit. Sincerity and pragmatism is a combination that leads to results. These are the methods that futurologists prescribe to solve our biggest problems. It is a more stoic perspective of progress which relieves the pressure of polarization without relinquishing our personal principles. They are smarter than the past generations, so they can see both sides of the issue. They did not have to clutter their mind with memorization. The computer in their pocket at all times can retrieve any information imaginable. Instead, these very well-educated men and women have spent a great amount of time learning how to learn. They intuitively embrace the ambiguity of our time because it is a skill that they learned from an early age. F. Scott Fitzgerald said, "The test of first rate intelligence is to hold two opposing ideas in mind and still have the ability to function." He could have written that about the millennial's relationship to the world today. To stoically rise above the turmoil of the future will be their crowning achievement.

Nate Silver predicted the 2012 election outcomes in all fifty states, an impressive feat. Yet he never claimed certainty, but he did claim confidence. There's a big difference. Twenty-first-century dilemmas are unique and complex. The best among us will be able to sort out the noise and solve problems. This will require incremental change and a nuanced approach. It will require ingenuity, creativity, and maybe, most importantly, curiosity. People feel safe in the arms of certainty, even if that certainty turns out to be completely wrong. That is a dangerous notion. Fitzgerald is saying that a decision will still need to be made but only after a contemplative journey. This is the leader's quest for the future. Facts are easy. Analysis can be done by computers. The melding of two powerful contradictory thoughts can be understood only by the human brain. So synthesis of the infinite subjective can finally lead us toward truth. Silver is one of the world's best predictors because he has aligned his model of the world under the statistical assumptions of the present, stating that that cause is not correlation and that neither lead to certainty. The paradigm of problem solving itself is under assault when certainty is unquestioned.

When we think of engineering, many times we equate it with Germany. German-born United States diplomat Henry Kissinger would disagree. He believed the Americans are the true engineers, born with the expectation that any problem, big or small, can be identified and solved with the right amount of time, energy, and money. "You are wrong," he says. "All of the world's great problems are not problems at all. They are dilemmas, and dilemmas cannot be solved." Problems are not going to be solved, only made better. No one is going to solve pollution or solve unemployment. We can only hope to improve. This is the task of the future. This is a skill that must be learned to lead in the future. To move forward, we must be pragmatic leaders that shed the baggage of partisanship, whatever psychological connection we have made which has crept into our system 1 cognitive processes. In a world of interdependent systems, represented most accurately by the Internet itself, zero sum outcomes based on ideologies acquired in dead cultural eras cannot be applied to our lives or our disciplines.

Few experts saw the financial collapse of 2008 coming. If you read a short chapter of *The Unwinding, An Inner History of the New America* by George Packer, it would seem to have been an absolute inevitability. The city of Tampa, for example, was sprawling, for no other reason than it was sprawling. Economists, who spent their lives preaching and theorizing, largely missed the signs. Hindsight may be 20-20, but how can we trust a group of quasi-scientists to fully understand something as complex as the world economy when a collection of narratives regarding bleakly average people lends us more insight than an encyclopedia of economic models and Laffer Curves? Besides the complexities of, say, evolution or climate change, is there anything as integrative as economics? These masters of the discipline are the geniuses of the economic world, but seemingly, once their opinions are formed they fall victim to the confirmation bias of their own beliefs. The dirty secret in economics is that there is more than one way to find equilibrium. Therefore, our greatest economists can disagree on just about everything. They are both right, and they are both wrong. It depends on the circumstance and point of view. The data that they are using is simply too big to assign causality.

Darrel Huff warned that not understanding causality and correlation could lead to disastrous effects in 1954. We as modern humans need to learn to resign to correlation, especially in a world that before long will rely on much more complex models that will require us to make decisions. Let's say that big data from Amazon servers found that the latest sales book on the market significantly increased profits for salespeople the following year. The human brain can understand that information. That book must have undoubtedly had unbelievable information and the power to motivate. The catch is that this was only and overwhelmingly true for those who bought the book on Tuesday afternoons! Given this information, it would be absurd to wait until Tuesday afternoon to buy the book. But how do we interpret that difference? Maybe we don't. Maybe we can't. The so-called Father of Virtual Reality, Jaron Lanier calls this, the Shower Knob Effect. Imagine you require an exact amount of water pressure and an exact water temperature. To complicate matters, there are one thousand knobs in the shower. None of them are marked, and each control, either hot or cold, or more or less pressure. The slightest turn may decrease pressure drastically, followed by a more dramatic turn, which increases temperature slightly. You are required to use all one thousand knobs to find your ideal setting. You will eventually get it right. You would falsely attribute your last few turns as the key to the puzzle. The truth, however, is that there are infinite ways that could have gotten you there.

Our path to the truth is the most veritable and viable method. This is called confirmation bias. It is a symptom of poor self-reflection. If we believe a decision to have been inept, we will search for that proof, and it will be found. In the modern age, no solution will be correct 100 percent of the time. Likewise, we will develop a solution bias to reaffirm what has been effective previously. Dilemmas will always leave room for critics to effectively counter very legitimate solutions. If our favorite talking head outlined talking points against a proposal, we could easily and wholeheartedly accept that position. If those same talking points crawled across the screen of our least favorite talking head, we could quite easily find a very well-articulated and reasoned acceptance of the proposal. The Platonic folds in our mind will always create an intuitive opinion. The leaders of tomorrow will have to understand the reasons for their opinion. Ambiguity is an issue that we will have to teach. Any one decision on any one issue will allow many parties to be at stake, and none having the panacea of a generation ago. Consensus can never be reached if individuals never adjust their own position to achieve the goals of the group. The group, many times, is larger than our field of vision. This is where the leader who is aware of the bigger picture needs to communicate the obfuscated goals. Everyone has a perspective, and that perspective is a very real component of the decision-making process of the future. Hearing people and people being heard is a component of leadership that will not soon go away. The group dynamics, the edification, and the perspective of the solution must be taught. Ambiguity and change are barely palatable to the average worker or citizen, especially those who were around when solutions were relatively easy. Consensus is no longer the goal, however. The many perspectives, openly shared, can move the needle. The awareness and the acceptance of the open process may even trump the decision. Eventually, the acceptance of ambiguity will become an evolved virtue.

There is a fable told of a farmer who remains stoic in the face of bad news or good. The loss of a horse eventually resulted in the gaining of twenty more. The broken leg of his son by one of the new wild horses resulted in the son missing a war that killed the entire able-bodied male population. Wall Street trader Nassim Nicholas Taleb updated this story in long form in his book *Fooled by Randomness*. He illustrated the point of the fealty of human confirmation bias in a case of a hypothetical dentist playing the stock market. Because the market tends to go down more often than it goes up in a given day, this opened the dentist up to the possibility of far more negative events in his life, even if the outcome of the day ended up positive. The proliferation of data and our constant monitoring makes our human brain connect patterns where they do not exist. The dentist goes home with a series of nonpleasurable feelings about the day's proceedings rather than happy about the positive outcome at day's end. He was fooled by randomness. We are all fooled by randomness. We do it unconsciously every day. It is the definition of prejudice. In ancient Greece, the economists of the day were philosophers. Instead of maximizing finance, they attempted to maximize happiness, or at least minimize anxiety.

Although the Internet has opened up nearly all knowledge for mankind, it has given us two very detrimental effects. One is that a new proof bias has been created. Just because we have access to all information in the world, we believe that we have the ability to organize it in our minds. This distorts the intention of the entire scientific process. As climatologist Michael Mann suggests, "Proof is for mathematical theorems and alcoholic beverages. It's not for science. Science works in evidence through best explanations and most credible theories." We believe that we can draw linear connections between events that give us cause and effect unequivocally. The second problem is the introduction of doubt. Formally, science is still a very slow-moving and bureaucratic process, which must wind its way through scholarly bodies that have been assigned authority. That is because the very definition of science is replication and understanding of the community who can understand it best. This leaves room for doubt. Examination of plausible alternatives is the only way to garner acceptance of a theory within the community. Now, because bits and pieces of those theories are available to the masses, there is a tendency to pick holes in them. The Internet allows the lone skeptic to have a voice the size of an entire community.

This is why we as a culture have actually gone backward with more information. Cynicism is confused with thoughtfulness. The sheer amount of data distracts from the big picture. Evolution was once taught as all but certainty. We determined that the process of evolution really does exist in the natural world. Our own personal religious beliefs could be formed around that fact. Today, a full one-third of Americans do not believe in evolution. Almost every earth or life scientist in the world agrees that evolution exists, to the tune of 99.85 percent. The dilemmas of the modern world are many and complicated. We enter the conversation of every given issue with our own confirmation bias. Instead of focusing on what can make us think, we focus on what can make us understand. We try to connect the dots where they apply. Mann developed the hockey stick graph, which mirrored the historical rise of humanity's use of fossil fuels with the last great temperature spike to illustrate the alarming, unnatural, and unprecedented rise in global temperature. The climatology community is in 97 percent agreement that mankind has had significant impact into the world's changing climate. Due to the 3 percent of doubters within the community, only 54 percent of Americans agree.

In the twentieth century, we introduced the social sciences into the conversation. Hypotheses regarding anthropology, sociology, and psychology were added to the list of what could be studied. The rise of the understanding of statistical significance allowed us to make determinations about human behavior. Still the sample population was finite. The Big Data of the modern era is much more complicated. There could never be any direct scientific data that "proved" a single case of lung cancer was ever caused by cigarettes. However, we came to believe that it was very likely that cigarettes could give you cancer. The larger issues like evolution, climate change, and economics cannot be studied through a single entity like the effects of tobacco on the human body. They are constantly changing dynamic factors, which are interconnected in ways much bigger than the human mind can comprehend. No one will be able to directly attribute a climate event to any actual event of a human, no matter how large. A hypothesis may be formed as to what happened, but universal agreement will never exist as long as there are actors on the other side with an agenda. It is very difficult for humans to understand that we are coming to the end of what we can passively and intuitively understand. The Quantum Moment, which began around 1927 according to philosopher Robert Crease and physicist Alfred Goldhaber, fundamentally challenged the way we define truth. Quantum theory had assigned a mathematical proof to determine that the world was uncertain and unfair. Humanity would need to reorganize around this novel idea. Its cultural applications sent the world spinning into the infinite subjective known as the postmodern period. Scientifically and statistically, the information collected through advanced algorithms of big data has finally caught up with the subatomic theory of a century ago.

Quantum theories lead to correlation which has been a scientific dead end in the past. Organizing the world's information, the exact quest of Google, is a messy process with lots of inconsistencies. The world's entire deductive math problems left over from the world of Newton have been solved. All the simple empirical issues, which can be linearly and incontrovertibly connected using causation, have been designed and tested. What is left is humanity in a metamodern world where all the world's information is delivered to our fingertips and the signal of truth is in constant battle with the proliferation of noise. Intelligence is nuance, which itself is more difficult to accept in a world of limited attention span. The Big Data world is the next realm for science and mathematics, but it only works within a culture which can embrace its strange method of communication. A generation must finally come to terms with the inevitable conclusions that an uncertain world is on the horizon. The goal will be intelligence and leadership which acts by depolarizing rather than denying the existence of a transformed world.

PART 2

THE SEVEN VALUES THAT WILL CHANGE THE WORLD

CHAPTER 9

ART AND EGO (PARTICIPATION)

The ancient Indian text, the *Bhagavad Gita*, opens in a metaphoric war between kingdoms. The Lord Krishna recruits the young Arjuna to drive his chariot into battle. Arjuna has reservations about the nature of war and second-guesses his teacher's request. Why would he see everyone he knows die in battle for a cause that he does not understand? Krishna explains to Arjuna that his own personal dharma, or that which aligns with the order of his circumstances on earth, requires not just contemplation but action. In today's western terms, Krishna would tell Arjuna that his special gifts (archery in his case) were required to fulfill his destiny (a rough English translation of *dharma*). The talents and gifts that each of us are given as individuals must be used to their fullest extent. The physical action of our gifts is required. It is our duty as humans. That is what we are here to do. Conquering the enemy within—lust, as he called it—is a form of inaction as it is an internal battle. So before we fight our metaphoric and external battles with action, we must first temper our actions with the inaction of combatting lust—or what we would today refer to as the ego.

We Americans glorify our freedom of the market, religion, keeping and bearing arms, or taming the land. Freedom is our enduring national character. Eleanor Roosevelt said, "Freedom makes a huge requirement of every human being. With freedom comes responsibility." The self-aware leader acknowledges our right to excess, hyperbole, extremism, and destruction, but this lust to satisfy the ego is a failure of responsibility. Exercising these freedoms might be necessary to establish our dharma, or in this case a realization of the self. Acting on our true nature is a virtue, but acting on our small and selfish understanding of our nature is an overreach. In *The War of Art*, Steven Pressfield calls this the battle between the ego and the self. The ego encompasses an exceptionally small portion of the self, yet this is where the corrosive agents of our being lurk. Remove the divisive and competitive nature of the ego, and the true goodness of human nature can emerge through the self.

Like Arjuna's circumstances, the metamodern world calls for us to have a bias toward action yet shed our ego as often as possible. Essentially, if you were born to do something, you have the responsibility to do it. We neglect the inspiration in our lives because of feelings of inferiority, hopelessness, or fear of vulnerability. Rock and roll legend Neil Young has said that when he gets an idea, he stops what he is doing to pay attention to it and "treats it nicely." The source of his art, in his mind, is a near physical entity, separate from his self or his ego. He has acted on behalf of the self, devoid of ego, to take responsibility and dutifully act on the gift of his art. There was never any guarantee of the fame and riches bestowed on Mr. Young. The fruit of labor in most cases, even for the great Neil Young, is the ability to produce the labor. For artists, the intrinsic value of the work is the gift. Finding your art—your dharma—and acting on it is your great responsibility. In this way, the artist is a simple conduit who dictates the gift.

Art, of course, is a metaphor, but it does imply a personal technique, flair, or competency, which only you as an individual can add to the actions of your calling. Many times, for humans, making the art is the easy part. It is when we are forced to communicate the work to those who we perceive as possibly being unreceptive which slow down our creative process. We can be artists, innovators, entrepreneurs, or artisans, but if we are afraid to share our work or our ideas, we will never be great ones. Connection with someone is the ideal in which we are trying to achieve but which will also nearly always generate disconnection. Dr. Brene Brown spent a decade trying to understand our fears of being disconnected by shame. She found that the healthiest among us, whom she called the wholehearted, had an absence of control of whom they thought "should" be in favor of who they are.

What the "wholehearted" classification in her research all had in common was that, by and large, they viewed their contributions as worthy because they, themselves had courage, compassion, and the ability to connect. Because of these traits, the proverbial artist can assume vulnerability, which according to Brown is the key attribute. She defines *vulnerability* as the ability to "put our ideas into the world with no assurance of acceptance or appreciation." Vulnerability has been an historical weakness of man. Situational inferiority, as well as its cousin, situational superiority, are both signs of an unhealthy ego. According to Peter Fuda and Richard Badham's 2011 *Harvard Business Review* article "Fire, Snowball, Mask, Movie," the ability to be vulnerable, which they call *mask*, trumps our ability to navigate situational roles. Authenticity and honesty, with the removal of the ego, builds trust, which enhances connection and is the ultimate goal of the artist.

So there is now power in vulnerability. No progress comes with the nonaction of invulnerability, while the criticism itself is not pointed at our being but a tiny dot within the self, called the ego. The title of Brown's book, called *Daring Greatly*, is taken from an excerpt of a speech given by President Theodore Roosevelt in which he lauds the man of action . . .

> It is not the critic who counts; not the man who points out how the strong man stumbles, or where the doer of deeds could have done better. The credit belongs to the man who is actually in the arena, whose face is marred by dust and sweat and blood; who strives valiantly; who errs, who comes short again and again because there is no effort without error and shortcoming; but who actually strive to do the deeds; who know great

enthusiasms, the great devotions; who spends himself in a worthy cause; who at best knows in the end triumph of high achievement, and who at worst, if he fails, at least fails while daring greatly, so that his place shall never be with the cold and timid souls who neither know victory nor defeat.

The "man in the arena" could be the embodiment of the perseverance of Arjuna. It could be Galileo, who took his telescope to Rome in 1611 to show the Papal Court the new mysteries of science. It could be Neil Young, who was told that his voice was strange and unmarketable, or Steve Jobs, who was told that the user experience could not be quantified and therefore was not an effective business model. Discomfort marks progress. If you are blending in, following orders, and appeasing the masses, then you are not doing the work of an artist; you are taking part in the status quo. The innovator and the entrepreneur must be out of touch with the mainstream. Neomarketing guru Seth Godin says, "Only when you make art that isn't for everyone do you have the chance to connect with someone." As Chris Guillebeau reminds us in his work *The Art of Non-Conformity*, in every aspect of our life, in every organization that we join or institution which we navigate, we will find "gatekeepers." These are the same people whom Pressfield would call the fundamentalists. Devoid of religious or political implications, these are people that think hierarchically and historically. They seek to control the world and restore balance to a time of imagined perfection. Their experience as an insider guards against the blasphemy of new ideas. In his book *David and Goliath*, Malcolm Gladwell told us that adopting unconventional strategies is the path to success against traditional gatekeepers. Rather than fight in hand-to-hand combat with a giant and an expert in the craft, David instead chose the element of surprise by shedding his heavy armor in favor of the agility of being equipped with only a sling shot.

David, of course, beat Goliath in the ancient duel, which became a parable for bravery and persistence. Gladwell explains that the lesson of David has been modernized with the advent of social science. If he were the guardian and gatekeeper of the rules of combat, David would have stood no chance against Goliath. Incumbent powerhouses are much more likely to win when the game is played on their terms. Strategy changes, however, are not their forte. By choosing the slingshot, David the underdog becomes David the bettor's favorite. He effectively entered a swordfight with a pistol. Gladwell cites social science findings that by using unconventional strategies against the more powerful tilt the scales statistically in favor of the underdog. The gatekeeper who rules by experience of the past still recognizes experience over ability, although the pace of the world is biased toward the capable and the competent. Meritocracy, then, is more attainable but only for those who can effectively disrupt.

Being a good employee or employer in today's world means something different than it did just ten or twenty years ago. Not only do you have to be an expert, a multitasker, and technologically proficient, you will need to be able to navigate in the complicated and layered environment of the vast human resources within and beyond the organization. Because every hiring manager is different and every position is different, they will prioritize the competencies they require differently. What they will all look for is a positive attitude, competence, and accountability. The modern business world talks about having an entrepreneurial spirit. Managers no longer have time to explain the details. What they need are intuitive leaders who make no excuses. What they need is the often identified but rarely defined attribute of having an internal locus of control. This attitude goes well beyond a common competency in a work environment to a complete viewpoint of the world around them. We must believe that we are in control of our own destiny. We can never be the victim of our own narrative.

Early in Kathleen Kelley Reardon's book *It's All Politics*, she uses an analogy of a man who has the sufficient work ethic and knowledge necessary for his field, yet he lacks the accompanying social and political skills that his company and nearly every company culture requires. The man she created is named Reginald Strongbrow. He is a generally good employee, and he works for any average medium or large sized firm. Due to his complete lack of interest or thought about his surroundings and his place within the company, he has become a beaten man. He is used as a scapegoat by other employees, who unabashedly exclude him from office activities. Reginald has an external locus of control. Everything negative that happens to him can be attributed to someone else. Reardon explains that everyone is at least 75 percent responsible for how they are treated in most situations. Subservience is just as toxic to the ego as Machiavellianism.

Only by understanding that we are the prime mover behind our relationships and events in our lives does that translate into any representation of power and respect. Power is sometimes the goal in politics, but neither power nor politics has to have negative connotation. Where there is power, there must be ethics. There are many forms of benign power, including expert power, referent power, and prestige power. Taken with a dose of self-awareness, social awareness, and empathy, these types of power can go a long way. This is a far cry from the Machiavellian and narcissistic stereotype of the word. Destructive and divisive politics can be the downfall of careers and entire companies. Taking accountability when blame should be assigned is a virtue to strong leadership. Being the scapegoat when no such blame exists is corrosive to mental health and only feeds the vicious cycle of victimhood. To be an artist requires upsetting the status quo yet subtly navigating the power structure. This requires connection with people. As more connections are formed, we have to be more aware of the group dynamics while mindfully examining the ego.

Having an internal locus of control is important for success in any discipline. Psychologist Carol Dweck explains a very similar phenomenon to the locus of control, which she calls the mind-set of success. Those with a fixed mind-set believe that their abilities are innate and static, and those with a growth mind-set believe that their abilities are the result of hard work, learning, and perseverance over time. Those with a fixed mind-set avoid failure first because it is seen as a repudiation of their intelligence. Those with growth mind-sets understand that failure is an inevitable predecessor of learning. The vulnerability, so important to Brown, is never surrendered for members of the fixed mindset category, and the personal accountability, which comes with our actions, is released to a third party of external phenomena for the external locus of control individuals.

Many of the necessities for success in the twenty-first century are an updated version of the theologic, sociologic, and economic ideas, which have propelled America for centuries. In the first decade of the twentieth century, German social theorist Max Weber identified the Protestant work ethic in his book *The Protestant Ethic and the Spirit of Capitalism*. For one thousand years, during the Dark Ages, the Holy Roman Church was an infallible and united institution for the Kingdom of God on earth. The responsibility for individual existence itself fell into the confines of the Church. The invention of the printing press allowed Martin Luther to spread his ideas on paper. The interpretation of God's Word was democratized to the individual, and Luther became the face of the great Protestant Reformation in Europe, which divided the church into new sects.

Just as Krishna taught Arjuna the meaning of fulfilling his dharma in the ancient world, Luther taught the western world of the sixteenth century the meaning of fulfilling its vocation. Vocation is from the Latin root for the word *calling*. It would have had only sacred and religious context a century earlier. The Protestant Reformation though, through the lens of new world Enlightenment, allowed man to branch out from the necessity of tying work to the church. Diligent work, separate from God, was for the first time, a sign of the grace of God. Productivity, success, and achievement were met with God's approval. The longer and harder we worked, the more we fell into God's favor. When the New World was settled, the mostly Protestant settlers carried this ethic to a new land. When Adam Smith was foretelling the future of capitalism, Thomas Jefferson was penning the future of democracy. Capitalism, Protestantism, and Democracy converged on a new continent where they could take on their own distinct character, devoid of the meddling of the old world, the old feudalism and monarchies, and the old Church. The farmers went to work, taking advantage of a new idea of personal property rights for the common man, with a tangible link between work and prosperity. The Industrial Revolution was on the horizon. The Protestant work ethic would be cemented as an American tradition, although the work itself would be constantly permutated. The individualism gained through Enlightenment required a responsibility to God of self-reliance. For the first time in the history of the Christian Church, the theology of prosperity was viewed favorably. Doing better economically brought you closer to God. Hard work attained a symbiotic virtue with righteousness and God, and we have never doubted it since.

One hundred twenty-five years ago, you would have worked for yourself. Almost everyone did. Those that did not were perceived as some form of indentured servant. The economy was local, economics was classical, and organizations were small. Scientific management had not yet been created. Using humans as cogs in the machine was not yet the mainstream. The entrepreneur's ability to meet their customer's needs and connect was all that they had. With no social safety and no mass production, art, rather than science, was the surest way to make a living. I am not suggesting that everyone ran around town with a paintbrush and a palette. I am suggesting that people were truly more connected to their work and accountable for how it made people feel. Webster's definition of *art* is "something that is created with imagination and skill and that is beautiful or that expresses important ideas or feelings." The twentieth century brought the greatest prosperity the world has ever known. Slowly, the butcher, baker, and candlestick maker went to work for someone else; function began to trump connection, and the wheels of the industrial society began to turn. Great art never died, but it became more difficult to practice as a vocation on a daily basis.

The twentieth century feared art because it had no direct connection with productivity. It was not safe, and it was not practical. The radio was invented and played approvingly in households, generated collectively from the European tradition and mass produced in an area in New York City called Tin Pan Alley. Meanwhile, the fringes of music were more disparate. Music not made on assembly lines or for the masses was gaining traction. Jazz was the embodiment of art. It was improvised and the only fine art created in America. Country and western took traditions of yodeling from northern Europe, and the steel guitar from Hawaii led to folk and bluegrass.

The African gospel traditions developed into rhythm and blues. The amalgamation, in time, led to rock and roll. The pioneers of rock and Roll, because of their skin color and their deviance from the safe and sweet sounds of symphony, were an instant affront to the establishment. But what was a threat in the industrial culture was also an opportunity. The late 1950s were the beginning of the first decade of the teenager. The oldest baby boomers were becoming marketable. *Rebel Without a Cause* was released in 1955 and signified a new social awakening in the years ahead. The corporate instinct seized this music and tamed it. The fearful quelled the revolution for some time, choosing to whitewash and produce only music that the masses could tolerate. Rock and roll had to be outsourced to Europe to be reintroduced. On a Sunday night, February 9, 1964, the Beatles played on Ed Sullivan. The United States sullied the spirit of rock and roll, but the Brits had mastered it. They brought the sound back home, and music and culture has never been the same since.

We can't all be groundbreaking musicians and artists, but we can strive for what connects people. A year after the Beatles took the stage on Ed Sullivan, a twenty-four-year-old Bob Dylan, who had made a name for himself as a folk singer, took the stage at the Newport Folk Festival. Adoring fans awaited his acoustic set as he strapped on his Fender Stratocaster guitar. Instead, Dylan plugged it in to an amplifier in front of an audience abjectly hostile to the electrification of music. Bob Dylan lost the lukewarm acceptance of most of the live audience that night. He disappointed thousands staring him in the face and won over millions yet to be born. America was shedding the collectivism that Whyte had chided a decade previous, and its prophets were our masters of art. Producing for the masses may have once made good business sense but now just leads to mediocrity. This gives opportunity for humans to do what they do, which is to be human and connect, as well as not fearing disconnect. The fear of art will again turn into the opportunity of art.

In the book of Matthew, the word *epiphany*, translated as "the vision of God," was the sudden realization of the manifestation of God (Jesus) as man. In the modern world, we learned epiphany one hundred years ago through one of the twentieth century's most revered writers, James Joyce. Joyce described epiphany not as an unattainable physical state of God but as a manifestation of great spiritual change. The artists and the philosophers of the ancient world looked to the nine muses to help them tell their story in the proper way. Homer begins his epics pleading to the muses for inspiration. During the Dark Ages the gift of creativity was unified with the existence of God under the belief of Divine Providence as proof of God's existence in the physical world. By the time of Joyce, we still revered the spirituality of epiphany, but we began to see its science.

As the story goes, the great ideas of history are understood suddenly and instantaneously as if being struck by an unknown force. Archimedes cried "Eureka" when he computed density, and Newton intuitively understood gravity when an apple fell from a tree. As Scott Berkun explains in *The Myths of Innovation*, the epiphany of innovation is serendipity sprung from the rigor of work. All of the creative and intuitive understanding of gravity captured by Newton, from the flight of the apple from the tree to the ground, was an epiphany of years of contemplation. It took Newton another twenty years to articulate what his brain captured in a mere instant. Isaac Newton is the father of modern science and one of the most consequential humans to ever walk the earth. He is most known to the world for his epiphany, although all epiphany is only possible first through action.

Ask any leader, from the avant-garde of the art world to the mainstream of corporate America, and they will all tell you that the greatest competitive advantage is innovation. To be an innovator, however, is to break free from the norms and sometimes even the culture that binds us. This is the piece de resistance of the art world and taboo for the business world. Dean Keith Simonton, in *Creativity in Science*, explains that the very fields where we seek and require innovation the most are the very places where we are least receptive. Congressional voting cycles increasingly favor the incumbent at historic rates of over 90 percent, while disapproval rates of Congress itself are at record lows (near single digits). While we would like to embrace the change required to surrender to uncertainty, we psychologically favor the known failures. The perceived eccentricity and its respective uneasiness pull us back to the safe and secure and its inevitable failure.

In the year 2000, Jeffrey Pfeffer and Robert I. Sutton had already documented the gap regarding what we know and what we do. The business world spends tens, if not hundreds, of billions of dollars a year acquiring knowledge through consultants. The prescription, inevitably, is strategy as a cost savings, cultural alignment, or revenue-generating mechanism. In other words, change is some form of innovation. Good consultants recommend organizational upheavals for long-term success, which quickly die in application. Bad consultants recommend small inconsequential updates, which affect no real change. Still, too often, these very same leaders hunger for innovation as ideas. The belief that innovation is simple epiphany, born of the semantics of consultants, is as dangerous to the management class as formulaic self-help rags to riches is for the working class. In other words, shortcuts of any kind are few and far between.

We make the mistake that all the inventions on earth have been created. Evolutionary biology teaches us that complexity is the inevitable trajectory of life on earth. Creativity and innovation is the connection of ideas that have never before been linked. This could be as simple as a new labeling system for the office or as complex as a breakthrough in nanotechnology. Sociobiologists would argue that when mankind hits a cognitive threshold—that is where complexity surpasses our brain's ability to understand itself—our intuition is to recoil into a reactionary aversion to innovation. Perhaps one thousand years of the Dark Ages was man's utopia on earth as the rigor and work of innovation was disconnected from our earthly responsibilities. In the ancient world, epiphany was a kiss from the gods. In the modern life, the sweat and toil of epiphany is of this world, a suffering blessed by the power of God.

The notion of the self-made man is as old as the republic itself. Hard work and striving for continuous improvement in life, work, and learning was the early path to the American dream. The term *self-made man* in America may originate from founding father Benjamin Franklin, but it was made famous by Fredrick Douglass, an escaped slave turned orator, author, and abolitionist. According to Douglass, if a man owes nothing to wealth, education, birth, relationships, or any other favoring conditions, the "good luck theory" of success is false. Success may be achieved via serendipitous circumstances, but it is the mental and/or physical work that is always indispensable from achievement. According to Douglass, "There is nothing good, great, or desirable . . . that does not come by some kind of labor."

From its start, America was a place where the self-made man of democracy and capitalism could exercise the insight of the spiritual understanding of man as master of his own fate. The Protestant work ethic in the infancy of capitalism meant physical exertion equated with the persistence of the family through an agrarian society. The idea of farmers and artisans being inseparable was a basic understanding of American life. The entrepreneurial craftsmen of the farm related to the candle maker, the printer, and the blacksmith in the city. The first version of the American self-made man was expiring in the late nineteenth century, however. The Industrial Revolution would change these small operations in every aspect of life to larger operations with small parts. By the time the Horatio Alger myth was popularized and the heat of the Industrial Revolution was already forecasting materialism, the middle-class morality of work ethic propagated by Douglass had already become the middle-class respectability of Alger based only on achievement. The "rags to riches" ideal of Alger was not as consumed with the honor of the man in the process of making it as much as the man who had made it, devoid of the process.

The industrial society of the twentieth century differentiated the United States as a modern empire minus the imperialism and colonialism indicative of recent centuries. Instead, capitalism and industrialism were its conduit. Even during the First World War, the Depression, and throughout the Second World War, consumption was seen as a vice to be avoided. As early as 1917, a brilliant Austrian-American, Edward Bernays, working in the service of President Woodrow Wilson, coined the term *public relations.* After reading *A General Introduction to Psychoanalysis* by Sigmund Freud, Bernays paved the road for public relations, marketing, and advertising, which would alter the consciousness of Americans for a century and beyond. The great American inventor, Charles Kettering, who graced the cover of *Time Magazine*, said in 1929, "The key to economic prosperity is the organized creation of dissatisfaction."

Adam Curtis made an award-winning and marathon-length documentary titled *The Century of the Self* in 2002, which placed Bernays at the center of a century of a society that has used large institutions and organizations to influence individual behaviors. Americans, even the middle and lower classes, were able to purchase what they desired rather than just what was required. Materialism was an undeniable aspect of twentieth-century American life. The ancient materialist philosophers viewed material as benign and without social implication but closely associated with the idea that all that exists can be seen and touched. Even the anticapitalists, usually known as socialists, believed that physical objects mattered to humanity. Whether the material was beneficial to society or egalitarian was not the point.

So a century of rhetoric began, coded, framed, and filtered through a new subconscious communication that euphemized propaganda. A new class of professionals emerged to sell on Wall Street for financiers, on Madison Avenue for advertisers, and on K Street for lobbyists. The size and scope of business forced owners to outsource operations to the new bureaucratic force of management. The institutions of finance, advertising, and government blended seamlessly with the media in the last years of the twentieth century and in the Internet age are nearly undistinguishable at first sight. In the age of rapid and vapid media consumption, we need to remember the reason the techniques of anxiety were created in the first place, which is to get us to commit further in the unrelenting and manufactured pursuit of dissatisfaction.

It's been a half century since we left the industrial economy, although all our lessons about life, liberty, and the pursuit of happiness have been established among the factory floors and crystallized there. There is no doubt that the machine that propelled the industrial economy blessed the world and, specifically, blessed the United States. Thomas Jefferson, perhaps our greatest thinker, foresaw a society distinct from the urbanization of Europe indefinitely, but he failed to see how the next manifestation of technology would lead to economies of scale and naturally denser pockets of urbanization. Jefferson was a contemporary of Adam Smith, neither of whom could have made predictions about the disruptions of the future. It is with the same distinct dissociation that our leaders of today fail to recognize what a severe turn in the economy we have taken and what it means for the future.

The paternalistic last half of the twentieth century was riding false hopes and predictions calculated by bloated pension calculations and erroneous lifespans of the Great Society of the 1960s. The collectivist and herding mentality of the middle third of the twentieth century created stability, it introduced materialism into society as an economic boom, and it stabilized the sins of inequality of the gilded age. We became individually what William Whyte called the Organization Man in 1956, which killed the rugged individualism of Teddy Roosevelt who championed the Man in the Arena. The creativity waned while the risk and the reward lay dormant. The Protestant ethic of work was being exercised but without its most important component: individual meaning. Advanced capitalism had been instituted in the United States, where the developed infrastructure relied on financial trickery, technology, efficiency, trade liberalization, debt, and denial. The tactics of advanced capitalism were squeezing the productivity out of the midcentury capitalism at the expense of a new generation.

Inevitably, we must return to equilibrium. As Reid Hoffman, founder of LinkedIn, says, "You were born an entrepreneur," which we often forget or never know. Micro financier and Nobel Peace Prize winner Muhammad Yunus reminds us, "All humans are entrepreneurs. When we were in the caves, we were self-employed . . . finding our food, feeding ourselves. That's where history began. As civilization came, we suppressed it. We became 'labor' because they stamped us, 'You are labor.' We forgot that we are entrepreneurs. Every company, even the great Amazon.com remembers that it is always day 1 for entrepreneurs . . . great companies are always evolving." A hypervigilance exists in Silicon Valley, which eventually trickles down to the rest of the working world. As Mr. Hoffman explains, a 2009 billboard in the Bay Area puts it bluntly: "One million people overseas can do your job. What makes you so special?" Ouch!

Entrepreneurship is back. It is true that small business is the life blood of the economy and that we still need the traditional entrepreneur to take the risks necessary to fill new niches in our economy. The role of the entrepreneur in big business is as vital as ever. It is also true that the sizes of our largest companies are shrinking and their half-lives are shortening. Experts on the life cycles will tell us that once an organization reaches success and maturity, they inevitably grow less risk-averse and less innovative. The spirit of the entrepreneur is replaced with compliance and rigidity. The entrepreneur in this sense is not a job title; it is a mind-set. Whether you are organizing the growth of a rooftop garden business, starting up a mustache grooming boutique, or working in middle management in corporate America, it is imperative that you identify with the individuality that you and you only can bring to the job at hand.

Pulitzer Prize–winning journalist and author Thomas Friedman says that in the modern world, in every job that we do, we need to "think like an artisan." Efficiency is cheap and a product of the economies of scale. Only by doing high-quality work with our own personal signature can we differentiate ourselves. In a world of checklists, our identities dissipate as the task becomes near robotic. In a world of common culture, such as a large organization, we deviate toward the perceived expected norms. Acting based on someone or some other group's expectation is an interruption of the ego. We must forge our personal identify within the new context. The artisan is cognizant of every brushstroke and attuned to how it will make people feel. So individualism is important—necessary even—given our ego is healthy. In the 1950s, Whyte criticized the Organization Man because "There is—or should be—a conflict between the individual and the organization. This denial is bad for the organization. It is worse for the individual . . . We are not hapless beings caught in the forces we can do little about . . . Organization has been made by man; it can be changed by man."

Whyte did not like that the ethos of the organization constricted and conflicted man's hopes and dreams. Whyte himself mourned the loss of the Protestant ethic. Even by the turn of the twentieth century, Whyte found that the ethic had "already been strained by reality. The country had changed. The ethic had not." Many of us will go out on our own to start a business, but the pure vision of entrepreneurship provides the unbridled power to create products, services, relationships, and organizations in their image. That is the power and vision of the ethic. Many more of us will work in organizations big and small. In this case, the ethic lies in the values of accountability, ownership, responsibility, and trust. These are all values for which we can take pride in as individuals, aside from our affiliation with organizations.

In *The Purple Cow*, Seth Godin picks up where Whyte left off. In Whyte's world of the 1950s, being an organization man was effective for success. Whyte did not argue that point; he just feared for the souls of the future. Godin takes it one step further. He modernizes the concept, claiming, as did Whyte, that we are still playing "follow the leader" en route to our next step up the corporate ladder, but the safe path is now the dangerous path to irrelevance. We conditioned our inner desires to relate to the mean of the group, whether it is the customer or coworkers. Chris Anderson introduced a concept called the Long Tail, which says that with modern distribution methods, even the extremes have the ability to compete with the mainstream. Who would have thought a decade ago that a show on the Internet could compete with a network? The reason, as Godin would argue, is that an artist's goal is to reach individuals, while a marketer is trying to reach the masses on the networks. It is a dying model.

That night in 1965, Bob Dylan had to make the decision to both disappoint and excite or to ameliorate and oblige. It was as if Krishna were there, whispering the sanctity of his personal dharma. Shakespeare may have recommended, "To thine own self be true." Dylan never cracked the top ten in US singles. He was never accepted by the masses but is revered in certain circles as the hero and the savior of American music in the twentieth century. *Rolling Stone Magazine*, the vestige of taste of recent musical history, asserts that his song "Like a Rolling Stone," performed in Newport that very night over fifty years ago, is the greatest rock and roll song ever recorded. Dylan took a path unpopular and risky. He chose "the road not taken" that Robert Frost had prescribed decades earlier . . .

> Two roads diverged in a wood, and I—
> I took the one less traveled by,
> And that has made all the difference.

Fortunately, the current generation does not have to anguish in decision. Two generations ago, we would have been lulled by the safety, security, and paternalism of the safe path. Dr. Brene Brown would say that Mr. Dylan left himself vulnerable that night in a way much more public than any of us ever will know. He surrendered his authentic self to immediate critics to fulfill his calling rather than exercise the appeasing comforts of the ego. The choice between the fruits of the Protestant work ethic and the ability to identify with your own personal calling is once again merging. Thomas Friedman espouses the mantra to "think like an artisan," but he also recommends "thinking like an immigrant." Globalization, technology, and a new digital abundance have reconfigured the intersection of artist and worker. *Forbes* contributor Glenn Llopis says immigrant thinking is an "earned serendipity," which is seeking good fortune through action rather than hoping for good fortune through inaction.

The personal responsibility revolution of the 1980s made little sacrifice for the adults. We tripled the national debt, lowered taxes, exploited the commons and the environment, raised education costs, lowered healthcare opportunities, gave high returns in the stock market, and outsourced jobs in return for cheap goods, all while patting ourselves on the back for escaping the malaise of the 1970's. The Contract with America of the 1990s was a reaffirmation of the 1985 State of the Union address by an overwhelmingly popular incumbent president. The federal budget had to be slashed in favor of outsourcing the duties to the state level. Inevitably and purposefully, this meant less government and less government programs. The rewards would be reaped by the masses already well into adulthood. The spoils would drastically alter the expectations of their children.

So we have learned the intersection of work ethic and artisanship firsthand in the modern world. We have Gene Simmons, author of *Me Inc.*, who teaches us to master business by being you. There is Reid Hoffman, author of *The Start Up of You*, who likens Friedman's understanding of immigrant thinking to the agile project management world of Silicon Valley where every project is now in "permanent beta mode." Tom Peters recommends promoting *The Brand Called You* by differentiating yourself through marketing schemes and networking. Daniel Pink told us about artisan/work ethic intersection as far back as 1997 in *Free Agent Nation*, where even before the proliferation of the Internet, we were seeing the mobility and freedom of a new class of workers who made contributions on their terms. The worker is once again personalizing work as the customer is personalizing the experience.

The personalized attributes of considering taste, beauty, and aesthetics is an opportunity in the postindustrial world. We have been surrounded by things void of meaning for so long that we forgot that materialism in the ancient sense is a philosophically neutral idea with real possible benefits to our humanity. In the postconsumer/postmaterialist world, we have the opportunity to make art based on experience. As we lose touch with the mass-produced items that propelled world economies for decades, we are reacquainting ourselves with the hand-made. We see the resurgence of farmer's markets and local merchandise. A century and a half ago, we indulged in aesthetics as a byproduct of the necessity of purchase. Today, the decision-making process to purchase goes beyond the rational components of traditional economical ideas of quality and cost. In the modern world, people are just as concerned with how a product, service, or experience makes them feel. They want a spiritual experience, via the Protestant work ethic but kissed by the muses.

CHAPTER 10

SOCIAL THEORY AND COOPERATION (PARTNERSHIP)

In 1996, as First Lady of the United States, Hillary Rodham Clinton titled her book in derivation of various African proverbs *It Takes a Village*. It was an examination of the forces outside of the family that contribute to a child's development. Predictably, to her critics, even suggesting that these forces existed was a rebuke to the sacredness of the family unit. It was an unpopular sentiment from an unpopular woman in some circles. It is also a straw man approach to the false choices of mindless political rhetoric. It was drivel to cement the then-recent Contract with America, a decades-long capstone to shrink government and abolish the New Deal for once and for all. To critics, this idea relinquished the responsibility of the nuclear family. It obviously takes a family to raise a child. The village can worry about its own problems . . .

The belief and understanding of the role of government will be a central theme of the twenty-first century. As of 1996, we were telling ourselves that social policy does not and should not have any effect on our children. The virtues of individualism won through the various incarnations of the Protestant ethic, along with the nurturing of the family, would insulate us from the effects of the abandonment of the social ethic. On the campaign trail in 2012, President Barack Obama cut to the heart of privilege . . . or lack thereof, by stating,

"If you were successful, somebody along the line gave you some help. There was a great teacher . . . Somebody helped to create this great American system . . . Somebody invested in roads and bridges. If you've got a business—you didn't build that. Somebody else made that happen." The sentiment was valid, but again, the ending left the door open for excessive criticism. The takeaway is, of course, the entrepreneurial spirit of America should be applauded and awarded, but it would also behoove us to examine the exact social contract which made us successful for decades.

The Republican Contract with America of 1994 reinforced the need to lower public capital (taxes) in favor of the modern individual. Just as our government officials pledged that we would require less government interference, public policy professor Robert Putnam professed the declining nature of social capital in the United States in his book *Bowling Alone* in the year 2000. Americans, he described, were no longer participants in their communities. Trust in institutions had waned. Civic, political, and religious affiliations were dwindling in participation. The community involvement of the 1960s ceded to private interests. Narcissism had gone viral under the guise of freedom and individuality. Just two generations ago, William Whyte had bemoaned the soul killing social ethic, and now Putnam was longing for its return.

It is no secret politically that Conservatives favor the free market over the infringements of government and Liberals favor the equity and meritocracy that the government can ideally impose over a free market, which innately favors the privileged. Francis Fukayama, a founding father of the neoconservative movement, dismisses the idea of man prospering alone and isolated. He rejects the ideas of Hume, Hobbes, and Rousseau that human cooperation evolved only after the modern nation state. Fukayama understands, as do biologists, sociobiologists, and evolutionary psychologists, that social networks are the primordial organization of humans. The Hobbesian Fallacy then, according to Fukayama, is that at some point, humans made a cognitive decision to band together for social and technological progress. By studying the primate world, we can conclude that the decision never existed. Humans were born to socialize.

We do not have thick skin, dense fur, strong teeth, or speed. We are the world's most successful animal because we can learn language and communicate. We can read the expressions and intentions on the face of our friends and enemies. We can divvy the chores where we each have specialties. We grew our food, organized our civilizations, and innovated based on the needs of our fellow man. Even by the late nineteenth century, Darwin's concept of "survival of the fittest" was advancing based on the capabilities of socialization and not evolution. The model of survival, even in the toughest times, not only invoked genetic predispositions but our inevitable predisposition to maximize our social stratification. That is why to not cede that at least a portion of your success has to be awarded to those that helped get you there is a political red herring, devoid of the true nature of the human experience.

We can believe that it is our will, possibly even with the help of God, to assist our neighbors because it is in our own self-interest. Philosopher David Hume tells the story of two corn farmers who have no personal allegiance outside of the fact that their harvests are offset. In the agrarian world, the farmers could each lose a portion of the fruits of their labor or band together in shared labor for the benefit of each individual. The idea of reciprocity, as philosopher Michael Taylor explains, is one of short-term altruism replaced by eventual long-term self-interest. Alexis de Tocqueville, while observing America in the early nineteenth century, saw this selflessness in action. He understood that it was that all Americans were beholden to the yet unnamed idea of the Protestant work ethic of the individual, but underneath, there was an uncalculated understanding of the benefits of reciprocity. As our towns turned into cities and our neighborhoods turned into communities, the American social ethic was formed.

Nature is who we are; freewill is what we learn about how to accept or reject our nature based on introducing new cognitive patterns to our brain. The remainder of our personhood is our nurturing, the environments where we learn to understand, interpret, and relate to the world around us. The conservative viewpoint is credible that the starting point is the nuclear family, but influence, even as children, is assisted outside of the sphere of parental control. Most likely, the inspiration of the book *It Takes a Village*, for Clinton, was the understanding of the spiritual idea of Ubuntu, prevalent in African philosophy. Various cultures in Africa understand that the human reinforcements of the social structure outside of the home affect the rearing, personal identification, and values of the individual. It is most commonly identified under the slogan "I am because we are," which subsequently became a documentary about the effects of the AIDS epidemic on the children of the African country Malawi.

So the outrage over Clinton's book is overdone, the criticism is categorical, and the implications real. We are who we are, at least in part, due to who we all are. Just as important as our identity, however, is our capabilities. Personal achievement is commendable, but true progress is bigger than oneself. What can be drawn from the social contract and applied to the world at large includes not just the benefits of the present but of all those that came before us in our endeavors. This includes the very real effects of our family, our ancestry, and our genetic predisposition but also the human history of discovery and innovation, which has made our own personal trek in this world possible. In a country with hundreds of millions and a world of billions who can all connect instantaneously with a push of a button in your pocket, it is naïve to believe that the world around us does not present us with context. It is infinitely more naïve to pretend that the countless small innovations throughout history have no bearing on our future potential.

The social contract in the United States, which is essentially the role of the individual versus the role of the state, is the central question in politics. Conservatives believe that personal responsibility should define the contract, while Liberals believe that a social responsibility exists at the behest of the state. In the middle and over time, we have come to an agreement of the role of the state. As free market denizens, we would not pool our money to hire our own private police force. Police protection was the role of government. For the most part, bridges, roads, and parks fall under the "commons" ownership of the citizens. We have determined that it is in our best interest to artificially lower prices on gasoline, corn, and cotton by government subsidies. We know education is the good of the highest value and highest return for the continuation of our economy and our social contract.

Harvard University was the first corporate charter ever given in the United States. It passed the litmus test of both having the ability to instill the personal attributes of higher learning to the individual while promoting real benefits to society. For decades and decades, universities at the state level were highly subsidized by the commons to promote the individual and continuity of the commons itself. That state support has eroded over the last generation and is predicted to become extinct. We have made a decision to eradicate the "commons" of higher education just as the privilege has become a near necessity. We have chosen to keep intact public education for the time being. Will a time come to withdraw this support? Historically, as citizens required higher levels of schooling for the public good, the burden rested on the government. Should the government fund higher education for the public good? Why are libraries public? Should we sell our waterways to the highest bidder? Should we privatize the fire departments and let houses burn if they are behind on their fire fees? Ideas surrounding public value versus the private cost shift with generations. Usually, the true recourse is never known until the following generation assumes their role as leaders.

Although the circumstances change, the question remains how should everyone act in relation to the individual? Those are the ramifications of public policy, which draw deeper and longer than the insipid nature of politics. What we did and how we organized affects what we do and how we organize! In 1968, ecologist Garrett Hardin revived a nineteenth-century idea known as the tragedy of the commons, which from an economist's perspective is the consummation or depletion of a resource based on personal interest in spite of public well-being. In the last decades of the twentieth century, the commons were under attack. Beginning with the Reagan Revolution and through the Contract with America, the commons were increasingly eroded. Void of the judgment as to the efficacy, the logic, or the morality of the new understanding of the commons, a new generation was left to only be accepting, ignorant, or adaptive.

We left the twentieth century with our proud Protestant ethic intact. In an historical moment of reflection on the individual, innovation had no biological context. Our greatest inventors surpassed our understanding of time. Newton knew that he had excelled inside the embrace of a series of equals throughout history. In a time of reflection on the individual, achievement, mastery, and excellence came from a source within. The tiny steps, attributed to family, friends, mentors, genetics, experience, education, and the gods, give way to the narcissism of personal achievement. Humility turns into entitlement in these epochs. It just so happened that right around the turn of the millennia, a phenomenon of technology was morphing the way we organized and communicated. The lone inventor could never again be devoid of her circumstances.

In a fast-paced world, progress requires communication, collaboration, and speed. The lone innovator of lore may still receive the gift of epiphany born of hard work, but the intricacies of mass collaboration are what move the world forward. In 1958, Leonard E. Read wrote an essay titled "I, Pencil." His intention was to take one of our most simple and useful products and document the global and mass production of human effort required in its manufacturing. The pencil requires cedar loggers and the graphite miners. It needs vulcanized oil to process the rubber eraser and the iron derivatives to make the metal band. It needs someone to transfer and manufacture these raw materials. Finally, the pencil manufacturer can accumulate the components and add the lacquer and glues to produce a finished product. Along the way, countless organizations touching thousands of people in support are responsible for a single pencil. This is what Read meant by the "family tree" of the pencil. The ancestors of any one product are multiple. Even with our most simple products, no one person in the world has the ability or capability to produce even one pencil from scratch. The intelligence of the pencil is embedded in the vast and unseen network of its life cycle.

"I, Pencil" was written during the last days of the Industrial Revolution. Since then, we hardly think about raw materials anymore. Little thought is given as to the origin of most products we use. Things used to be simpler. We mined the silver, the gold, the lead, and the coal, and they had a function. We cut down trees and understood that they would become books. The silica would become glass. We formed industries around raw materials. We witnessed the fact that things turned into things. You may have never heard of Leadville, Colorado, but 130 years ago, it was the second most populous town in the state. Doc Holliday escaped Tombstone and found a haven in the bustling mining town. Its rise and fall coincided with the mining industry. Oscar Wilde claims to have seen a sign hanging above a piano in a saloon there which read, "Please don't shoot the pianist. He is doing his best." It was the first in a string of rugged mining towns that eastern settlers would find as they made their way across the Great Plains.

Seventy-five miles to the Northwest of Leadville is an area sacred to the Native Ute Indians. Today, Glenwood Springs is home to the world's largest natural hot springs pool. Steam rises from this honorary town square amid the picturesque backdrop of the Rocky Mountains. It began as a coal mining town, but Walter Devereux saw the opportunity for tourism for the super wealthy during the turn of the twentieth century. It is credited with the birthplace of the teddy bear during a stay by Teddy Roosevelt in 1905 at the historic Hotel Colorado. In between these two towns born of two distinct natural resources, you can find a third. Aspen is the quaintest, tame, and isolated of these three mining towns of the Old West. Now it boasts the most expensive real estate prices in the country. It turned out that the mountains were the resource. Some of the best skiing in the world and the highest fashions can be found in a town of barely seven thousand people. It feels like a small neighborhood without outside influence. Promotion is not welcome. With careful searching you may find a tiny placard of the golden arches hiding a two story McDonald's.

The origin of these towns, like most all across America, was the nonrenewable resource. Once the earth was scorched, the land became stale, the purpose for being there had to change. People migrated to areas based on the land. They stayed because of the lasting industries that formed around it. Fortunately, all three of these places still prosper in a modern purpose. Raw materials as an industry is not what it once was. The new raw material is data, and data never dries up like an oil well. It is the most scalable material ever created. Simultaneously, intellectual property is the new industrial complex. We do not need to build giant factories and stake out large swaths of land. We need only to collect information. Money is changing hands whether we see it or not. If you are using a service online and not paying for it, you are not the customer; you are the product. It may not be that far in the future that companies list data as an asset on their balance sheet.

Industry used to leverage capabilities to produce what was wanted. Precious metals were extracted, shipped, sold, fabricated, sold, and then sold back to the individual. Mining data is much simpler and much more effective. The competency lies in convincing the population to share everything. Predictive analytics in data sometimes know your next purchase. Based on the tracking of your spending habits, the department store Target may even know you are pregnant before you do. The new mining town is the server room in a data center, and business is booming. The old West did not have the conveniences of our modern infrastructure, but the precursor to our modern highway system was the railways. In a great and untamed land, the "commons" was not yet a reticent aspect of our lives. The maturation of the Industrial Revolution by the twentieth century, allowed us to build an infrastructure that met our water, waste, electric, energy, communication, and entertainment needs in the comfort of our own homes.

In its very short existence, the Internet—and more specifically and recently—the social network, have become the vehicle of mass and instant communication via various mediums with anyone in the world instantaneously. Facebook, among others, has quantified the previously unseen networks behind "I, Pencil." Because connection has always been the way we progress with ideas, products, and innovation, social networks themselves are the next generation version of the public utility. Just like we use the roads and bridges for our personal use and, in turn, public good, we use the pipelines of the Internet and the interfaces of social media to store our most valued asset of the twenty-first century—our network. The hidden aggrandizement of the possibilities of the human network behind the pencil have been illuminated and distributed to anyone with a small computer in their pocket. The commodity called the Internet is increasingly becoming viewed as a utility.

The idea behind "I, Pencil" has always been to showcase the interconnectedness of the vast monetary system, which we call the economy. We must remember that economics is a social science based on rational choice and behavior. In the realm of politics, we disassociate beliefs between the social and the economic. The organization of society determines the organization of the economy and vice versa. In the 1950s, when "I, Pencil" was conceived, we had a vibrant and closed economy with a bright future. By the 1980s, a new idea was introduced that would affect both society and a stalling economy. Neoliberalism was based on classical economics and a new understanding of personal freedoms and global trade. In the same decade, our largest and most diverse generation in US history was born. These new personal freedoms of international economics awakened a generation of parents to not only the virtues of individualism but of a new world of economic hypercompetiveness. They were called helicopter parents out of the social necessity for eventual economic success of their children or, more aptly, the fear of not succeeding. These children were reared from the repercussions of market-based fear and individualism to create and thrive in a new world of interconnectedness.

That generation grew to quietly rebel against their parents, who preferred to "bowl alone" not because they had any particular interest in reclusion. The social fabric shifted by the end of the millennia because a new economic competition demanded sole attention to "your" interests and "your" families. Economics had clearly changed our social identities. Our idea of the commons from another generation was being privatized. Opportunity in private affairs and influence in public policy was shifting from young to old. Education, the great equalizer, was becoming at worst unaffordable and at best accessible only through an inevitable lifetime of debt. Inequality, by the old system of economic measurement, was increasing, and pure capital was ever meandering toward the 1 percent. The American

Dream of economic outperformance of our parents was surrendered to the yet-to-be-measured productivity of overt connectedness. The economic structure has very recently changed the social structure. The new capabilities of technical sociality, particularly of social media, would soon return the favor.

The exploitation of the shared resources of the pencil was lamented by Hardin in the *Tragedy of the Commons*. Although first identified in 1986 by Carol M. Rose, the Internet age has propelled the inverse of Hardin's idea known as the *Comedy of the Commons*. Much of the way we connect and, hence, share, innovate, learn, and produce is absolutely free in the modern world. We have a whole new domain, which may be ascribed to the commons. The melancholy dissipation of our old understanding of the commons cedes to a virtual and renewable replenishment of ideas. The comedy is the benign and positive interjection of resources for the good of the community rather than the detriment. The entire history of humanity, propelled by sociality, has found explicit networks to overtly contribute altruistically. A new era of mass partnership has renegotiated the social contract, even though the stalwart economists still operate under a model from another century.

Reciprocity, the reason why Hume understood that two farmers could find mutual interest within self-interest, was a key element in the agrarian economy. At the height of the industrial economy, reciprocity had little bearing on the economy, although it may have had an impact on the social ethic. In today's world, we have the ability and the honor to take advantage of both. This concept is still novel to the individual, unsettling to the businessman, rejected by the politician but embraced as the order of nature by today's youth. Value to the individual and, to the whole, in the modern world is not a Machiavellian or divisive "mine versus thine" idea. Economics has been called a monetary system of the "coincidence of wants." The modern world has removed some of those wants into the space of the commons. The secretive, strategic, and divisive ideas of win-lose scenarios are being replaced. In the modern world, even our competition can sometimes be our partner. If we run a company and find groundbreaking methods to keep employees safe, why not share the method with the competition? It is the right thing to do, and the altruism could be beneficial in the future with absolutely no cost to the individual or the company.

The past one hundred years have been marked by companies hoarding most of their proprietary knowledge. This conventional wisdom is dying. Open-source technologies are not a fad; they are an evolution of culture. Even research and development power house Procter & Gamble outsources a significant amount of their innovation to anyone with a good idea on the Internet. The modern company must conclude that there are a lot smarter people not working inside the company than within. The right mix of open sourcing and guarding key proprietary information will be the key to leveraging success. According to Don Tapscott and Anthony D. Williams, authors of *Wikinomics*, "These new collaborations will not only serve commercial interests, they will help people aspire to public-spirited ventures like cure genetic diseases, predict global climate change, and find new planets and stars." Perhaps not coincidentally, this coincides with a young culture who views transparency, openness, and even privacy much differently. A majority of those 18–29 view Edward Snowden, who leaked classified US documents in the name of transparency, as a hero. This viewpoint tends to erode as we consult the gatekeepers of traditional institutions.

Much like the emergence from the Dark Ages a half millennium ago, a new era of humanity is shunning hierarchy in favor of enlightenment. Information in all regards is increasingly accessible. The employee, who retreats within their walls and becomes self-reliant within their company, department, or pay grade, will decrease. For the first time in history, the young people are the authorities. They understand the technologies that will propel us forward even if they do not yet know what *forward* means. In other words, this generation is on the cusp of enlightening a population. Openness has changed industries from media, entertainment, and software, but that is just the beginning. Resistance to these ideas in this era is the enemy of progress. The music industry was not interested in iTunes. The phone companies were not interested in wireless technologies, Kodak was not interested in digital photography, and car companies were not interested in fuel efficiency. The list goes on and on. It is now an "adapt or die" world. Some organizations never learn and hang on to the status quo to the bitter end. Many times, the necessary change is a scary leap of faith that is simply beyond their leader's field of vision.

Rob McEwen's back was against the wall in the late 1990s. He was heading Goldcorp, a Canadian gold-mining company, and things were not going well. The company was in debt, strikes were brewing, and there was no indication that the half-century-old mine would ever produce anything substantial again. As a last ditch effort, McEwen doubled down on test drilling. To his surprise, there were indications that the mine still had vast reserves, yet his geologists still had little luck extracting the treasure. His resources were depleting, and his options were running out. During an MIT conference regarding Linux, open-source software that allows users to develop and modify operating systems, McEwen had a revolutionary and controversial idea which would change his life forever. He bucked the conventional wisdom of proprietary data governance and released every detail of the site. He offered the Goldcorp Challenge, which offered a total of $575,000 for insight into the best excavating areas of the mine. An interdisciplinary array of professionals and students offered advice and quickly turned a $100-million mine into a $9-billion-dollar industry powerhouse. McEwen took the leap of faith and reached outside of his organization to make it stronger.

Outsourcing is a relic of the neoliberal economy, especially as it refers to offshoring in the global economy. The next sourcing evolution has been crowdsourcing, which aligns the individual need to contribute and the business or community goals. The best known example of crowdsourcing is the build and maintenance of *Wikipedia*. This site began as an open-source platform, which encouraged amateurs to share information regarding a subject and remains so today. The *Encyclopedia Britannica* was the undisputed champion of reference books. They employed a team of experts to publish a text beyond reproach. The lone expert and academic toiled away, finding insight into every subject comprehensible in a grade-school report. There the printed pages sat on shelves, mostly collecting dust. *Nature* magazine performed a study comparing the veracity of scientific entries between *Britannica* and *Wikipedia*, which began to shine a light on the power of *Wikipedia*. *Britannica* was found to have three discrepancies to *Wikipedia*'s four, a very slight difference. The crux being that by nature, *Wikipedia* is a self-correcting machine. The average posting is updated several times and an MIT study found that the average obscenity placed in the *Wiki* text will be removed in under two minutes. Unlike encyclopedia text, *Wikipedia* is constantly in flux, constantly searching for more credibility.

No one believed in the power of participation until everyone began to participate. What is Facebook and Twitter but valuable content which people are compelled to share? The 2010s will go down as the decade of sharing. Social networking has become a staple of culture like the Internet, television, and radio before it. An entire generation has just shown up on a new medium, and the results have been astounding. This is the idea of participation web 2.0. The lone expert may be outdated. The average eight-year-old football fan could predict the outcome of an NFL game just as well as the expert on TV. The true insight can now be found in groups as James Surowieki's explained in his 2004 book *The Wisdom of Crowds*. Here is a brief excerpt from a fitting source, *Wikipedia*: "The opening anecdote relates Francis Galton's surprise that the crowd at a county fair accurately guessed the weight of an ox when their individual guesses were averaged (the average was closer to the ox's true butchered weight than the estimates of most crowd members, and also closer than any of the separate estimates made by cattle experts."

The new organization of human behavior, which the participatory web offers, has transcended culture and has already reached all areas of our lives. Howard Rheingold has called the convergence of communication technologies to amplify human potential a revolution of Smartmobs. The web inspired values adopted by a new generation of meritocracy, transparency, freedom, and community can be used to build more connected cultures within our organizations and institutions. High-powered corporate consultants such as Christine Comaford illustrate the power and connection of the team building possibilities of "smart tribes" in the modern business environment.

Various open models give citizens a collaborative platform to share their ideas, report issues, find like-minded volunteers, and track civic progress. Where we once shifted our burdens to the commons, we now have the capabilities to shift our possibilities to the commons. The collective wisdom embedded in our networks surpasses even our experts.

Even today cutting-edge breakthroughs in academia are bottlenecked through the slow-moving process of verification rather than the sharing of peers to replicate. Review processes are tedious, access to the work is costly, and the distribution of the knowledge is small. In the middle of the nineteenth-century US navy commander Matthew Fontaine Maury collected a multidisciplinary array of data from every ship in which he came in contact. His work *The Physical Geography of the Sea* fundamentally changed the way ships sailed the ocean. He collected data, which was counterintuitive to the greatest sailors of the day. This data collection was again an affront to traditional expertise. Many merchants were open to the idea, however, and were grateful for Maury and his team's insights. Science had come to the seas, and its teacher was the social network of those who had sailed the waters prior. Over 150 years ago, Maury had learned what many experts have still failed to learn today. Opening information is the only true scientific method. A lifetime of learning is at your fingertips. Maury himself said it best: "Thus the young mariner instead of groping his way along until the lights of experience should come to him . . . would here find, at once, that he had already the experience of a thousand navigators to guide him."

Open-source ideology in the information age is the reciprocity ideology of the agrarian age. We give what we as individuals can offer for a future return on our investment, which cannot be easily quantified now or in the future. Any attempt to quantify the relationship diminishes the authenticity of the human interaction. We are now virtual cogs in a series of networks. The only way to connect at levels, which ensure reciprocity is by building a reputation capital. The only way to build a reputation capital is to participate in the new world of the commons. The cynicism of the modern age has rendered the broadcast nature of media, advertising, marketing, public relations, and sales suspect to doubt. Trust, in any form, is built through long-term connection and reliability. Savvy fact checkers can now validate information instantly. Whereas once stretching the truth could bring short and potentially long-term successes, it is now a recipe for reputational suicide.

Ownership of land and property was the ultimate goal of peasants attempting to free themselves from the subservience of their feudal lords. The intersection of the Enlightenment and new ideas of democracy, including the pursuit of life and liberty, was a drastic alteration in the course of human events. The long game of the constant and continuous collection of material and ideas over centuries, is finally realizing its true capabilities. In economics, there is a term called *idling capacity*, which is the ratio of capacity to actual utilization. Just a few short years ago, our possessions, ideas, and resources were mostly relegated to die or excel inside a sphere of influence where we had firsthand and personal communication. The virtual world has unleashed an unforeseen and exponential series of possibilities to enlighten new capacitance in our lives. Because of our quest for materialism and ownership, we were inefficient with our material and virtual or ideological possessions. The lack of ability to communicate our capacities to the entities, which could maximize the effects, has held us back as a community, civilization, and world.

For our possessions, which we no longer need or want, we can access Freecycle.com. On Swaptree.com, we can find out what goods we can trade for material that we no longer require. Shareable.com embraces the sharing transformation said to be a "worldview and practice to experience a new and enlivening way to be in the world." Philosopher John Stuart Mill coined the term *marketplace of ideas* in 1859. He said that essentially, ideas will be prioritized in society based on their relevance. Reddit.com posts content based on a bulletin board organization of user submissions. Mill's marketplace has always been highly inefficient. Only recently can the proper connections be made to maximize our collaborations. Social theorist Jeremy Rifkin, in *The Zero Marginal Cost Society*, explains that technology has recently made it inefficient to expand economic progress in some cases. In its wake lies a new possibility of organization, which trumps economic interest. Rifkin says that by connecting in new ways, we are able to lower the cost of communication, energy, logistics, production, distribution, goods, and services. This disruption inevitably will change our lifestyles and our priorities.

The sharing economy that has surfaced has allowed us to reimagine the inefficient idling capacity in our lives. What we already own can be rented when we are not using it. Our houses (Airbnb.com), our cars (Relayrides.com), and everything else we own (Zilok.com). Most of what we own is in use a fraction of the time. From power saws to popcorn makers, some items in our lives would have been more efficient to rent rather than purchase. Before the availability of the redistribution of resources via connection on the Internet, this economy would have been impossible. Nonprofit organizations and businesses like Zipcar.com are molding to a more mature version of the sharing economy. Instead of leasing one car, which may be utilized 5 percent of the day, we have access to a fleet of vehicles to use at our disposal, thus increasing the capacity of the fleet as a whole and driving down individual cost. In the future of self-driving vehicles, instead of an average of two cars owned per family, we may only require two cars per block if they are used and organized efficiently.

We can share our toys (Toyrentals.com). We can connect land owners with farmers who can use the land more efficiently (Sharedearth.com). We can use collective wisdom to better understand our health through the sharing of information (Patientslikeme.com). These are enterprises that are not easily measured in our traditional economic models yet provide real value to people's lives. New York University professor Clay Shirky calls these new opportunities a cognitive surplus. The wisdom collected by groups of people is finally being harnessed. We are using open-source software produced for free by experts who seek a mutual interest for providing free use in return. Even large companies like IBM, which relied on proprietary information as strategy, have embraced and invested in the crowdsourcing openness of the internet to the tune of billions of dollars.

Crowdfunding such as Kickstarter.com and Gofundme.com have allowed us to broadcast our ideas as never before. Kiva.org allows us contribute small microloans to individuals around the world. Donations to crowdfunding could simply be a form of charity based on exceptional ideas. We could get incentivized to assist with funding based on the reward which it brings. Using crowdfunding, we have the ability to sell equity of our ideas to those around the world with the cognitive surplus, talent, and connections to meet our self-interest. This has always been the method of capitalism, which is to support self-interest by promoting mutual interest. It has always, however, been veiled inside of the disorderly understanding of the economy. Relationships based on production have turned into relationships based on connection to leverage capabilities.

We are consuming in new ways. During the Enlightenment, we began rejecting the communal lives of feudalism for good reason. John Lock stated that private property was a basic human right. For hundreds of years, we have organized based on this new world understanding. We now live in a postindustrial and increasingly postmaterial world. We no longer buy the physical goods of books, movies, and music. We instead choose to enter agreements for use and access on their particular platforms (think HBO, Apple, Amazon, and Netflix). Even the retail, healthcare, education, and restaurant industries, to name a few, which were nearly solely based on products and services, have ushered in the "experience economy." Good products and good services are not enough. Customers must connect with the people offering the goods and services.

We tend to believe that the old-fashioned business of sales is dead, and in a sense, it is. Door-to-door or used-car salesmen can no longer prey on the victims of economic or information asymmetry. Technology has opened up the floodgates of information. As author Daniel Pink has taught us, we have gone from *Caveat Emptor* to *Caveat Venditor,* or from a long history of "buyer beware" to "seller beware." The great power shift in business has been a knowledgeable consumer. The prey has become the predator. What does that mean for the sales industry? Approximately one in nine Americans work directly in sales. Surprisingly, there is not any significant historical change. What has changed are the skills that the new sales world requires. The extroverted and braggadocio depiction of the historical salesman stereotype is diminishing. Pounding the pavement to bend an ear has become a Zen exercise in listening to customer requirements. Empathy has melded with influence. Dale Carnegie's *How to Win Friends and Influence People* was written nearly eighty years ago, but it is as pertinent as ever. The power of praise, humility, and honesty goes a long way in an ever-more-cynical world.

Sales guru Joe Girard's Law of 250 explains how the human capability to intimately know 250 people can quickly become exponential, as each and every one of those 250 people, in turn, have a similarly sized network. Social media now allows us to maximize the benefits of those relationships that were never before available to us. We have quantified the ability to turn social capital into market capital and vice versa. This entirely new understanding of our social structuring, which in previous generations took decades or centuries to shape, has drastically shifted in just a few short years of mass and mobile social media. We had an economic revolution in the 1930s, a cultural revolution in the 1960s, and a political revolution in the 1980s. In the 1930s and 1980s, we could point directly to public policy to explain new shifts in social structuring. In the 1960s, we spoke of these new reactive structures as counterculture. Today, with the realities of modern communication technology, we realize they are just glimpses of a bright new future that does not just seek to accompany mainstream economics, politics, business, and culture but to merge and forever change it.

CHAPTER 11

PSYCHOLOGY AND MOTIVATION (PERSONALIZATION)

In the mid-nineteenth century, 90 percent of white male workers were in business for themselves (a necessary differentiation due to the existence of slavery and limited women in the workforce). Large business consisted of three or four employees. This means that artisans, laborers, merchants, and farmers were mostly classified under the same category: entrepreneurs. Even without the modern status quo of two years of preschool, thirteen years of formal education, four more of college, possibly grad school, certifications, mentorships, internships, workshops, and corporate learning, these men of the Republic of the Self-Employed, the United States, somehow figured out how to educate themselves and run a business. The work was personal and intuitive. The harder one worked and the more connected with it he became, usually the better his quality of life. By the early twentieth century, the Industrial Revolution changed the nature of work throughout the world. Under a new discipline called scientific management, workers began abandoning their craft for a spot in the assembly line. The once proud and skilled artisan was now trading his time for money. The science of streamlining work was made famous by Henry Ford, who made the automobile available to the masses, including his own employees. He had such contempt for their intelligence that he once wondered out loud, "Why is it that whenever I ask for a pair of hands, a brain comes attached?" The assembly line zapped our collective passions and demanded robotlike compliance. Instead of going to work to learn a trade to provide a purpose, we began going to high school to fit into the new constraints of the industrial era.

The industrial mindset taught us how to follow the rules in the new civilized world. Technology had designed machines to improve productivity, but scientific management concerned itself with the repetitive tasks that humans could now do which could not yet be mechanized. In order to control and inspire in this environment, scientific managers looked to the ideas of a group of psychologists called behaviorists, who defined the psychology of management in its scientific infancy. Their method was observable behavior, corrected either positively or negatively by the appropriate stimuli. Behaviorist psychologists like B. F. Skinner needed only to watch to document reinforcements. Classical conditioning experts like Ivan Pavlov took this approach to modify behavior with external rewards and punishments. The cognitive psychology wonks can be left to study the brain. Motivation, after all, is difficult to document by observation. What can we dangle in front of employees to immediately garner production, what punishments can we offer to bestow compliance, and how will those employees react? This was the red meat for the behaviorist management movement, identified by answering the idiom "the carrot or the stick" as a metaphor for a donkey fearing the punishment of a beating or striving for the reward of food.

In 1934, Russian psychologist Lev Vygotsky wrote *Thought and Language*, which laid the groundwork for a philosophic challenge to the pedagogical foundations of the behaviorist movement. As his ideas matured, the tradition was revived by psychologist Jean Piaget under the name constructionism or the closely related term *constructivism*. The ideas behind behaviorism outsourced all productivity to the instruction and organization of the (management, ruling, teaching) class. The means of production lied with the accountability of the elite using their external controls and commands. The new traditions posited that the only true motivation cannot be dictated by a class that by definition offers no true connection to the work at hand.

The motivation that is most effective lies inside the cognitive functions of the individual. Constructionists believed that there was an innate suffocation that had stunted human potential tied to behaviorist dogma. Constructionist ideology saw mankind not as a gadget to be perfected by an outside force but an internal struggle to psychologically align the necessary forces for their own personal triumph.

Abraham Maslow turned the science of management into the art of management in 1943 with *A Theory of Human Motivation*. Maslow injected a psychotherapeutic hierarchy of needs that examined the grand ideas of the Enlightenment as the basis of motivation. Thomas Hobbes's 1651 work *Leviathan* saw civilization as a brutish existence whereas a pessimistic natural state of humankind required a strong and absolute sovereign to temper humanity's natural state. Rousseau, one of history's foremost Enlightenment political minds, said, "Nothing is so gentle as man in his primitive state." Maslow, in the tradition of the constructionists, was erroring on the side of optimism in the human spirit. He said, "Freud gave us the sick half of psychology and we must now fill it with the healthy half." Not only was he the conduit to later constructivism, but he is considered the grandfather of the positive psychology movement altogether. It was Maslow who first saw motivation as Enlightenment philosophers saw freedom, as a state of mind rather than an externally controlled gadget.

By 1960, Douglas McGregor had formulated what he called Theory X versus Theory Y motivation styles in *The Human Side of Enterprise*, a work fifty years ahead of its time. It simply and perfectly illustrates a fundamental difference in viewpoint between the industrial world and the dynamics of industry for the future. He states an assumption, whereby Theory X managers assume employees to be unmotivated, lazy, and in need of constant direction and discipline. This was in line with the dogma of behaviorist management style, which did not apply the lessons of Maslow. Theory Y managers assume workers possess the necessary talents for greatness, accountability, and internal motivation to perform at their highest level. Maslow's hierarchy of needs assumed pivotal and necessary benchmarks for human greatness based on a pyramid of morally superior needs. Basic human needs must be met before any stability can hoped to be attained. Only when these needs are met may humanity search for love and belonging, which enables us to explore the unlimited possibilities of the human condition. Goodness lies within a system that peaks only when the full potential of the individual is realized.

McGregor called nourishing the harmonies of this natural hierarchy the Theory Y perspective. Essentially, his position is that the starting point of unlocking motivation assumes that a magical mix of virtue and productivity based on psychological and philosophical truths of optimism will result from treating employees with humanity. The behaviorist tradition viewed employees as interchangeable cogs in the machinery of production. Still, eight years later, in 1968, Fredrick Herzberg asked, *"One more time, how do you motivate employees?"* Herzberg said that Maslow was correct, but there were two independent systems working in duality as they relate to job satisfaction and motivation. He said there were "hygiene factors," to which there were expected to be a minimal set of environmental circumstances required to remove the notion of job dissatisfaction completely. Similarly, Maslow had a similar understanding of hygiene factors, which he called deficiency needs, whereby entrance to the higher-level needs are blocked until these needs are satisfied. Lower-level states on the hierarchy of needs are akin to a poorly developed technology or the lack of a vital tool. This is what has been called Maslow's Hammer. If our needs at a certain level of the pyramid are never met, we end up using the wrong tools to solve the wrong problems. In 1962, in *Toward a Psychology of Being*, Maslow said, "I suppose it is tempting, if the only tool you have is a hammer, to treat everything as if it were a nail."

Herzberg talked about what would later be defined as the psychological contract between an employee and an employer. The hygiene factors in one era could wear off or be subjected to a form of hedonic adaptation whereas what we believe to be our basic needs would forever expand. This would be the starting point for positive psychologists three decades later. Motivating factors, however, are fairly stable. Job enrichment is a pursuit of filling the highest levels of Maslow's hierarchy, which is a personal interpretation of achievement, mastery, and recognition. Money, the ultimate extrinsic motivator, has been found to have no effect on happiness after about $75,000 per year. Dan Arielly, in *Predictably Irrational* in 2008, finally ended the long-fought behaviorist versus constructionist battle. He proved that there is a social currency, never before measured, which displaces our rational idea that money is our main motivator. Arielly related a series of experiments which show that injecting money into a situation previously guided by internal motivations actually causes people to rescind the favor. Once we tie a financial calculation to our time, we intuitively associate it with an extrinsic motivator, which in some cases is deemed less important. This phenomenon has implications from management to economics to religion.

Working conditions in the late nineteenth century were deplorable. By 1906, Upton Sinclair exposed corruption, unsanitary food, and labor exploitation with *The Jungle*, depicting the turn-of-the-century Chicago meatpacking industry. Even Ford Motor Company, perhaps the ideal middle class job by midcentury had a 370 percent turnover in 1913, and most employees had quit in the first week. The Adamson Act of 1916 established the rules for overtime pay and normalized eight-hour workdays. Regulations required business to conform to laws that allowed workers to reclaim their dignity lost since entering the factories. Henry Ford eventually realized that if fair and decent wages for the workforce was a requirement, they may as well make enough to be customers. By the 1950s, the conversation of labor exploitation had become the conservation of corporate paternalism. William Whyte derided the new ethic of collectivism in 1956 with *The Organization Man*. A drastic change had taken place in a half a century. The organization was embracing the employee for long-term mutual success, and the employee was inherently loyal to the organization. As the Industrial Revolution entered its last and strongest phase, the philosophers, poets, sociologists, and theorists wondered what had happened to individualism.

In 1958, John Kenneth Galbraith explained the phenomenon as the *Affluent Society*. His economic metaphor was "The rooms have been furnished." In other words, a (relatively) equal society had been built based on the values of collectivism. We, as Americans, could check off the box for the basic needs of comfort and safety. Never before had a society built such a universal affluence in relation to the history of the world. A new baseline was set as for the requirements of workers and citizens going forward. The "Affluent Society" gave us confidence to build the "Great Society" under Lyndon Johnson in the next decade, which was aimed at further equality and a safety net from the scarcity and poverty, which was all too familiar in annals of history. New ideas of equality and Liberalism with a definite capital *L* only reinforced the psychological contract between employee and employer. American idealism and optimism left no reason to question the trajectory of progress and growth.

So an era emerged with baby boomers entering the workforce in droves to organizations which projected growth. There was cheap education and plenty of well-paying jobs regardless of education levels. Skill sets remained static for decades, pension plans were a given, and efficiency still mattered less than quality. The ongoing cold war had not yet opened half the world to trade nor had technology perfected the global supply chain. When Alvin Toffler wrote *Future Shock* in 1970, which predicted change on the horizon of a postindustrial society, it seemed to be an outline of the warnings of Galbraith twelve years earlier. The inflation and stagnation of the 1970s led to an economic and cultural malaise defined in postmodern philosophy as cynical, pessimistic, and decadent. The promises of the demand side economics were no longer working. The rooms had been filled, and the status quo was no longer working. The reorganization required was a neoliberal economic revolution, which abandoned the demand-side of economics for the supply-side. This newfound freedom returned the possibilities of growth to the Baby Boomer Generation. The goal of the United States had always been growth, of course, but the economic success in the midcentury was its offspring. The 1980s turned to financial trickery and efficiency as its only grandchild.

Neoliberalism opened the United States up to the inevitabilities of the world economy. It laid the groundwork for companies like Wal-Mart to leverage global supply chains for competitive advantage at once in rural china and the rural United States. It ended pensions, lowered wages, raised education prices, privatized, leveraged, and commoditized. It also lowered prices and allowed the middle classes access to the substantial financial gains available to those who turned the corner safe with a pension and 401k plan, still safe in the paternalism of the organization but leveraging the future based on a dead economic model. The early 1980s awoken the world to whispers of inconsistencies of the social contracts of the future. Unfortunately, the new growth of the 1980s and 1990s was not based on new innovations, which is a form of psychological optimism, but by focusing nearly exclusively on the art and science of efficiency in strategy and operation. Consultants, mergers, and acquisitions became popular vernacular as Wall Street became mainstream business. Bain Capital opened for business in 1984 and corporate strategy reprioritized. American businesses began a twenty-year-long commitment to cutting costs and not being taken over by a competitor or a group of venture capitalists. It put the American economy on the defensive. Quality measures began to spread. Six Sigma process improvement methods saved General Electric billions of dollars. We learned how to manage every dollar in our organizations. Risk management began as a legal department and spread throughout the firm, which finally found a home in the IT department. We were doing everything we could to survive at the expense of our employees.

Eventually, the quality measures put in place had served their purpose. Organizations are committed to continuous improvement, but as Harvard professor and strategy expert Michael E. Porter reminds us, "Operational effectiveness is not strategy." Years ago, the old, venerable companies could easily position themselves to succeed for decades. This is what strategy was about. In today's environment, no company is safe with a constant strategy for the short and long-term. The last and final cycle of positioning was clinging tightly to only strict operational effectiveness at the expense of innovation, namely Six Sigma, which calls for 99.99966 percent of products to be manufactured without a defect. By the 1990s and 2000s, this is where our companies put their focus. Looking back, we now realize the 2000s are known as the lost generation for human resources. We forgot to personalize, mostly because personalization is difficult to quantify, which is what was lost in the age of efficiency. The psychological contract had been signed by a generation who had won leadership through attrition and tasked to motivate the way they had learned. The ugliness of the beast of the efficient organization had to be endured because of the "golden handcuffs" of safety, security, and pension, which lay in wait at the end of a career. As a new generation arrived in the workforce without the golden handcuffs which bound the psychological contract, they were expected to naturally assimilate themselves into a foreign culture with incentives that simply did not apply to them.

Companies were so busy improving that they forgot about developing. No one had noticed that between 1985 and 2005, the number of Americans that were satisfied with the way life was treating them decreased by 30 percent. This was due in large part to their situation at work. Famous Gallup polls from 2011–2012 showed only 13 percent of employees are actively engaged at work. Sixty-three percent of employees are disengaged, and 24 percent are actively disengaged. At the very moment where we need the most dynamic employees who are motivated to do their job, we were focused on hundredths of percentage points of operational effectiveness. Most companies have just recently learned that the area of most opportunity lies in their employees. Sixty percent of variance between employees can be attributed to lack of proper motivation. In the last century, the greatest assets were infrastructure and brand. As the half-lives of our great companies continue to erode, that mind-set will change. Dissatisfaction has increased at work as the pace of change at work has accelerated. Younger generations have never seen the nostalgic "good old days," which older generations have romanticized. The young are the mice in the parable "Who Moved My Cheese?" by Spencer Johnson. In this story, cheese represents anything trying to be achieved in life. Two mice and two little people are dropped in the maze with the clear goal to find their "cheese." Both the mice and the little people sporadically find cheese and get by until finally they find enough cheese where they can stop exploring the maze on a daily basis. Time goes by until one day, they look around and they are out of cheese. The little people are shocked. They did not see the signs that the cheese was running out. They are paralyzed and angry. This was *their* cheese. Who moved my cheese? Meanwhile, the mice continued unfazed on their journey in search of new cheese.

In other words, the young understand that their current employment is not lifelong. There is no reward of pension for making it thirty years with the same company. The average young person will spend less than three years at their current job. Every time they do find the cheese, they understand that a series of plans need to be made for when the cheese finally runs out, which it will. Constant change is the only constant in the new world of work. The older generations may be harder workers by their definition, but working hard at the expense of progress in their own self development is its own form of complacency. Our youngest generation at work today is the first generation of true free agents. They pick up skills at various jobs and move on. This perceived lack of loyalty also makes the older generations angry, many of which are retirement eligible and may able to cash in a pension which the young will never receive. There is no reciprocal loyalty from the organization and younger generations accept that fact. It does not make them angry, but it does make them pragmatic. Therefore, we can finally remove the artificial motivators still compelling the majority of leaders across the spectrum of our various organizations and institutions. It is not effective for the future if we are to refuse a half century of science learned since Herzberg. The era of the broad and reciprocal contract as a motivating factor is long since gone. As much as the generation of our current leaders rejected the paternalism that the golden handcuffs brought, they still wore them. The figurative handcuffs certainly seemed restrictive to the younger generations because they were no longer golden.

There was a "Pygmalion effect," as defined by University of California, Riverside professor Robert Rosenthal, beginning in the early 1980s whereas a new generation did not have to conform to the higher expectations that a more efficient world demanded, it was already their baseline. Similarly, the "Flynn effect," based on the research of New Zealand professor James Flynn has found that IQ scores have risen by as much as fifteen points across the world since the 1930s. Both researchers determined that the higher levels of expectations cause higher levels of results. Thanks to a wide variety of contributing factors, it is now a personal world. In 1978, the Stanford Research Institute did a study, the "Effect of Baby Boomers on American Society." The Baby Boomer Generation, as the Millennial Generation is now, was just about to reach its point in ascension in leadership in American society. Demographics were the observational method used to categorize prior to this study. Using what was called assessments on values and lifestyles, or VALS, demographic categorization could be transformed to psychographic interpretation. It identified the motivational tendency called *inner directed*, which would supposedly define the generation but was actually just a suppressed form of human inclination. The distinction between physical characteristics and the way people thought had begun. Psychographics then became the dispersion of various ideas in terms of postmodern philosophy without a coherent grand strategy forward. It is science's job to hierarchically rank the psychographic needs of the individual based on how close they come to self-actualization, which is ultimate fulfillment of personal potential. VALS inevitably change. Whereas baby boomers were suspicious of government since the Vietnam War and Watergate, a new ideology surfaced that rejected government for the private sector that had lavished them with predetermined excess based on the combined technologies of government support over their entire lives.

The VALS of millennials do not border on this level of ideology, but it was business, not government, that had limited their opportunities. They became adults when young adult wages were at historic lows although they were the highest-educated and brightest generation alive. Healthcare rates were high because they had to subsidize the elderly. They paid Medicare and Social Security even though it was not funded for them, and those using it had paid sometimes hundreds of thousands less than they were using. Education has skyrocketed and stunted any hope to accrue wealth and encourage spending due to the trillion-dollar debt incurred. Our fault was not neoliberalism in itself, which was an idea inevitable to spur the economy when the room was full and technology and innovation needed time to develop new patterns. Our problem was that we did not learn the lessons of motivation, which psychologists had been spreading for decades. Our fail safe was the economic equivalent of pessimism in the form of efficiency, which allowed our organizations to limp through a period of malaise as an intermediary. The grand narratives of the road to personal freedom in life and work as interpreted by Maslow are finally accessible. The freedom of the worker, fought and won by the young baby boomers, has finally been realized. They, however, decided to keep the paternalistic perks of pension, 401k, cheap education, government subsidy, a social safety net, paid internships, and corporate education. The next generation is exactly free, but they ask that you not judge their freedom when you question their loyalty.

What they ask for is the freedom of motivation lost so long ago when the industrialists overtook the artisans, when science interjected with the personal connection that humanity associated with their job. There were no pension or social safety nets but an invisible ring of economies around every personal transaction. The only contract they signed was intuitive and hypothetical based on the not-yet-named Self-Determination Theory developed by Edward Deci in the 1970s. Deci suggested that competence (mastery), relatedness (connection), and autonomy (self-sufficiency) are universal motivating factors for humans. However, Deci identified something spectacular that would not have been recorded two decades earlier. In conjunction with the self-esteem movement and postmodern thinking of the unique individual, "intrinsic motivation," according to Deci, was not universal but subjective. Deci's studies on the motivation of the individual reinforced the unproven rhetoric of the Greek philosophers, the Roman Stoics, the heretics of the Enlightenment, and the recently forgotten Pragmatist philosophers. Over a century prior to Deci's work, philosopher Soren Kierkegaard defined *despair* as abandoning the true self. Social scientists were slowly putting together the pieces of truth of two millennia of philosophy and applying it to the constructs of our daily life. Deci contended that extrinsic motivators only diluted the only true motivator, which comes from within.

A new generation was raised on the subtle self-actualized needs, which science had presented for years before their birth yet business had outright rejected until very recently. Productivity is that which always grows economies. The next advancement of productivity will not be stricter micromanaging or the next ingenious quality initiatives. The next advancement will be a self-managed organization that can best exploit the personal capabilities of the individual. Capturing the energy and enthusiasm of natural human inclination will translate to better profits and happier customers. With constant digital media at our disposal 24/7, the work-life balance is quickly becoming the work-life convergence. Allowing the human as maker to do what makes him happy will add productivity without the inconvenience of balancing efficiency. Advances in productivity will make up for the small lapses in efficiency; technology will determine that aspect. As technology becomes increasingly at the center of our lives, it is important to remember the emotion at the heart of what makes us most human, empathy. No other emotion has allowed us to climb up the evolutionary ladder faster. Empathy gave pause to enlightened ancient generals just as it provides guidance to modern parents. Many have learned the tools to authentically explain the outcomes of the negative actions of their children in terms of the feelings of the transgressed. This is a different lesson than the previous generation taught of correcting transgressions without explanations. Children are now taught the ramifications of their actions on others from an earlier age. We are less likely to hit our kids when we can understand them and when they can understand us. As Stephen Covey, author of the *7 Habits of Highly Effective People*, suggests in habit number 5, "First seek to understand, then to be understood." Empathy is the cornerstone for emotional intelligence, the foundation for unlocking motivation, communication, collaboration, and understanding.

The greatest computer ever built, the human brain has an intuitive ability to interpret emotion on a human face regardless of cultural barriers. The greatest machine IBM can build cannot. In an age of technology, to be human is our biggest asset. Psychologist Jean Piaget, the original constructionist, proposed that the goal of education is overcoming egocentricism both intellectually and emotionally. In other words, overcoming our own ignorance and selfishness is what we ultimately strive for as humans and hope to pass on to our offspring, and empathy is at least 50 percent of it. The transparency that modern technology brings shines light on the character and authenticity of our true self at work. If people do not connect emotionally to brands, products, or employees, they will go somewhere where they do. The experience economy is not about cheaper or easier in many cases. It is about the feeling that the customer experiences from the product, services, and people that a company represents. As Dan Arielly has proven, there is no amount of efficiency that can quantify the cost and reward of individual attention. Money is irrational when it comes to an individual making a personal connection with a cause, movement, or idea.

In the book *Drive*, Pink outlines that tangible awards led to decreased intrinsic motivation in 128 experiments on the subject, not to mention the fact that ethics, creativity, and performance also decrease. The measure of productivity, just two decades ago, was determined by the amount of efficiency saved. This equation has changed to what Robert Greene, author of *Mastery*, has described as "the greatest power of mankind is for everyone to move towards their inclinations." This is the deliberate action of Covey's seventh habit called sharpening the saw. We must develop and nourish our own high-level skills and development constantly based on our innate capabilities and our unbridled curiosities. Neuroscience author Christine Comaford has determined that we must simply speak to the evolved part of the brain. Twentieth-century management had kept employees in what she refers to as the critter state, or what blogger and marketer Seth Godin would call the lizard brain. The discipline of psychology has evolved much the way the brain itself has evolved. What began as a study of the ancient inclinations of the prehuman brain has become a study of the more recently developed and intellectual aspect of our brains. It has been just a few decades since the emergence of the study of positive psychology. The physiological ramifications of the mental state of happiness are just now beginning to be understood. It just so happens that the lessons learned in fostering a happy environment at work lead to the conditions that will differentiate a good company from a great company. The same personal joy derived from connection to work gives people satisfaction at home. Sigmund Freud's view of happiness was simply "work and love."

Hungarian psychologist Mihaly Csikszentmihalyi developed the concept of "flow," which understood the alternate state of intense curiosity, creativity, learning, and immersion by which humans enter a hypnotic state of ecstasy. Csikszentmihalyi used creative people in demanding jobs to determine periods of intense engagement with the task at hand. He determined that there is no greater unleashing of the human potential than an individual who is highly skilled and highly challenged. It is the mindful act of dealing completely with the present even if the task is preparing for the future or examining the past. This act of ecstasy is a learned method of controlling consciousness reminiscent of the Stoic philosopher Marcus Aurelius, who was not armed with scientific validity but intuitive knowledge through the state of flow critical to the immersive learning of ancient philosophers. Flow not only provides untapped learning potential and creation to the subject at hand but allows us to rise up Maslow's pyramid to the state of self-actualization. It enables us to become more of our self, while at once losing the anxiety associated with being different. It is a magical formula, funneled through science, by what Csikszentmihalyi called psychic energy.

Psychologist Martin Seligman, often called the Father of Positive Psychology, says, "More happiness causes more productivity and higher income." We spent the last one hundred years denying this inclination because it was never proven. As Maynard Webb has said in *Rebooting Work*, the onus of all development, be it personal or professional, has shifted toward the responsibility of the individual. In the midcentury, the company shaped the employee in their image. The next steps were micromanagement, process management, and risk management. We had devolved from homogeneity of the paternalistic age to automaticity of the efficiency age. As social science and business author Daniel Pink explains, there is a gap between what science now knows and what business is doing. The cognitive psychologists have been able to make very good cases that many businesses are on the wrong trajectory. Individuals, especially the young, have an intuitive grasp on what will be important. In terms of Herzberg's vocabulary, money is not a motivating factor. It is a hygiene factor for up to $75,000 per year. What is important is an environment that allows for an update in the psychological contract. The contract is no longer safety as a hygiene factor and security as a motivating factor but money as a hygiene factor and growth as a motivating factor. Motivating factors have finally and inevitably converged with the science of those in the realm of positive psychology and its predecessors.

A very personal world is where we find ourselves. Digitization and social media influences have only exacerbated the need for individuality. Jeremy Rifkin, in his 2011 book, *The Third Industrial Revolution* prophesizes a time in the near future where the individual will produce most of their own energy and manufacturing using yet to be developed technologies. Thomas Friedman, world-class global economist, says that globalization 3.0 is already here. The personal digital technologies have shifted the responsibilities from other people (bank tellers) to machines (ATMs) to individuals (Applepay or bitcoin). Peter Aceto is the CEO for Tangerine Bank of Canada. He has developed a reputation of understanding the personal touch, even in the banking industry. So much so that he has developed the reputation as "the Social CEO." He wrote a foreword for the Ted Coine and Mark Babbitt book *A World Gone Social*, which explicitly outlines the reasoning and staying power of social media in business. Aceto begins the foreword stating, "I would rather engage in a Twitter conversation with a single customer than see our company attempt to attract the attention of millions in a coveted Super Bowl commercial." Aceto understands the "leap of faith" required for the social age. Customers and employees require everything to be personal. A brand must connect with an individual above and beyond the rational understanding of value based on cost and convenience and even quality. The experience of the interaction is now what is important. We always assume humans to be rational agents who will make carefully weighed decisions based on a spreadsheet of calculations. The truth is that their business will usually be given to those who give the best experience. In October of 1936, Dale Carnegie published *How to Win Friends and Influence People* and has since sold over fifteen million copies. The simple answer to Mr. Carnegie's thesis is to make it personal. Leaders like Peter Aceto understand the connecting power of social media. It allows direct access to anyone in the world—instantly.

The cold rationalism of Master of Business Administration (MBA) takeovers a generation ago has ceded to the personal touch of individuality. Younger MBAs seek smaller firms to practice softer skills. Mature companies are looking to wisdom from Master of Fine Arts (MFA) to develop the spiritual side of their business. The road to efficiency is an asymptote that plateaus or becomes invisible to the naked eye. Research today would discover that the market is saturated with blenders. There is an abundance of low-cost high-quality blenders for sale. Doubling the engineering budget to perfect the blender is fruitless. The blender has already been perfected, and the distribution chain is flawless. What to do? Race to the bottom to find a way to make the very cheapest blender on the market all while maintaining some level of quality? That is nearly impossible. The only thing to do is design in order to establish a personal connection. Perhaps it is a blender that is horizontal rather than vertical, 100 percent childproof, sleek, and unique. Design acknowledges the uniqueness of a product just as service acknowledges the uniqueness of an individual. According to the London Business School, for every percent invested in design, a company's sales and profits rises by 3 to 4 percent. Business acumen is trending in the trajectory of the Chinese metaphysical art of Feng Shui to understand the harmony in the environment based on personal connection rather than simply function or price.

The final frontier of psychology is the final frontier of management, marketing, sales, and countless other departments and industries that are just waiting for the bean counters to use the new math. Awakening the engagement from our employees and customers is truly the next great battle in the ongoing struggle to make our organizations and institutions more human. As we rely on technology more and more, there will be an increasing need for the personal touches in everything we do. The old structures give lip service to the theory but can never truly manage to justify the difficult changes, which would inevitably follow. Truly embracing these ideals means complete changes in incentive and accountability structure throughout the organization but, more importantly, changes in the way the individual lives and works. The patterns of motivation gaps are being studied by educators, futurologists, and economists, not to mention psychologists and philosophers. Happiness and well-being is the most personal endeavor we will encounter. As Brendan Burchard in *The Motivation Manifesto* has said, "By deeply contemplating higher aims, we energize ourselves to pursue them." The richness found in the mundane can be justified if it can be tied to a personal experience. Einstein was compelled by the merger of religion and science that facilitated individual freedom. This was a sacred combination intuitively known to mankind since "Know Thyself" was written on the forecourt at the Temple of Apollo in ancient Greece to which we are just now applying our modern scientific standards.

CHAPTER 12

PHILOSOPHY AND EDUCATION (PEDAGOGY)

Literacy began in Mesopotamia, often called the cradle of civilization for that reason. Even five thousand years ago, the ability to read and write in the Tigris-Euphrates river valley, from Sumeria to Babylon and from Assyria to Akkadia, was an important virtue for men and women. The pre-alphabetic cuneiform pictographs of language began here. At least one thousand characters representing language was gradually reduced as the Bronze Age came to a close. Scribal schools rose in the valley, bearing ancient texts protected by the new guardians of physical knowledge. The ability to collect, disseminate, and decipher knowledge was the key to societal advancement even in man's first civilization. The modern idea of education first began with the rigor of a scribe trying to understand the human capabilities of syllabary and phonetics. The architects of the written word were naturally the architects of all pedagogy, or what is known as simply the practice of education.

As the Bronze Age became the Iron Age, a new educational movement was imminent in the Greek settlement of Miletus, Ionia, in modern-day Turkey. Here at the crossroads of the East, Asia Minor, Mesopotamia, Egypt, and just over the Aegean Sea from Athens, the philosopher was born. His embodiment was Thales of Miletus, the most prominent knowledge seeker in the Ionian Period of the enlightenment of humanity. The lore and mysticism of the Greek gods no longer satisfied man's curiosity. The great understandings of science and philosophy, which had seemed beyond human comprehension and left to the realm of the gods, suddenly seemed knowable. Zeus and Poseidon were no longer a representation of earthly and heavenly knowledge. This Greek way of thinking was the first building block to true ideological progress in the west. This period paved the way for Greeks to lay the foundation for all of western culture, no doubt with the influx of diversity from throughout the known world.

Prior to the "Ionian enchantment," as sociobiologist Edward O. Wilson has called it, knowledge was simply what was known from the past. The past was ancient folklore for the purpose of mental and physical survival in an unforgiving world. Philosophy, or the love of wisdom, was an introduction into reflective, critical, and objective profiles of the world. Thales introduced the scientific method two thousand years before it was defined. In the centuries to follow, the Greeks produced under the tutelage of Socrates, Plato, and Aristotle the basis of philosophy and education, which still shapes our culture today. Before Socrates, pedagogy, translated from Greek as "to lead the child," meant training in the beliefs passed down through the centuries. To the amusement of the young, he spent his time questioning all that claimed to be known. For these questions, he was accused and charged with impiety and corrupting the youth, a crime punishable by death, for which he was allowed to self-dose the poisonous hemlock.

Socrates's method of corrupting the youth by asking questions to stir critical thinking has become the apex for advanced learning and the foundation for all education to this day. His martyrdom proved to be a demarcation point in history and an impetus for his student Plato and, shortly thereafter, Aristotle to treat philosophy as a method to find truths from logic negotiated within the confines of the human mind. The physical properties of the earth were not attributed to an incomprehensible notion of the gods but to laws that were knowable. The analogy of Plato's Cave relates consciousness to the circumstances of who we are and to what we are exposed. Education frees us from what Plato called *doxa*, or opinion. The cave is the metaphor for the mind. Doxa is the noise and falsehoods that we begin to accept as we are indoctrinated into society. Gradually, humanity was accepting Plato's dialectic method of introducing opposing viewpoints and learning through discourse and reason.

Plato's student Aristotle leveraged a science out of the deductive reasoning of the human mind. For Aristotle, education was not an intense understanding of one field to the detriment of knowledge to another; it was the unifying and connecting source that spanned the wide array of the scientific principles. Education was not about learning for the sake of knowing; it was about learning for the sake of thinking. To Aristotle, the ability to be critical was the highest form of human knowledge. Today, the American Association of University Professors (AAUP) calls critical thinking the "hallmark of American education." In 1605, Francis Bacon defined *critical thinking* as "a desire to seek, patience to doubt, fondness to meditate, slowness to assert, readiness to consider, carefulness to dispose and set in order, and hatred for every kind of imposture." It is and has always been employing our full cognitive abilities through the spectrum of reasoning to find truth beyond our intellectual fallacies.

The root and purpose of philosophy and education was argued to be truth, but it was also goodness. Where Socrates sought to curb the hubris of politics and ethics in society, Aristotle sought to define it. In *Politics*, he explores the relationship between the citizen and the state in society. In *Nichomachean Ethics*, he explains how the individual should best live. The pursuit of this knowledge was surely the way forward, but education and science was still in its infancy. Soon Aristotle's "Ethics" would merge with the burgeoning Christian sensibilities of the West. Although his hopes for the possibilities of the future remained Romantic, he was the first Realist of the philosophical traditions. Some of the laws that he proposed for society were setting a marriage age, killing all deformed children, keeping children cold for preparation in military service, keeping children inside the home until age seven, and beating and disgracing anyone saying or doing anything forbidden in society.

The Romans adopted the teachings of the Greeks and built an empire where all roads led and the sun never set. What the Romans lacked in philosophy they made up in oratory, engineering, and governance. Three centuries later, and in opposition to Aristotle's realism, Roman philosopher Marcus Tullius Cicero conjured the birth of Romanticism philosophy. He questioned situational ethics and human understanding of morals in *On Duties*. He espoused the divinity of the human condition and opposed the inhumane treatment of slaves. He contemplated the earnestness of businessmen, the role of immigrants and women, and to his demise, the relationship of the emperor to the empire. For these questions, he met the same fate as Socrates, only Cicero's head and hands were removed and displayed in the Roman Forum as a warning of dissent.

Dissention had not been favorable to philosophers until St. Augustine of Hippo. The emperor Constantine had begun the transition of the future of the Roman Empire back to the Ionia, the birthplace of philosophy, at Constantinople. The Visigoths had sieged Rome in AD 410, and according to eighteenth-century historian Edward Gibbon in *The Decline and Fall of the Roman Empire*, many Romans pointed the finger of destruction toward Christianity, a strange and new mystical religion out of the Hebrew monolithic tradition of Yahweh. Many Romans felt that the spectrum of the gods, revived and mutated from the Greek tradition, was forsaken in the name of a single God and his son Jesus Christ. St. Augustine's theological contributions to Christianity were many, but his philosophy of the City of God, alive in the hearts of Christians, connected a civilization in deterioration.

Jesus had said, "Render unto Caesar the things that are Caesar's, and unto God the things that are God's." A shared Christian culture of collectivism, poverty, and simplicity was a stark contrast from the decadence of the Roman Empire. The Dark Ages froze time under the guise of utopia and transformed the western world. Theocracy and monarchy began to merge. Civilization found mankind in a replica of the pre-Socratic era of philosophy where questions were unwelcome. The philosophical formation of Christianity was a rejection of the values of barbarism of the ancient world. It was the antidote for the greed, materialism, and selfishness of an empire on the decline. Perhaps for the better, or maybe just the sanity of humankind, the City of God cast a shadow over progress. Stirring were the philosophers to rekindle the critical analysis of the ancients.

Out of the Dark Ages a church-centered, mostly illiterate, and pre–printing press society formed the mystical understanding of the seven liberal arts in education. The two layers of liberal arts consisted of the Trivium, or the ancient arts espoused by the Romans of grammar, rhetoric, and logic. Grammar was the use and understanding of language and speech. Rhetoric was the art of persuasion and influence through oratory and writing. Logic was the methods that guided us to truths deduced through a God-centered universe. The path of the second layer, called the Quadrivium, was a more advanced level of the model, which usually equated with a naïve version of science. These subjects consisted of simple arithmetic; the spatial relationships of geometry; the sounds, patterns, and rhythms of music; and astronomy, which was the primitive understanding of the natural sciences embodied by a metaphysical version of physics.

True education was understood to be a crossroads of art and science. Science sought man's objective truths while the arts sought the subjective truths. By the Renaissance, the Trivium was replaced with a new and broad understanding of the humanities. God's Divine Providence of all aspects of humanity was being challenged by a new era of philosophers, who at first tried to keep it intact. Although Christian theology remained important to Enlightenment culture, the liberal arts began to incorporate theology into the Trivium rather than let it be its guide. The long period of the Middle Ages was termed the Dark Ages because of superstition and stagnation. The reintroduction of the classics elicited a spirit of progress, which was labeled heresy by a church that was unaccustomed to dissent. The dialectic argument against the church decoding every new piece of information was growing. The idea of progress was resurrected.

Aristotle's deductive reasoning helped explain the logic of ethics and politics of the arts of the Trivium and offered mathematical proof of the irrefutable logic of arithmetic and geometry of the Quadrivium. Not until the father of modern science, Francis Bacon, did the world understand that in a growing domain of complexities, simple deduction and reasoning of the human mind, isolated from the physical and social world, was insufficient. Man needed to explore the world to progress. He invented inductive reasoning for which we apply likelihood of an event being true. This was the beginning of the scientific method as we know it today. Bacon posited that testing events in nature properly can lead to new understandings of the world. He constructed a "ladder of the intellect," which incorporated the components of the new era of knowledge. With inductive reasoning, we test observations that are empirical—that is, gathered scientifically—but alas, based on sensory experience of an individual.

Because the individual is tied to his subjective experiences, we cannot get the same fundamental truths from induction that we can from deduction, but that journey of the pursuit of knowledge is where education is reclaimed. If humanity were to move forward and fully embrace the inductive reasoning of the scientific method, the individual would have to remove his personal doxa, according to Plato. Bacon named the four idols that kept prisoners in their allegorical cave. They were pertinent 1,800 years ago in Athens, 400 years ago in England, and just as relevant today. He said that man harbored fallacies, which hindered the scientific method. The first idol was the tribe. As humans, we possess natural bias, furthered by rhetoric, prejudice, stereotype, and exaggeration based on our surrounding social environment. We have idols of the cave, which is both our nurture and nature, idiosyncrasies, rearing, birth order, and habits. The idols of the marketplace affect our language, location, interpretations, speech, and meaning. The idols of the theater are politics and ideas especially pertaining to the media and marketing of the modern era.

The challenge of humanity is that enlightenment and progress demand us to examine these freedoms. Critical thinking was a giant leap forward, stipulating that we first analyze ourselves to get to the true nature of science. The new manifestation of liberal arts allowed mankind to pursue its true possibilities. By definition, a liberal education was meant to be liberating. It was literally freeing us from our ignorance of the world but also about the capabilities of ignorance within ourselves as individuals. A macro shift from centuries of collectivism to the individual ideas of empiricism was underway.

Although concerned more with politics and ethics than Bacon, John Lock proposed that natural law was "self-evident" to the individual. There was no deductive manor to prescribe the rights and needs of man, especially within the framework of an evolving method of governing. Empiricism was a belief that superseded the infancy of the sciences and quickly caught on to the art of human affairs.

Locke recalled the philosophy of Cicero to end the oligarchy of power resting with the few. He reminded humanity that the idea of freedom, law, equality, and justice were more powerful than any one man. Morality could be expressed as a law of nature or the grace of God, beyond the man-made paradigms that had trapped man for so long. Realism as a philosophy dated back to at least the book of Leviticus of the Old Testament or ethics as prescribed by Aristotle. Both lessons offered static solutions in an ancient realm. Locke offered the possibilities of a world beyond the divinity of a monarchy. He championed a world of liberty, equality, and democracy. The ideas of philosophy could and should be shared with the masses. The manifestations of the three arts of the Trivium introduced the world to the United States of America. The "logic" was guided by the philosophy of John Locke, the "rhetoric" by the propaganda of Thomas Paine, and the "grammar" by the phrasing of Thomas Jefferson.

Democracy, in no hyperbolic terms, changed the world. This new and foreign system of government gave farmers in an agrarian society the same power as the nobility. Because of its democratic and liberal tradition, American decided immediately that educated masses was the key to social and economic prosperity. The cornerstone of the Enlightenment was still the naïve understanding that all is knowable, but gradually, in the United States and around the western world, the Romantic period was fading. The realities of the modern industrial world redistributed our understandings of the merits of philosophy. America was, as of yet, not credited with anything novel besides its mere existence. The "whole man" education of the seven liberal arts was renewed with the revolutionary spirit and persevered in education as well as the Order of the Freemason, which had been practicing classical knowledge since the fourteenth century. America had bestowed the world with new ideas based on

Enlightenment values, but the young nation had not yet produced a cohesive and original epistemology to differentiate itself.

The origin of metaphysics may be traced back to the dualistic idea of consciousness and matter of Ancient Indian philosophy known as Samkhya. Aristotle understood metaphysics as the ability to collect information through the senses to gain knowledge. The logical outcome of the existential questions, which metaphysics attempted to answer, was a centuries-long delve into the ancient Quadrivium. The science of arithmetic, geometry, music, and astronomy was finally being discovered after medieval metaphysics tried to answer them with cosmology, astrology, and alchemy. As the first modern scientists began to practice new methods such as empiricism, the ancient ideas of consciousness were reexamined by a slew of European philosophers. The rationalists, in the vein of Descartes ("I think, therefore I am"), had served their purpose of enlightenment by appealing to reason rather than dogma.

The traditional understanding of metaphysics was breaking down. Immanuel Kant offered the *Critique of Pure Reason* in 1781, which shifted mankind's view of philosophy forever. He said that human experience must be introduced into metaphysics as fiercely as rationalism. He also posited that the true nature of the world is unknowable in an objective sense because it is viewed through the filters of the individual. This was a fundamental change from the perpetual battle to seek the ultimate truth through philosophy. The concurrent scientific revolution was disproving the teachings of history's greatest thinkers. Science told us that half of the liberal arts, the Quadrivium, was no longer a philosophy or a belief system. The arts of the Trivium, however, are innately personal. Kant exposed philosophy to its future, fading as a profession of the past and blending into the complexities of the modern world.

At Harvard University in the 1870s, a discussion group formed who called themselves the Metaphysical Club. Among the members of this group were future US Supreme Court Justice Oliver Wendell Holmes, mathematician Charles Sanders Pierce, and the Father of American Psychology, William James. What united them all was philosophy and education. Here, in a dorm room in Cambridge,

Massachusetts, the United States had finally produced its own unique and original branch of philosophy that could only exist in the modern philosophical epoch introduced by Kant. It came to be known as Pragmatism. These new Pragmatists believed that the historical exploration of the perfect philosophy was not a useful endeavor. Pragmatism was about how we think and not necessarily what we think. William James said that Pragmatism is not a philosophy because that connotes a belief system. It is the application based on experience. Humans have the ability to put rational thoughts into situational context.

So the metaphysics of time and space apply to this radical new version of empiricism. In the early seventeenth century, Sir Edward Coke, known as the greatest legal mind in England, said, "Reason is the life of the law." In *The Common Law*, written in 1881 by Metaphysical Club member and future justice Oliver Wendell Holmes, he refuted Coke's statement by declaring, "The life of the law has not been logic, it has been experience." He explained experience as "the felt necessities of the time." In other words, strict adherence to rationality is not static, nor is it sufficient, even in the pivotal matter of the law. James said, "To get at truth, we must study experience itself." Effectively, what we experience is only comprehended through what we as individuals have experienced. Truth is not always objective; it is, by definition, simply experience. It is a fluid concept devoid of philosophy. What the Americans had introduced was the ideology of not having an ideology, which was a breakthrough in philosophy.

These ideas could be applied to the education of the new and expanding disciplines. The three subjects of the Trivium had become the humanities. As the humanities incorporated the scientific method, we could finally bridge the quantifiable properties of the Quadrivium to the art of human affairs under the new title of the "social sciences." As we applied more scientific rigor and specialization to the disciplines, they became less attainable to the average individual. Because of this new hurdle to education, the early twentieth-century Pragmatists, led by John Dewey, offered a modern solution for education. To Dewey, the ancient quest for certainty of the philosopher had ended. The static constructs of truths imparted by centuries of philosophers had always become embattled ideas in light of new information. The Pragmatists believed we should move forward in education despite philosophy, not in conjunction with it.

Simultaneously, as the disciplines in academia began growing in number and making it more difficult for a unified liberal arts curriculum to sustain, the market forces of the Industrial Revolution demanded more intense learning in the vocations. Universities grew and expanded yet left little room for the consilience of their prior form. John Dewey believed "School has no moral end but to share in social life." Education was not based on divine teachings or reasoning discovered and applied in different eras; it was an active and critical endeavor into the demands of modern society. Morality is defined by the current social context and may only progress through education. The true definition of the ancient liberal arts was understood to be moral progress for the value of society. By becoming the "whole man" through the experience of education, the dualism of sociality and individuality unite. The result is closer to the quest for truth than the deductive reasoning of even the great philosophers.

By the mid-twentieth century, America's great contribution to philosophy was on the decline. Pragmatism was a morally relative belief system, which had attacked longstanding customs, ideas, and traditions of society including—but not limited to—education, religion, and patriotism. Dissidents described it as a subjective and experimental way to think, which claimed that the bias of the present obfuscated the long-held traditions of western culture. In the epoch of the conservative and conforming society of the 1950s, searching for new truths based on experience was dangerous. This apolitical version of conservatism posited that the truths had already been uncovered. Morality was adherence to these incontrovertible facts. Education was again an exercise in the rote learning of the past. The experience of the individual faded into the social ethic of conformity.

Dewey cared about the social value of education because he believed, as did Jefferson, that an educated populace contributed to a healthy democracy. Populism, the belief that the common people should have direct access to government has collided with elitism since the formation of the republic. Elitism, in the vein of Alexander Hamilton, believes that the common people shall elect the elite to maintain a government by their consent. The idea is that the educational requirements to make the dire policy decisions are simply not accessible to ordinary citizens. Political office, like every other profession over the past century, has become increasingly complex. The part-time job of the citizen farmer as a representative of the people has become an exercise in navigating political action committees, lobbyist groups, nonprofit organizations, as well as grassroots activism to discern consent. Populism is, of course, ideal, but for populism to be successful, we must have learned masses. That is, by definition, the contradiction and the conundrum.

Just a few decades ago, the United States educational system was the envy of the world. Our adults currently heading for retirement are the most educated citizens on the planet for their age group. Currently, our educational system does not break the top twenty in the world. In those few decades since our educational decline, we have opted for more specialized vocation, whether it be white-collar or blue-collar. to the detriment of true knowledge. We have confused productive members of society with replaceable cogs in a bureaucratic machine. Correct answers replaced curiosity, critical thinking, and discovery. The neoliberal forces of global hypercompetiveness have forced us to abandon the moral benefits in education in place of the purely financial return on investment. The staggering high inflation of higher education costs is a direct result of the forces that caused us to abandon a full education in the first place.

American academic and writer Louis Menand has said, "Liberal Arts is the pursuit of knowledge without any vocational utility, any financial reward, or ideological purpose." This is a great ideal and perhaps even a truth. The role of the modern Pragmatist, should any still exist, is to define the individual and the social experience of a generation. The extreme nature of the inflation of the price of higher education paired with the state government's continued unwillingness to subsidize it has caused challenges to the populist understanding of democracy. Should the lower and middle classes elect to pursue postsecondary education, the practical reason would be a return on investment. The reason education can be priced so high to begin with is that it has been effective at churning out the obedient masses for fifty years. We are wary to change education even as the world changes around it.

The seven liberal arts have a modern version, which exists within the confines of a critical education. Unfortunately, most curricula in the United States can be deduced into the rote learning of test preparation. We have based teacher's worth and student's future on standardized tests. It is the application of old methods to new models when what we really need the application of new methods to old models. It has become not economically feasible to pursue the education that is required to be creative at the exact time that creativity is in demand. This is the counterintuitive reality of the early twenty-first century. The vast majority of the populace has the financial obligation not to pursue their strengths but to determine the most cost effective return on investment. Education has sadly been reduced to a financial equation devoid of moral and social implications.

The limitations of education in the modern world are presumably economic. Inevitably, the bliss and catharsis of education that allow the elite freedom to pursue critical analysis perpetuate de facto elitism. William Deresiewicz, in his book *Excellent Sheep*, debunks the idea of a true modern liberal education, even at elite institutions such as Harvard. Deresiewicz claims that in order to even gain admittance at one of these universities, one must first not only excel on standardized tests but prove competence in a host of various activities. Once there, the pressure is so great to compete in an elite pool of talent that it leads directly to the waning of individuality and diversity. The goal of the university thus becomes maximization of the future economic value of the individual in order to become successful donors after graduation. Character building is a distant second to vocation, primarily in the lucrative financial sector where many elite grads now head.

What we teach and the way we teach it in schools have changed little in the past fifty years. However, obtaining excellent test scores, earning stellar grades, and participating in organized extracurricular activities are now the baseline for college admittance. Homework increases with advanced timelines throughout elementary school. "Helicopter parents" ensure assignments are completed nightly rather than the responsibility resting upon the child. "Tiger moms" enforce the Asian practice of treating the school day as a prerequisite to the real learning enforced at home and with private tutors. The hyperefficiency, which we have injected into all aspects surrounding learning, has been an exercise in training rather than the true and deep learning. The goal of American education has become regurgitating information to pass a multiple choice test graded by computers. Even with the urgency and rational economic incentive of modern America, we have fallen from our number-one world status of just a short time ago. We relinquished true learning and critical thinking in name of able measurement. As of 2009, the United States did not even register in the top twenty countries in the world for education.

What happened to American education? Because of a variety of forces, we squeezed all the juice out of an outdated model more suited for the factory workers and the middle managers of the 1950s. Instead of making a pragmatic strategic pivot by relating to the current environment, we just did a lot more of what we used to do. The result was a disenfranchisement from the classic virtues of education. The only pragmatic approach taken was how to navigate the soaring costs of education to negotiate documentation of proof of learning through a degree relevant to a hiring manager. Jean Piaget, who tackled education from a psychologist's perspective and was perhaps the most universally recognized contributor to education in the twentieth century, would have been disappointed at this inevitable outcome. In 1934, he said, "Only education is capable of saving our societies from possible collapse, whether violent or gradual." By the end of the twentieth century, the mandates of the social power of education was withering and clinging to the values of another time.

So naturally, we look for a scapegoat for the failing status of an institution that, given the character of the American people over history, should be a self-correcting model. The teachers' unions are too greedy/not paid enough! The parents are too/insufficiently involved! There is no common core/too much symmetry in education! The advanced kids/average kids are keeping my kids behind! Politics, both national and local, have infiltrated our idea of what is required to the detriment of the individual and the curriculum. We believe that more resources, money, diversity, smaller class size, etc., is the key to our children navigating the competitive edge to the next level of education and, hence, the next closer spot to gaining the competitive edge in the future industry of their choice. If we are to truly progress in education, we must divert from our prescribed paths and look to the models that have maintained allegiance to a true method of learning.

In her book *The Smartest Kids in the World*, Amanda Ripley investigates those countries that have surpassed the United States in terms of true education. Her barometer is the Program for International Student Assessment (PISA) scores, which, according to the Organization for Economic Co-operation and Development (OECD), is not a test of rote memorization similar to an American multiple-choice test but a problem-solving measure that seeks to invoke creativity required in the complex modern world. In 2009, Finland was the pinnacle of international education. It had been a cold and rural nonfactor in international learning until quite recently. How did Finland not only significantly overtake the United States in terms of educational prowess, let alone the entire world? Was it because of the singular and nonstop focus on education drawn from the Asian world? Was it because of the possibilities and experimental leverage of Eastern Europe in countries such as Poland that had made dramatic international strides in education?

Finland excelled not because of its internal insistence on the return on investment of education. It did not continue to insist on the quantity of education to the detriment of the quality. In fact, as it turned out, Finland was not so much different from the United States in terms of students. It spanned the spectrum of jocks to burnouts throughout the socioeconomic range. Unlike the Asian education culture, Finns had other values besides the myopic interests of schooling. The school day was very average. Homework was not excessive. In fact, at first glance, nothing pointed to exceptional in the entire curriculum. What was missing was cultural context. Teaching is among, if not the most, noble profession in the entire country. Yet among modern elite in the United States, teaching is a profession of low pay and low status. In Finland, ten out of ten teachers graduate in the top one-third of their class. In the United States, those results are but a fraction.

Finnish teachers are among the most educated class in the world. They are exalted in society, and that reverence is clearly visibly communicated to students via culture. In Northern Europe, educators have become elevated to the status of doctors and lawyers in the United States. As Ripley notes, we try to "reverse-engineer" teachers in the United States through incentives and rewards. We are so infatuated with the process, policies, and politics of education that we have forgotten that well-trained teachers are the secret to unlocking educational capabilities. They are able to carry the message that the student's responsibilities are that of the students and not the parents. The rigor must be accountable to the individual. Character is manifested through effort. There are many world-class pockets of education within the United States but many more that accept low expectations. World-class democracies understand that there are inextricable links to the weakest constituents and societal health. This is the apex of education, according to Piaget, and the singular definition, according to Dewey. Finland knows what we have forgotten.

Fortunately, there are signs of progress that the metaphysical realm of education is still vibrant. The ancient curiosity that propelled all learning for centuries had become a static buffet with occasional indications of progress. In 1927, William Heard Kilpatrick, in *Education for a Changing Civilization*, cemented the Pragmatic legacy of John Dewey by completely individualizing education based on the "project approach" to learning. This new theory of project-based learning was a radical process of discovery independent of the theoretical lectures aimed at presenting and interpreting ideas of the past. Project learning, especially when coordinated with other individuals, gives context to the true nature of the need for the project and allows the individual to access the heights of their individual aptitudes and interests. Discovery, which is at the heart of the history of critical thinking, is given the opportunity to blossom.

Kilpatrick introduced a curriculum behind Dewey's insistence on learning through experience. Project-based learning begins with a broad base of knowledge, which challenges students to problem solve through projects. Working together in teams and challenging the understanding of a leader-led course opposed putting the instructor at the center of the learning. If all knowledge comes from experience, then theoretical constructs will not move us closer to the truth. Real-world problems require real-world solutions. Education, especially under the mounting pressure of the digital world, will inevitably transform from teacher-led to teacher-facilitated. Immersion, which is the state of experience, is the next evolution of deep learning. Schools and universities all around the country are beginning to come to this realization, which had died for decades. The private Olin College of Engineering is one such school that is committed to the curriculum of a project-based curriculum.

For years, companies have been hiring business students. Peter Capelli of the Wharton School of Business, in *Why Good People Can't Get Jobs*, identifies the cultural and bureaucratic nature of the perceived skills gap in modern America. These homogeneous business school students are essentially a product of an IT department algorithm. Senior managers want emotionally intelligent, critical-thinking, problem-solving, question-asking, and innovative thinkers ready for hire. Middle managers are concerned with safe and experienced productive employees who will not question the status quo. Hiring managers are even more consumed with erring on the side of hiring safe as opposed to hiring for greatness. Because of this built-in risk management strategy, the exact qualities which most leaders in organizations claim that they require and are in short supply of are the exact qualities that their organization is overtly rejecting. This disconnect will be completely evident in the years to come as business strategy begins to release itself from its rationalistic urges.

So because of the complexities of the modern world and because of the new demands of creativity and innovation in business, the liberal arts are making a resurgence not just for social conscience but for economic prosperity. The ramifications of the goodness derived from education can now be measured. The social sciences tell us that education gives us a better opportunity to, in turn, educate our own kids. Utilitarian philosophy would advocate the communal prosperity of higher volunteerism, job satisfaction, healthy choices, pay and benefits, and in turn, tax revenue through higher education. The pragmatic understanding of the liberal arts must be adjusted for every new era. In the modern world, we have the "blended learning" of the capabilities of social media and the Internet along with project-based learning, as well as the personalized restructuring, which technology can offer in the future. However, the method in which we learn, as in the words of John Dewey from last century have never been more prescient, "Facts—may become irrelevant—what will never become irrelevant is teaching 'problem solving,' as it is the only discipline as useful in the present as it is in the future." This is critical thinking for the ages.

CHAPTER 13

ECOLOGY AND CAPITALISM (PURPOSE)

Out of the great philosophical traditions emerging in the nineteenth century, the Pragmatists explored the interdisciplinary experiences of humans to find objective truth. The Existential Philosophers explored the subjective truth of the authenticity of the individual. The Existentialists relied on the singular state of being. The essence of what it means to be human can only be defined inside the singular consciousness of the individual. Whatever label or understanding applied by an outside force distorts the context and the nature of the soul. A central theme to the existential experience is anxiety. The existential implication of anxiety manifests itself through experience of life, which by definition cannot be shared. The experience of consciousness leaves us alone in a world where we are left to believe in only our own authenticity. Meaning is thus derived through existence alone. The great existential questions of the meaning of life posed and defined through the art and science of philosophy through the ages was handed over to the individual to define. Whether from the religious or secular traditions, the essence of the individual defined one's unique purpose.

Because of the introduction of anxiety into the definition of existential philosophy, it is not unreasonable that these ideas lent themselves well as a merger into the field of psychoanalysis.

Psychiatrist and holocaust survivor Viktor Frankl wrote one of the most important books of the twentieth century. In *Man's Search for Meaning*, Frankl introduced logotherapy as a technique based on man's primary force, which is the search for meaning. Man creates meaning by what he makes and experiences, as well as the manner by which he perceives these actions. Again, drawing on the metaphor of Plato's Cave, Frankl likens logotherapy to ophthalmology. He says, "A painter tries to convey to us a picture of the world as he sees it, an ophthalmologist tries to enable us to see the world as it really is . . . so that the whole spectrum of meaning and values becomes conscious and visible to him . . . actually, truth imposes itself and needs no intervention." Frankl was interested in the spiritual counseling of the freedom of the individual to find his own morality barometer. He believed that the depth of man's search was obfuscated with grandeurs of influence, affluence, hedonism, and materialism. Man's unhappiness was neuroses primarily of a spiritual disorder.

To get to meaning and purpose requires the individual to explore the depths of her own nature and consciousness. Because of the very personal nature of the journey, freedom is an essential component of the subjective requirements of meaning. According to Frankl, "Freedom, however, is not the last word. Freedom is only part of the story and half of the truth." Freedom is actually degenerative and corrosive if not properly checked and balanced by responsibility. Frankl believed in the duality so much that he recommended building a Statue of Responsibility on the West Coast of the United Sates to balance the idea of freedom exalted through responsibility. Part of that responsibility is to seek to lower the division between what one is and what one is to become. This tension of freedom and responsibility is "inherent in the human being and therefore indispensable to mental well-being." Logotherapy is essentially a medium by which an individual can explore his own "responsibleness," the outcomes of who, what, and why will become self-evident in time. It is then that by participating in life, through action, can the education gained of personal meaning through logotherapy flourish.

Because of the subjective nature of truth in existentialism, meaning is not universal, but the shared experience of culture can help to develop our interpretations. From the secular humanist tradition, cognitive psychologist Dan Dennet finds that education appeals to the informed consent of a strong democracy gained through understanding religion as a biological construct of culture. According to secular traditional understandings of religions, they are universally designed by natural selection no differently than the evolution of a barnyard animal. Because they have adapted to various cultures throughout millennia, they are the lens through which we view meaning within a culture. As religious scholars such as Reza Aslan remind us, all religions are purposefully ambiguous. Religion does not form culture, but rather, culture interprets religion. Even though religious doctrine is considered sacred, the ambiguity of semantics and time allows the injection of the difference in interpretation. From the perspective of the religious faithful, Pastor Rick Warren has sold over thirty million copies of his book *A Purpose Driven Life* in recent years. Warren's central question is not so different from the existential understanding of purpose void of religious context. Like Frankl, he prescribes responsibility through the freedom of questioning, "What are you going to do with what you are given?"

Whereas Frankl believed in the power of the purpose motive for humanity, Freud, the pleasure motive, and Nietzsche, the power motive, the second half of the twentieth century solidified the misdirected profit motive as a near religious attainment. In 1759, Adam Smith published *The Theory of Moral Sentiments*, which laid the groundwork for *The Wealth of Nations*, written less than twenty years later, which has been used to explain the inherent morality of the public good of the selfishness of capitalism. Rationalist philosophy assumed that two parties who mutually entered an agreement would have their own personal benefits or else the agreement would have never been reached. In other words, supply and demand is a benevolent exercise in the organization of resources. So began modern capitalism, a framework that has allowed extreme poverty to diminish from 85 percent of the world's population during Smith's time to just 16 percent today. The per capita world income is up 1,000 percent since 1800. The per capita American income is up by 10,000 percent. With a few bumps and bruises along the way, the notion of capitalism was a healthy ideal into the 1950s and beyond. The morality of the purpose motive was still somewhat intact.

A global ideological Cold War between the capitalists in the West and the communists in the East lasted most of the second half of the twentieth century. The Marxist-Socialist worldview sought to bring private property to the public domain. The freedom and opportunity won through rebellion and revolution was being attacked via the economic system of capitalism. The American way of life, as well as that of the entire western world, had evolved and flourished through the imbedded values which capitalism signified. Our proud Protestant ethic was tied to our economic system. Our stewards of capitalism ensured that prior to the Cold War, the benevolence of the system was seldom questioned. As Marc Gafni, author of *Your Unique Self*, explains, "Lifting people out of poverty was never the conscious intention of business, it was the byproduct of a business well enacted." The Cold War gave us a conscious motive to react and defend its righteousness sometimes to a fault. Our purpose, bound within the limits of a moral framework of capitalist understanding, was usurped by an ideology too consumed with conceptual warfare. We took capitalism to an extreme to perpetuate our worldview at the expense of ourselves, and we lost our way as stewards to man's greatest economic system.

As social stratification increases, self-promotion is an intellectual version of narcissism, which has become economically necessary to attach to our identity. More competition and less loyalty leads to a very simple equation of self-reliance that when not properly cultivated may lead to the decadent version of the self. Although the cure for narcissism is a connection to others, relating to others on an intellectual and emotional basis is not necessarily transcendent. The spirituality of our values lies not within our selfish and worldly short-term needs. *Logos* is best translated from the Greek interpretation of "I say" and is interpreted broadly and simplistically as the personal interpretation of the world at large. The Gospel of John attaches *logos* to divinity. Later St. Justin Martyr bridged the philosophy of the Greeks to the divinity of the triumvirate of the body (*soma*), the soul (*psyche*), and the spirit (*pneuma*) of early Christianity. Three forces converged on the individual. The body was the most prescient and shallow. The soul nourished the connection of the individual through the human capabilities of empathy. The spirit is the overreaching purpose of being devoid of religious doctrine.

The ancients called upon the essential nature of the elements of earth, air, water, wind, and fire, namely the geosphere. Ecology informs our understandings of the web of life through an intricate nexus known as the biosphere. Jesuit priest Pierre Teilhard de Chardin, in his book *The Phenomenon of Man*, imagines the next evolution of human consciousness as the Noosphere, or the apex of human understanding. Teilhard believed that the patterns of humanity embraced a Darwinian spirit directly in line with Christian ideals. By accepting a purer consciousness of spirit, merged with the growing truths of modern science, a new spiritual consciousness would be formed. The highest level of human understanding, or pneuma, as Justin Martyr would have exclaimed, was only possible outside the mundane of the human experience. The values that prevail, it turns out, were not anointed through financial wizardry of the twentieth century but carefully cultivated through ancient knowledge and surrogated to the messengers of purpose throughout the ages.

In the twentieth century, we had lost touch with the social and economic implications of our spiritual values. The myth of Narcissus describes a hunter who was led to a pool of water and frozen by the reflection of his own beauty. In the late nineteenth century, the prevenient arbiters of post-Victorian values had already conducted timeless works of art prophesizing the corrosive spiritual effects that narcissism would accompany. Oscar Wilde updated the Narcissus story in *The Picture of Dorian Gray* as a Faustian choice between inner and outer beauty. By the time Gray had realized the implications of his hedonism at the expense of morality, he also comes to the conclusion that his attempt to reclaim his inner beauty is just another attempt at vanity. In the mid-nineteenth century, the whaling industry propelled the economy. New Bedford, Massachusetts, the center of the whaling industry, was called the City That Lit the World. Whale oil could be used for candles, cooking oil, or lubrication of machinery, and it was big business in a dark world before crude oil and kerosene. It is within this economy that Herman Melville created Ahab, Captain of the Pequod, a wealthy forty-year veteran of the glory days of the whaling industry.

Melville called his masterpiece *Moby Dick* after the great white whale who had taken Ahab's leg years before. Out of revenge rather than fortune, Ahab seeks the "fiery hunt" once again in search of Moby Dick. Ahab was not a contemplative man. His years of success in possibly the world's most exciting, utilitarian, and modern career had left him spiritually bankrupt. His lack of self-awareness, as told by a crew member and narrator Ishmael, had caused his physical and spiritual death as well as the sinking of the Pequod. His anger, his failures, and his very nature are reflected symbolically in the menacing depiction of the whale. Melville uses this unenlightened man as an allegory to evil as an embodiment from the past. His namesake is that of King Ahab of the Old Testament of the Bible. Melville uses allusion, which reflects qualities of the great and tragic characters throughout the history of literature. Ishmael, the mystical narrator and Pequod crewmember, is able to describe the demise of Ahab. The myth of Narcissus, he describes, "is the key to it all."

Narcissism researcher Jean Twenge, along with W. Keith Campbell, in *The Narcissism Epidemic*, claims that the very spirituality that Ahab lacked, we have been attempting to treat with self-esteem rather than humility. According to Twenge, in trying to stamp out aggression and materialism and build empathy and spirituality by "trying to build a society that celebrates high self-esteem, self-expression, and loving yourself . . . Americans have inadvertently created more narcissists—and a culture that brings out more narcissistic behavior in all of us." Throughout history, narcissism was infection of the soul, but we learned how to treat it as a remedy in the twentieth century. According to Twenge, self-esteem is such a foreign notion in the East that some cultures do not even have a word for it. Studies have found that narcissism has skyrocketed in recent decades, in large part because we are trying to cure it with a derivative of narcissism itself. We are taught that self-esteem increases success, yet Twenge finds no correlation. In fact, in the United States, the ethnic group with the lowest self-esteem, Asian Americans, has the best performance and potential. From an international perspective, Twenge finds, "We're number one in thinking we're number one," which inevitably perpetuates the affliction.

In a competitive world, we are taught that self-promotion is a prerequisite to success. When potential job applicants may reach the hundreds or the thousands, it is inevitable to assume that more self-esteem will lead to better self-promotion and better self-promotion will lead to better opportunities. To take this formula one step further and tie happiness to success, we have believed that higher self-esteem leads to greater success. Greater success will inevitably lead to happiness and the freedom to pursue our ideals. According to happiness researcher Shawn Achor, success does not lead to happiness and is, in fact, quite the opposite. Achor concludes, in unison with similar studies worldwide, that happiness is an interpretation of reality, which transcends socioeconomic status worldwide. Happiness comes before success and may be its greatest indicator. A measured version of esteem stemming from accomplishment is healthy. Injecting self-esteem before accomplishment to drive success is corrosive. The human brain is, however, still our most complex machine. As John Milton wrote in *Paradise Lost*, "The mind is its own place, and in itself can make a heaven of a hell, a hell of a heaven."

Through Achor's studies, he has found that we can literally retrain our brains to begin to seek out happiness in the world regardless of age. Because of the potential of neuroplasticity in our brains and the elasticity of our temperament and our beliefs, our understandings can literally be reprogrammed. Prior to these breakthroughs in the field of cognitive psychology, which have primarily come in the last decade, we would find that traditionally happiness increases into our thirties. In November 2015, a study by Twenge found that this trend was reversing. Those over thirty were not as happy as they once were and those under thirty were happier than they have ever been. A popular meme by Tim Urban on WaitbutWhy.com suggests why Generation Y, whom are mostly still under thirty at this point, are so unhappy. Urban depicts happiness as a formula where Happiness = Reality – Expectations. Although a simple quantification of a complex psychological understanding, Urban may not be far off. A version of this formula has been used to identify high suicide rates in places that report high levels of happiness.

Urban is recounting the various yarns told about the entitlement and spiritual vacancy that have infiltrated the souls of the youth of the world. Twenge literally wrote the book on the narcissism, laziness, and entitlement of the modern American youth. She called it *Generation Me: Why Today's Young Americans are More Confident, Assertive, Entitled, and More Miserable Than Ever Before.* Her 2015 findings are a reversal of her popular opinion that has infiltrated popular understanding of our youngest adult generation. She explains these strange findings as follows: "Our current culture of pervasive technology, attention-seeking, and fleeting relationships is exciting and stimulating for teens and young adults, but may not provide the stability and sense of community that mature adults require." Instead of offering the possibility that she misinterpreted her original findings or admit inexplicability, she has again chosen to demean by rationalizing their happiness as naivety and immaturity. Instead of viewing their happiness as the base of the building block of personal, civic, economic, and spiritual growth and a generational shift in rebuke of institutional narcissism, it is instead just further proof of their bottomless narcissism.

The hole in Twenge's argument is not because she has not collected accurate information or presented accurate depictions of linear inevitabilities but because she relies on the twentieth century notion of behaviorism predicting the future. Yes, narcissism has run rampant for decades, and yes, Generation Y was raised with a more-than-healthy dose, but the convergence of technology, economics, and global awareness has changed the consciousness of a generation. Positive psychologists have essentially been studying the most spiritually healthy people in society scientifically. This has been the quest for spiritual leaders for thousands of years, but the data is not yet two decades old. There is yet a lot to learn. Fortunately, there are indicators that the culture of narcissism is in remission, even if the self-aggrandizement of social media continues. Positive psychology, the last frontier of the discipline, is shedding light on the errors of our ways every day. These lessons affect our youth, if only indirectly, because of our acceptance or rejection of these ideas.

Jim Tankersley, *Washington Post* economic columnist, has been an advocate for placing the blame on the "narcissism epidemic" and its various scourges at the feet of the Baby Boomer generation. He has even gone so far as to say, "Baby boomers are what's wrong with America's economy." Tankersley says that every politician agrees that lowering the benefits for this generation is off the table even though they will collect tens or hundreds of thousands of dollars more than they put in. They burned fossil fuels at low prices, accrued pensions which stall research and development, saddled us with debt, and left us with inflated education, poor jobs, and cheap goods. The justification for the continuity and increase in the levels of economic success despite changing circumstances was not the individual examples of narcissism found by researchers counting "selfies" on Facebook pages but a mass hysteria of entitlement for which an entire generation is unaware, much less remorseful. Of course the younger generations are happier. The Great Recession culminating in 2008 reset the barometer. By 2013, the middle class owning stocks, homes, and businesses was down. The artificial economy was over. That year, the peer-reviewed journal of Social Psychological and Personality Science found that the long trend of increasing materialism and decreasing empathy was reversing.

Materialism is the vehicle on which narcissism rides. As we incrementally and inevitably enter the postmaterialist world, our consciousness will inevitably expose the goodness possible. The financial recovery actually sped up inequality, but it also allowed a generation to redefine their expectations. For fifty years, we lived in a world where we believed that the treadmill of consumerism was a vehicle to climb the mountains of satisfaction. So although Tim Urban has all the disdain for youth as Twenge, he seems to have been accurate in his assessment of the generic formula of Happiness = Reality – Expectations. There is another explanation, however. Shawn Achor defines *happiness* as pleasure combined with deeper feelings of meaning and purpose. Traditional psychology would measure the decrease of expectations after the recession. Positive psychologists would measure the increase in meaning and purpose that was the result of a material tragedy. That is where the spiritual shift lies.

At one time, seventy thousand New Englanders were employed by the whaling industry. There were Ahabs and Ishmaels much more mortal, who relied on the oil of whales not just for their uses but for the safety, security, and prosperity of their families. Fortunately, we no longer have to kill to heat. By the 1940s the blue and sperm whales were near extinction. Not until 1986 did the mantra "Save the Whales" enter our lexicon on a wide scale as the international community finally conceded that their preservation was important. Most of the whales are gone, yet their lack of resurgence is primarily due to overfishing. In the waters where the Pequod would have sailed, fish such as cod, haddock, hake, and flounder have decreased as much as 95 percent in the last decade alone. On this frontier is where sustainability battles the ego. William Destler of the Rochester Institute of Technology says, "Everyone thinks they have the right to unlimited clean water, natural resources, oil, and gas beyond a reasonable amount because they pay for it." If anyone suggests any free market infringement of a monetary transaction in defense of the earth, it is an infringement on their rights. Freedom without responsibility leads to an unhealthy ego and a corrupted soul.

Killing whales for oil seems like a barbaric process for lighting the world just as depleting the world of ancient fossil fuels for energy to the detriment of the climate and biosphere will seem very soon. The march of progress of the western world has increased man's separation with nature. Sufi mystic Llewellyn Vaughn-Lee says that the human disconnect with the natural world occurred when the monolithic God of the Old Testament suppressed the polytheistic gods and goddesses of creation. In these traditions, we were the guardians of the earth because the gods were representations of nature. The book of Genesis instructed man to have dominion over the earth. The one true God was relegated to heaven and could not be found in the natural world as before, so we became more careless as we could not offend God by disrespecting nature. Technological progress inevitably leads us away from nature, and we forget that it is the basis of our sustainability as a species.

Catholic Priest Thomas Berry said that the Enlightenment understanding of owning land only further separated the self from nature. The flowers, birds, and bees were mechanisms of human dominance. The American "manifest destiny" to tame the land between the Pacific and Atlantic Ocean was a materialist conquest that further removed the spirituality from the land. Berry said, "We never experienced the land as Native Americans did . . . we always asked what can we do with the land, rather than, how can we cherish and preserve the land." Before his death in 2009 at age ninety-four, he mourned the idea that we are in the sixth extinction period in the history of the world. The last period happened sixty-five million years ago. There have been seven glacial cycles in the past 650,000 years. The last ice age ended less than ten thousand years ago. Since that time the earth has been warming in large part due to man's existence and progress. Scientists have known that the release of greenhouse gases will cause the earth to heat since the nineteenth century.

We have seen sea levels rise seventeen centimeters in the last one hundred years. That amount of elevation is now happening in a decade. Global temperatures are rising as was inevitable. The warmest twenty years on record have occurred since 1981. The oceans are warming as well, causing glaciers to melt at the poles. Our waters are becoming more acidic, extreme weather events are multiplying, and snow cover is decreasing. The Intergovernmental Panel on Climate Change (IPCC) has said, "Scientific evidence for warming of the climate system is unequivocal." At the bottom of the website at Climate. nasa.gov, you will find the words *Scientific Consensus* followed by the statement, "97% of climate scientists agree that climate-warming trends over the past century are very likely due to human activities, and most of the leading scientific organizations worldwide have issued public statements endorsing this position." In the name of progress and comfort, we did not act as stewards of the natural earth. The void of a spiritual understanding of ecology in our society is quickly becoming a series of tangible issues. The spiritual price has been paid. Soon we will have to view these issues not as idealistic hand wringing but in very practical terms. A 2013 *Nature Magazine* study estimates that the price of methane released from melting ice caps could cost the world economy $60 trillion.

Jainist Monk Satish Kumar outlines the three dimensions of ecology from the Hindu traditions. The path to spirituality is three-fold, and enlightenment is achieved by understanding the soul, society, and the soil. By engaging in *tapas*, or self-discipline, to achieve self-knowledge, we can gain more fulfillment by surrendering our ego. By practicing *yajna*, the ritual that represents replenishment to the earth, we acknowledge its vital necessity to our life force. Humanity has been blessed with great constructs of knowledge throughout the ages. Cultivating generosity, or *dana*, is the alms which we must pay for our blessings. Many times we can find three dimensions to our sacred understandings. The Greeks believed in truth, goodness, and beauty; the ancient Chinese Confucians believed in the triad of humanity, heaven, and earth. The Christian faith divides God into the Father, the Son, and the Holy Spirit. The United States Constitution extols life, liberty, and the pursuit of happiness. New Age spirituality highlights the mind, body, and spirit as the path to enlightenment. What we require from our spirituality as a culture transcends the self or society. It is a connection to the earth, obligation from our ancestors, and responsibility to our children.

Native Americans have a much more metaphysical understanding of existence. The Shoshone believed in three distinct natures of the soul. The social ethic encouraged respect, hospitality, honor, courage, and honesty. The main difference from our understanding of spirituality is their version of subsistence. In the Native American tradition, individual and societal needs of the present were balanced by the sustainability of the seventh generation to come. The Great Law of the Iroquois suggests, "In every deliberation, we must consider the impact of the seventh generation . . . even if it requires having skin as thick as the bark of a pine." Modernity has enveloped us very suddenly. Just one hundred years ago, President Teddy Roosevelt, military leader and environmental activist, said, "To waste, to destroy our natural resources, to skin and exhaust the land instead of using it so as to increase its usefulness, will result in undermining in the days of our children the very prosperity which we ought by right hand down to them amplified and developed."

Twentieth-century American theologian Reinhold Niebuhr said, "Nothing that is worth doing can be achieved in our lifetime; therefore, we must be saved by hope." Faith, hope, and optimism for the future is something that we owe our children. Instead of following this advice throughout the twentieth century, we developed what *The Sustainability Generation* author Mark Coleman has called generational entitlement. We were corrupted by the collective ego, which is a recipe for unhappiness. The process was documented in Tim Kasser's 2003 book *The High Price of Materialism*. As a psychologist, Kasser claims that the profit motive was the most powerful force of the last half of the twentieth century. Its constant pull to economically raise consumer spending through marketing, commercialization, and heightened materialism had an inverse relationship with prosocial values, such as empathy for all creation. We lost touch with our intrinsic values in place of external resources. In the end, we were left with a less vital society, degraded personal well-being, and a less sustainable world.

According to the Buddhist tradition, the cure is mindfulness. Thich Nhat Hanh, a Buddhist monk of Vietnamese descent and author of over one hundred books, says the cure to this malaise is a collective awakening. He writes in *The Bells of Mindfulness*, "We have to hear the bells of mindfulness that are sounding all across the planet. We have to start learning how to live in such a way that a future will be possible for our children and our grandchildren." Mindfulness is the practice of introducing well-being into our consciousness. The "joy of being" concentrates attention to the moment. Unhealthy egos can never truly be mindful because the present is always a poor substitute for the possibilities of a moment which never comes. Feeding the future of the ego in absence of the present is an inauthentic path to spirituality. Mindfulness declares that the possibilities of the future relies on our consciousness at the moment. We must alter our idea of success. If we achieve our goals void of the mindfulness of our ideals, we will look back at a trail of unhappiness.

The Buddha taught the term *dukkha* to mean "suffering," which is man's natural state. The idea of seeking happiness is elusive. We need to cultivate the joy of being, a form of happiness that does not depend on what happens. The Four Noble Truths of Buddhism speak of the truth, the origin, the cessation, and finally the path of liberation from dukkha. The Noble Path itself is eightfold. Displaying the "right" wisdom and ethics are, of course, central to the teaching. Effort and mindfulness are also among the core tenets. In his book *The Master and his Emissary*, Iain McGilchrist explores the duality of the brain in human history. Beginning with the Enlightenment, we switched our primary functions to the left brain, which assumes the more rational interpretation of our consciousness has discounted our spiritual being. The progress of the twentieth century had only streamlined this transition. The noble values of truth, beauty, authenticity, consciousness, experience, and humanity were ideas lost in time. Our great hope is that the inadequacies of our material prospects and the heightened connection to enlightened ideas can heal the moral deficiencies of capitalism in disarray.

The complexity of the world is always multiplying. As we learn more about the intricate nature of ecosystems and that the honeybee is a key component to the global food supply, we realize how delicate and fragile even the smallest components are. Waking up from our individualism to a state of interdependence, even on a global scale, is humanitarian; it is not spiritual. Recognizing the earth as a life source for ourselves and everyone on it is a start. Understanding the ethereal obligation to our ancestors and descendants is true logotherapy. The trappings of the ego-self blurred our vision for decades. As the industrial world stalled, we began to exploit future generations and our natural resources through debt. The capitalism that pulled the world out of poverty had developed an inclination for leveraging debt and creating value, which was inexplicable. The Noble Path in Buddhism is sometimes called the middle way. It is finding the balance of extremes. It is balancing freedom with responsibility.

According to economist Umair Haque, the version of capitalism of the last decades of the twentieth century accrued what he calls *thin value*. Our financial goals were intact, but we were borrowing from our future and the sustainability of the planet in ways that we have a difficult time quantifying. For instance, Haque says a hamburger costs roughly $3, but the cost to society is closer to $30. There is a subsidy for the land as well as water use for cows; the code allows for tax breaks for even our largest corporations, a healthcare subsidy for the consumer, and a government subsidy of entitlements for the minimum wage worker making the burger. The cost is real, but the responsibility is absent. The debt is accrued but never calculated. It is not necessarily out of selfishness or greed but, many times, just plain ignorance. This ignorance has been the cornerstone of our growth. The GDP grows as the national debt grows. Our great spiritual battle will not be the redistribution of wealth but the redistribution of value. What capitalism requires are the very foundations that we all require. It turns out that the cornerstones that uplift humanity spiritually also are beginning to uplift capitalism economically.

Our business schools have spent decades talking about position, differentiation, competitive advantage, economies of scale, and efficiency. The result has been a gradual atrophy of morale and profits from the traditional vanguards of industry. Business is waking up to the altruistic opportunities of enlightenment. Business is becoming conscious and mindful in new and compelling traditions. Raj Sisodia, a thought leader in the "conscious capitalism" movement, has found that between 1996–2006 companies that displayed new principles of capitalism returned over 1,000 percent for investors versus an S & P 500 average of 122 percent. Likewise, Haque studied 250 companies and found that even by 2011, 90 percent still retained values from the twentieth century. If someone invested $1 million into those companies in the year 2000, the return on investment would have only been 80 percent in 2011. If that same person would have put that same amount in a portfolio that valued conscious capitalism, she would have been returned 300 percent of the investment.

The result of capitalism waking up to its true possibilities is counterintuitive to everything we know about the macroeconomic system. In the modern world, once the realization that the profit motive is primary, all parties lose their connection. Entrepreneurs and artists connect by displaying a purpose, but companies too often rely on the performance value of their products or service. Inherent in the purpose must be a mindfulness of the repercussions of all actions at every level of business. In 1970, free market zealot Milton Friedman claimed, "The social responsibility of business is to increase its profits." Friedman was the forefather of the values that took down the stock market in 2008. The notion of corporate social responsibility was nonexistent. To Friedman, any philanthropic gesture on the part of business was theft from the profits of investors. It was their responsibility to then turn their profits into the social good individually, if they so chose. This disconnection from the individuals working for the company, its customers, and the community it serves has been apparent and purposeful. This notion of hyperrationality usually leaves us with a shell of a company and with repercussions to the individual.

Conscious capitalism is not the ruination of our greatest method of economic organization. To the victors will still go the spoils, but the great successes must learn that equity is the path. John Mackey, CEO of Whole Foods, is a self-described free market capitalist libertarian. A generation ago, in business, the self-interested and, therefore, moral path for libertarians was fulfilling the rational egoism of success. It was a success for the individual and the company for the short term. Mackey's company caps executive pay at nineteen times the average salary not because he has any socialist inclination in his bones but because he knows the greatest competitive advantage he can add is an employee committed to the purpose beyond the paycheck. Mackey has adopted a very Zen Buddhist culture at Whole Foods, which suggests the plethora of models of traditional business is becoming extinct. In other words, the key to profit is to allow employees to make decisions based on purpose over profit. The result is a grocery chain that leads the market in profitability per square foot. Duplication of this feat has been impossible. Success is a result of connection. The connection at Whole Foods is a result of the mindfulness at every level of the business.

Capitalism's new winners are mindful at their core. The downfall of the "goodness" of capitalism was trying to eschew short-term profits at the expense of mission and values. Injecting mindfulness still acknowledges short-term necessities yet holds steadfast in the faith that the path to success ultimately lies in integrity. Surveys have found that 80 percent of execs would cut research and development to make sure they met their quarterly goals, even if it would result in a long-term devaluation of the company. The measurement process for which we regard the health of the business has been tainted. James Collins's 2001 book *Good to Great* highlights companies that had risen exponentially beyond the average profitable company. At the turn of the millennium, Collins highlighted a group of companies that were leveraging profit based on the cornerstones of another era. He studied 1,435 companies and found 11 to be truly great. Among the greats, he described Phillip Morris, Circuit City, Fannie Mae, and Wells Fargo. These were the stalwarts of prosperity of just a decade and a half ago. Today, their value has significantly diminished, their assets liquidated, or their reputation crumbled. We have already entered a new era.

The mission and values statements of a generation ago were begrudgingly honored after the company strategy had already dishonored them. Out-of-touch companies try to reverse engineer purpose by quantifying customer feelings and then putting policies into place to combat negative answers. Modern strategy is not mandating compliance to values but centering the business around them. Purpose in this environment is not limited to a departmental scorecard. Internal metrics give us reason to disassociate ourselves from our true purpose. Google's mantra is Don't Be Evil. They have built an empire on disavowing division, competition, hoarding, and competitive advantage. They are the only company on the Internet that actively searches for better ways to get you to another website. Umair Haque says, "Where the 20th century business was waging war—Google is waging peace." We were attempting to appease the customer and reward the shareholder to the detriment of both. In the modern world, the customer expects to be delighted *and* be intrinsically rewarded for doing business with a company that stands for something besides the value of the transaction.

Harvard professor and corporate strategy expert Michael E. Porter wrote an article in the *Harvard Business Review* introducing a new notion in an article he entitled "Creating Shared Value" in 2011. This article was monumental in introducing the power of responsibility to the mainstream corporate world. Management guru Peter Drucker had already began talking about the untapped value of purpose in the 1989 article from the same periodical titled "What Business Can Learn from Non-Profits." In the last few years, completely new sectors of business have formed based on the prophecies of Drucker. The cold, calculating, fearful, and stress-driven companies have embraced the altruism and nurturing of well-being of what Muhammad Yunus calls the fourth sector business. What we have learned in a complex world is that our biggest problems will not be solved by continuing with the same version of capitalism. It has been said that the world's toughest problems are easily solvable yet not cost effective so, therefore, insurmountable. The fourth sector company is not charitable, private, or public. It exists and excels because of its capability to do good works and makes profit in doing so.

So purpose, which is closely linked to happiness, not only provides benefits for the individual but also acts like a catalyst to the organization of our cause. The result is not only increased productivity but increased profit from the Zen-like connection that the input of connection of the individual has on the connection to the customer as a form of output. The purpose itself—hopefully, given it is a righteous one—continues beyond the transaction itself. As the author of twenty-three books, management PHD Wayne Visser may have written more about corporate social responsibility (CSR) than anyone. He traces the roots of the idea to be a risk-based expectation where companies allocated resources to social causes as a compliance item detached from the meaning of the cause. Slowly, philanthropy became involved with responsibility, and the company began to identify with a charitable cause and based programs around it. The next step was promotion driven. The company partnered the program with their public relations department and attempted to develop an image of altruism. Strategic social responsibility is product-driven. It injects the purpose into the product in order to obtain financial returns. The new version of CSR is not going after ethical consumers but building a fully ethical model in all facets of business.

The responsibility of a modern enlightened business then is to essentially fulfill the Hippocratic Oath upheld by doctors for 2,500 years, the spirit of which is to "first do no harm."

Mindfulness is intent on examining the true repercussions of our actions. Companies that display these values have more content employees. According to *Fortune Magazine*, the best companies to work for also outpaced the S & P 500 by 300 percent from 1997 to 2011. Eighty-eight percent of employees now seek employers with CSR values. Volunteerism of the millennial generation is higher than all others according to Pew Research. A new generation has awoken to sustainability of the earth but also the virtues of health, responsibility, freedom, equality, balance, and responsibility. This new enlightenment of culture has caused business to quickly and drastically reorganize its priorities. Economics had turned into the religion of the United States for forty years. We surrounded our purpose at its alter but were ultimately left unfulfilled. We now worry about locally grown, pesticide-free, fairly traded, made from recycled material, and the treatment and care of the producer. Just as the book of Matthew of the New Testament was a radical departure from the culture of war and tribalism in first-century Palestine, we can proceed knowing that the values of our great religions now have the science to merge with our great secular traditions. The negativity of competition has given way to the power of purpose. The great conduit for human progress is growing more conscious to fall in line with the values of a new generation.

CHAPTER 14

MYTHOLOGY AND LEADERSHIP (POWER SHIFT)

Joseph Campbell may have been the wisest man of the twentieth century. In an age consumed with science, Campbell relentlessly pursued and advocated the use of the timeless mythology of mankind to pursue our greatest truths. His trademark slogan was Follow Your Bliss as the key to a fulfilling life. He said, "When you follow your bliss, you put yourself on a kind of track that has been there all the while waiting for you, and the life you ought to be living is the one you are living. When you can see that, you begin to meet people who are in the field of your bliss, and they open doors to you. I say, follow your bliss and don't be afraid, and doors will open where you didn't know they were going to be. If you follow your bliss, doors will open for you that wouldn't have opened for anyone else." This is the mark of true faith, coming from a man who believed that God was just a metaphor for transcendental thought. He also said, "I don't have to have faith, I have experience." In reality, he had both, just probably not the faith to which we were accustomed. Campbell died in 1987. The following year, Paulo Coelho published *The Alchemist* in his native Portuguese, and it has since been translated into more languages than any book written by a living author. In the story, Coelho's hero meets King Melchizedek, an Old Testament reference who signifies the wisdom of a high priest. His advice is similar to

Campbell's, stating, "When you want something, all the universe conspires in helping you to achieve it." *The Alchemist* is a book of myth, exactly the genre to which Campbell devoted his life.

Myth is the primordial motivator of man. By the twentieth century, mythology, in its ancient form, had died. Campbell's bliss was presenting myths as universal cultural requirements that never die but just mutate into new forms. With every new level of evolution in the human psyche, myth must transcend what we are able to know. Hope, faith, bliss, and joy may become more accessible with the practice of meditation or the application of the new science of positive psychology, but the state itself is peace with the unknowable. Myth transcends space and time. The subconscious dreams of Sigmund Freud are private myths of the individual, and the archetypal myths of Carl Jung are what he called public dreams of society. According to Campbell, the monomyth is the grand narrative that unites all cultures and all of their heroes throughout history. The mystics and the shamans follow the same rules as the great religions. Gilgamesh, Osiris, Buddha, Jesus, and even the shepherd Santiago in *The Alchemist* adhere to the same world order. To better understand the impulses of myth in the present world requires us to understand its triggers from the past.

As man walked out of the savannahs of Africa to hunt and gather food, it had occurred to him that the perpetuation of life rested on the requirement of killing. Early societies had no sociological basis or even the understanding that they were different from the rest of nature. They were just one of the creatures evolving and adapting to secure continuity of existence by the predatory nature of the animal kingdom. The goal of existence was not well planned. It mainly involved eating. As the human mind evolved, the notion of death as a finite and necessary tragedy had borne the ritual, which was the earthly manifestation of myth, no doubt, in its first monomythic form. The circle of life, of killing, which is but an instinct in the animal world, is a moral choice for man, albeit a choice which will mean death. The ritual cleansed man of the shame of ending the life of what he may have considered his equals. It was solemn thanks for the continuity of existence. The mythological symbol was, of course, the Ouroboros, a version of the snake eating its own tail. Man was eating himself, in a sense. Catharsis was acknowledging nature as it was. As we pray to God today in thanks for our food as ritual, thanking the animal for its food was a very personal gesture that connected two beings. Man, alone and isolated in a world against nature, was the one and only battle. Mythology, as it has always been, is how we make sense of it.

About ten thousand years ago, the nomadic nature of man began to be questioned. The agrarian world emerged, now settled through the technology of the seed, and inevitably led to civilization. Permanence on a piece of land led to new paradigms. The danger of the natural world transformed into the danger posed by conquest in the static physical world. The nimble nomads had little value for material possessions. In the agrarian societies, possessions became livelihoods. Material, consisting of the sum of vegetation, animals, homes, and tools, as well as the new technologies conceived through the intermingling of trade meant tangible value to warring neighbors for the first time. War was the new inevitability of nature. Tribal enemies coveted all conceivable possessions. Sin as we know it did not yet exist. Nature was still the law, and nature did not concern itself with the ethics of conquest. The myth of survival had transformed from unification with nature to devotion to a new ruling class system, which could protect the masses against invasion. Religion had met its turning point as devotion to God through the natural world to devotion of the gods based on the sociological structure of society. The symbolism, however, dictated the power base of the new world, reliant on plants, and the hope and faith of favorable weather to enrich the harvest. The fertility of the sun and rain in the hands of the gods renewed the earthly ritual, but myth itself evolved to the sphere of the heavenly. Millennia later, when mankind was first shifting to a monotheistic future, the Old and New Testament of the Bible still adhered to the importance of the plant as myth. Isaiah 11:1 of the Old Testament, written in approximately the eighth-century BC, states, "A shoot will come up from the stump of Jesse; from his roots a Branch will bear fruit."

Writing developed in the three thousand years before Christ, which initiated a new period in human development and mythology. Man could now metaphorically represent the natural and rational world with mythology and capture the sentiment in perpetuity with written language. The shoot of Jesse was at once a branch, which supplied fruit for nourishment and life in the physical world, as well as a representation of the promise of future generations. Over the last few hundred years BC, mankind began to concern itself not with the conquest from its neighbors but with the sincere possibilities of mankind devoted to enrichment rather than fear. The Greeks were the foundation for the worldly abilities of cognition and potential it posed for mankind. Progress required leadership. Leadership in the new rational world of the Greeks was a dissection of the various methods of persuasion conceivable to the human mind. Aristotle called it the ethos, pathos, and logos. Ethos is the credibility that was required to be heard, pathos was the passion that went along with it, but the logos cemented credibility as long as the argument was compatible to the led in rational terms. This formula is still easily identifiable. The logos can be highly subjective and situational, but it ultimately must have some form of rationality grounded in human thought to be effective. Its polar opposite is the mythos, which is the irrational curmudgeon that can see beauty as truth or fundamentalism as law. The power of rational laws of the persuaded cede only to invisible laws of myth.

About half of the world still adheres to one of the Abrahamic religions, meaning Judaism, Christianity, or Islam. A traditional etiologist would concern herself with the systematic study of origins, especially as it pertains to myth. Today etiology would be concerned with the study of causation in a complex system such as weather patterns or, more likely, the human body. The vast unknown of the heterogeneous pathologies of the human system is still a great question of the human condition. The causes, interactions, deficiencies, risks, and cures of individual maladies are still in their infancy. The human life span has nearly doubled in the last one hundred years despite the limited knowledge of the intricacies of the individual human body. We know certainly, as a matter of science, what works broadly and effectively. The etiologists study what works on the individual level and why. Mythology is still the aquifer of the misunderstood from which we drink. Climatologist Michael Mann speaks to etiology in terms of climate change. Direct causation is our intuitive understanding of the world. Systematic causation disrupts both our logos and our mythos. In some cases, according to Mann, rising temperatures are actually connected to colder temperatures in some parts of the world. Climate change is not a binary system but a complex and interdependent set of circumstances that can be easily and understandably misunderstood. There is an inherent duality of the world, which leads to systematic restructuring. As technologist Jaron Lanier explains, "Every food leads to famine . . . every medicine is poison." Through the eyes of the system, goodness depends not on the beholder but when and how the beholder chooses to view it. Humanity's perspective is at the center of the continuum, just as Hamlet said, "There is nothing either good or bad, but thinking makes it so."

This is the state of mythology in the metamodern world. The mythological symbol for the metamodern would be the Roman symbol of Janus, looking to both the future and the past as a two-headed god staring in opposite directions. Janus represented the transition caused by the pulling in opposite directions. The sum of the struggle may ultimately be not balance as truth but the understanding that the tension of the polarity is where the truth lies. The Eastern tradition describes the parable of the blind men and elephant. Each of the touches of the blind men triggers experience of a different sensory truth as they are assigned to examine different parts of the elephant. Although their truth is very real and indistinguishably objective, it is just a part of the whole of the ultimate truth. This is the reductionist thinking left over from the Industrial Revolution. Each blind man was certain of his own unique and indistinguishable feature of the elephant. The very idea that the whole of the elephant lay outside the realm of their sensory understanding is an allegory to the lack of holistic thinking applied in the modern world. Feedback loops, which are existent in every system, are more toxic today than ever, as we not only select the feedback loops already compatible with our worldview but we are subjected to a group of friends and algorithms that promulgate our preconceived and negative notions. Simultaneously, entertainment sources disguised as media thrive on the negative loop. The vicious cycle, never before possible, consists of watching a network individually designed for anger and designed exactly to exercise the anger they created with further justification of the original anger. It is a brilliant strategy to confuse an otherwise savvy navigant of the systems of the world.

Mythological archetypes never die. Their relevance is eternal, but their cousin, the prototype, must be constantly revolutionized. The organization and increased complexity in society led to new requirements in leadership and new interpretations of myth. Fredric Laloux, in *Reinventing Organizations*, classifies epochs in terms of the maturity of the human mind. He uses the blueprint of developmental psychology in the tradition of Piaget to dismantle the prototypes of previous eras. Prior to fifteen thousand years ago, mankind, he says, was in the state of a newborn baby. The rituals of the hunter/gatherer followed by the chiefdoms of the new agrarian world responded mythologically as would a child of no more than five. The notion of past, present, and future; fixed morality; and group dynamics prior to the Enlightenment period equated developmentally with a modern human of six or seven years of age. Progress in the Enlightenment was defined by going into the world and questioning authority and scientific status quos. From this period of wonder the Great Divergence springs, replacing the archaic models of the past. By incorporating what we have learned from the paradigms of the twentieth century, mankind, according to Laloux, may finally be able to interpret the mythology of the history of the world through the eyes of a fully developed adult. In other words, we are on the precipice of a new Enlightenment to renew the archetype and eschew the prototypes of the recent past.

Capitalism, organized effectively through the Industrial Revolution, drove the inflection point of exponential progress in human achievement by the twentieth century. The Victorian idea of the limiting nature of the "white-collar clerk," as understood by Melville, Dickens, Poe, and Whitman, was considered in juxtaposition with the entrepreneur, artisan, and laborer who could showcase tangible results. As business became more complex, by the 1890s, these clerks were being grouped together into small departments. Fredrick Taylor, who would come to revolutionize managerial leadership in the first decades of the twentieth century, was born into a world where even by 1860, 40 percent of Boston residents had jobs that would have been considered nonmanual. A new class of leader rose, called the manager. The ethics of scientific management called for stripping bare the mythos of the notion of work. Mythology is the opposite of measuring, and Taylor designed the entire system exactly around quantification. Sometime later, American novelist John Dos Passos described Taylor's death: "On the morning of his fifty-ninth birthday, when the nurse went into his room to look at him at four thirty, he was dead with his watch in his hand." Peter Drucker, the heir to the Taylor tradition and the most respected and possibly quoted management guru of the twentieth century, cemented the new hierarchy by stating, "The productivity of work is not the responsibility of the worker but of the manager." Drucker may have sympathized with the plight of the knowledge worker. These were the higher-skilled former blue-collar worker, who, in his opinion, was not intellectual enough to join the management class. Drucker still had the same disdain for workers who had fueled Taylor's life work decades prior.

The appeal of the ethos, pathos, and logos of leadership was negative, and the mythos did not exist during this period. Taylor said, "There is not a single worker who does not devote a considerable part of his time to studying just how slowly he can work and still convince his employer that he is going at a good pace." A half-century later, the Drucker mentality was still "Never mind your happiness, do your duty." This genius and visionary also said, "We can say with certainty—or 90 percent probability—that the new industries that are about to be born will have nothing to do with information." Drucker could not even fathom a scenario just a few decades ago where an information economy was even slightly probable. Of course, the new industries are exactly aligned with information, yet very little has changed regarding the organization structure that Drucker espoused.

Leadership is still very much an egotistic, bureaucratic, deterministic, and mechanistic exercise in power. The archetype morphed into one where a homogeneous reinforcement of the status quo was the appealing narrative of the hero leader. The "hero's journey," the timeless and universal call to participate in life courageously, has been for some time thwarted due to risk management triggers of an unnatural system.

Out of the third millennia BC, we find perhaps the first hero ever recorded: Gilgamesh, the Sumerian king who terrorized his own people through fear. Control was the cornerstone of power and leadership and prominently remains so today. Gilgamesh found that all his attempts at worldly achievements were met with disappointment and dissatisfaction. Only by the cruel king departing his comfort zone via an epic journey is he able to return home with new and sacred wisdom. Homer's *The Odyssey* begins by finding the warrior-king Odysseus recovering from the effects of the Trojan War on the island of Ogygia with the goddess Calypso. Here on the island he finds all his worldly desires being met. Odysseus is lulled into a fog of safety and security in trade for his freedom. His departure from the island, through the dangers of the Mediterranean, is the quintessential hero's journey to the abyss and back. Progress through action is the culmination of this journey, complete only upon returning home. Odysseus's wife Athena, meanwhile, concludes that he should have returned home a hero from war by this time. She sends their son Telemachus on the "father's journey," which is essentially the coming-of-age tale, to bring Odysseus home. Jung described the hero as demonstrating values of the culture by transcending them. The journey is the collection of experiences that give us character. According to Campbell in his masterpiece, *Hero with a Thousand Faces*, the culmination of the hero's journey is not just on the return home but what Campbell calls the application of the boon. The journey is over only when the hero finally applies the lessons learned.

Campbell, when referring to roughly the period when Taylor was formulating scientific management, said, "The world is different today than it was 50 years ago, but the inward life of man is exactly the same." In other words, the men on the assembly line being measured by Taylor had the same yearnings for freedom, which man has always had. The scientific management revolution happened because it was exactly what was required at the time. Fortunately, the nature of work—or at least the nature of the work in which we now strive—seeks to appease our irrational urges. Just as the modernist artists made it new by exploring a new ethos of rebellion, new opportunities for catharsis entered our culture. Rock and roll opened a vein to exercise the demons in the tradition of Lord Byron. Bob Dylan was the Bohemian countercultural poet; the Rolling Stones brought a new intensity and hedonism, which had previously been suffocated, and it allowed the dangerous and Romantic heroics of Jim Morrison to "Break on Through to the Other Side." David Bowie became a perfect idol of the surreal role-playing of the postmodern period. Culture had advanced so that the sum of consciousness had grown immune to traditional myth. The value of myth had not eroded; we just began to access it in new and unusual ways.

The novel *Ulysses*, first published in its entirety in 1922 by James Joyce, has been proclaimed a masterpiece and is considered one of the greatest novels of the twentieth century. Prior to Ulysses, the story of the hero was told precisely to define and embellish the heroic qualities. Joyce goes to great lengths to draw parallels between the great Hellenic epic of *The Odyssey* with *Ulysses*. Our hero, Leopold Bloom, is no king or war hero, yet he is much more complex. Odysseus's journey home lasted ten years, which was recounted in epic fashion. Bloom's journey lasted one day, June 16, 1904, in Dublin. Joyce spent 265,000 words in sometimes a stream-of-consciousness prose relating the circumstances of an epic of one long and relatively inconsequential day. Stephen Dedalus, reprised from Joyce's earlier work, *A Portrait of an Artist as a Young Man*, represents Telemachus of *The Odyssey*, who is wrestling with his own journey of coming of age. Joyce introduced the "new hero" in a complex world of celebrity and new information systems. Joycean scholar and translator Stuart Gilbert called Bloom a polyphonic hero, who can be seen and heard from multiple points of view rather than the monologic viewpoint of the narrator. This is a truer representation of the nature of modern identity. Bloom can be identified as a father, son, husband, friend, citizen, and employee. He is compassionate to animals, sympathetic to people, and is a generally helpful and caring person. He is not cunning or calculated and finds himself sexually flawed in a poor marriage with an unfaithful wife.

To Joyce, the mythological dreams of the individual were as prescient as ever. One didn't have to return to his native land to proclaim his rightful position as the king of Ithaca as did Odysseus. Bloom just had to return to his middle-class home in the hyperrational world of the early twentieth century. The mundane actions of daily life, if embraced spiritually and for purposes beyond oneself, can be the journey. The hero's journey has always been the metaphor for personal growth; Joyce just reintroduced it to a culture that required more explicative understanding. Joyce's "new hero" meant hope that grand narratives and epic masculine journeys can be placed alongside Leopold Bloom, who displayed feminine qualities of compassion and empathy and was seen cooking and doing laundry. Short interpretations of the heroism of hypermasculine kings and generals pulling society forward through charisma and power was always a shallow half-truth. By the postmodern period, the idea that the bureaucratic and hierarchic centralized power even existed was due to what C. Wright Mills called lack of sociological imagination. Power of the individual eroded due to acquiescence to position power conjugated by the man-made bureaucracies of what he called the power elite in 1956. The loss of imagination in society is Campbell's worst nightmare as well; although he believed that it was impossible to suppress our mythic nature, it just takes other forms. As the sociologists and beatniks warned about the new power structures in unique ways, it was exercised in culture by revolution in the 1960s.

By the 1970s, neoliberal libertarian fervor to eliminate the centrally planned with the decentralized natural systems, especially as it pertained to the economy, was underway. The natural organization of society by the 1970s had become organized around women's rights, civil rights, and animal rights, which had fragmented and focused on certain natural rights that had not been explicitly addressed by John Locke and Thomas Jefferson two hundred years prior. Barbara Kellerman, in her book *The End of Leadership*, said that the women's liberation movement changed the entire nature of the world. Seventy percent of mothers now earn their own money, whereas for two thousand years, a male-dominated society had only given women power through the social contract of marriage. The virtue ethics of goodness extolled by Plato and Confucius had lost priority to the Machiavellian notion of power up to that point. As Kellerman explains, explicit power of the authoritarian has been declining for eight hundred years since the Magna Carta was signed. It has been three hundred years since the "divine right of kings" was undermined and 240 years since Thomas Paine wrote the pamphlet "Common Sense" prior to the American Revolution. As early as 1970, Robert Townsend began to critique that outdated notion of traditional hierarchies in *Up the Organization*. The realities of the complex and interdependent systems of the world demanded less central control. Mankind had grown accustomed to reacting against any attempt at authoritarianism that was not warranted.

In *The Starfish and the Spider*, Ori Brafman and Rod Beckstrom explain our resistance to conform to the natural systems of the world. They say, "Humans make order so we assume that the natural tendency of the universe is hierarchy." Top-down leadership is very orderly; it just happens to not be very effective. Decentralization and lack of position power as a strategy seems completely counterintuitive to our notion of effectiveness. It is not without precedent in history. The Aztecs were slaughtered by the Spanish due to their hierarchical nature. When the Spaniards turned their attention to the Apache, they found their offensives actually made the Apache stronger. The Apache were fighting an asymmetric war that made no sense to the Spanish but somehow proved quite effective. In *Antifragile*, Nicholas Nassim Taleb asks the question "What's the opposite of fragile?" He says *antifragile* is the answer. Strong would be the phoenix rising from the ashes after an attack. Antifragility is like the Hydra, a monster that grows two heads back for every one that is cut off. Revolutionary war officer Francis Marion led a small unit designed to be nimble enough to disrupt the large body of British troops. They were designed to quickly attack and just as quickly disperse back into the swamps in guerilla fashion. British reaction made them more susceptible to further attacks. For years, the United States fought the war on terror with shock and awe, which has led to new versions of the exercise of the antifragile nature of terrorist networks. The notion that power, might, and bravado may contribute to weakness is a phenomenon that we as a society have not yet come to terms with.

Cultural anthropologist Tom Nevins says that the Apache were a nuisance until 1914. Their demise as a threat to government was an ingenious task of giving the formless form. The small, nomadic, and decentralized Apache were given cattle by the US government. Their mythological distribution of power was all that needed to be disrupted. Once resources were introduced into their society, the Apache began to organize themselves hierarchically, which finally made them a controllable force. Around the same period, Taylor injected an artificial layer of bureaucracy of the management class, which had rendered astonishing results. By the 1980s, the virtue of the command and control legacy of centralization began to be questioned for the first time, at least in the west. A Fremont, California, General Motors plant, known for poor quality, absenteeism, and hostile worker relations, closed. Meanwhile, Toyota declared that they could right the ship and rehired the former GM employees in the very same plant to make their vehicles. American conventional wisdom stated that the Japanese management methods would not translate to American culture or to the American worker. Within three years, the plant was 60 percent more productive than it had been under GM. The Japanese model of removing management nearly completely resulted in huge increases. The great fear of management is that their removal will cripple the system. The truth is that their exit will cripple the system that they have manually installed. When GM hired management spies to infiltrate the plant, they expected to enter a free-rein culture of unaccountability with the removal of the management class. What they found was that the new structures, which systematically called upon the mastery of workers, were a more powerful overseer than any management dynamic that GM could muster.

In recent years, many management experts have begun to understand that there is not a lot of science that can be attributed to the multibillion-dollar leadership industry. Barbara Kellerman has stated, "Leadership industry has failed over its roughly forty year history to in any meaningful way improve the human condition . . . the rise of leadership as an object of our collective fascination has coincided precisely with the decline of leadership in our collective estimation." Over this period, the goal of every educational institution from Harvard University to corporate training is to develop more effective leaders. Leadership itself is no longer a result of mastery but a discipline unto itself. The universal themes include, trust, truth, integrity, authenticity, accountability, empathy, and a host of others. Kellerman's point is that every objective study to measure leaders' effectiveness has an inverse relation to the amount of leadership training we are giving. In a world that truly is intuitive and authentic, injecting the verbiage of authenticity or credibility when its underlying systems are not is more toxic than ignoring them. Jeffery Pfeffer, in *Leadership BS*, says, "The feel good leadership industry for which every leader follows is no match for the toxic workplaces that are inevitable in the modern business climate." Pfeffer says that all the attributes the leadership industry espouses, from *culture builder*, *nuanced, sincere, trustworthy*, etc., will in reality be interpreted as *soft*, *calm, uninspired*, and *not forceful*. The sad truth is that within the framework of organizations today that have not progressed structurally in decades, the sum of all of the best leadership qualities from the leadership industry translate to weakness. The old guard who still runs our organizations will deem that person "not leadership material." "So," says Pfeffer, "go home and throw out all of your leadership books . . . or better yet give them to career competitors."

While the cynicism is counterproductive, the pragmatic nature of his argument has a point. Leadership books highlight an ideal that, more often than not, has very little practical application. The leadership industry walks the fine line between self-help and science that may distort fact from fiction. The myths from the leadership industry can be very toxic. The heroic leader who changed culture and inspired dramatic progress decades ago most likely should not be replicated in the present. Attributing success to a checklist from another time and place is a highly volatile endeavor. Pfeffer says, "Most organizations are still mired in myth . . . but [myths] are worse than useless." Self-deprecation, a go to self-help strategy, is only effective if you have first succeeded. If you haven't, it becomes a sad form of pessimism. Narcissism, it is said, is a quick path to the end of a career. The truth is that it is one of the biggest predictors of success. selfish behavior, the mark of a toxic leader, is really the norm. So leaders became leaders not by their professed code of ethics but most likely by the antithesis of the message of the leadership industry. The implications are clear, acting in your own self-interest temporarily to put yourself into a position to make changes (which is rare) or taking the hero's journey, which would make Joseph Campbell proud. Answering the call to battle to fight for your true beliefs may very well get you fired. At the very least, it will get you banished to a strange world where your credibility is diminished. If you survive and return home to act on your newfound information, then you have completed the hero's journey. The millennial generation has the possibility to distribute millions of new Leopold Blooms into the world.

Leadership, organization, power, and mythology evoke different ideas across time. The ideal of the strong leader is being replaced by the focused facilitator, or as Brafman and Beckstrom call them, the catalysts. The trajectory of evolution proceeds without the rabid fervor of ideology adherent to a dying system. Prior to 1960, McGregor's revolutionary Theory X of motivation leaders assumed human nature was behaviorally similar to Pavlov's dog. McGregor suggested in Theory Y that it was possible for intrinsic motivation to exist within the worker. Years later, William Ouchi introduced Theory Z, which not only espoused the rational internal satisfaction of Y but the mythological harmony called *wa* from the Japanese tradition. Theory Z adopted the notion that a less hierarchic and more general design for organizations would better connect the individual with the culture. In the tradition of the Renaissance man, Joseph Campbell proudly called himself a generalist. He perceived grand truths through the whole rather than the narrow. In his opinion, specialization can never transcend. As work and life blend, the well-rounded optimism is nobler than the narrow-minded pessimism. Theory Z required long-term commitment to excellence from an employee who would constantly retrain and work in different areas of the business to understand systematic issues and individual perspectives. The Theory Z worker is the human manifestation of systematic evolution. The organization is turned on its head, traditional leadership methods are questioned, the vacuum of power is destroyed, and the myth is spiritual rather than dogmatic.

In *Cubed*, Nikal Saval points to the ideas of Dutch strategic thinker Erik Veldhoen, who has succinctly modernized Ouchi's ideas since they were presented in the early 1980s. Digitization has brought the knowledge worker, whom Drucker held in contempt in the 1960s, into the role of management. The inevitable trajectory of the flattening of organizations was seen as a usurpation of the means of production when it is essentially an optimization of leadership decentralized. Drucker, whose viewpoint is still very similar to many leaders of today, makes a fundamental error with self-management. They believe that it is only an irrational drive of the individual toward freedom in the liberal tradition, but they fail to see that it is a libertarian self-organizing mechanism, which has been driving the soul of conservativism for forty years. Veldhoen's conclusion, as is Barbara Kellerman's, is that the management class as we know it today is becoming obsolete. Although we berate the postmodernists as cynics and nihilists, they were right about one thing: the changing of culture disrupts power structures, which lead to new imbalances that we could not have planned. Decades ago, Drucker put the onus of productivity on the manager. This artificial structure shifted accountability fully to the manager, leaving the worker purposefully ignorant and unaccountable. In a mechanistic world of the factory floor, this was not only acceptable but ideal. In the twenty-first century, this idea is counterproductive at best.

Procrustes, the son of Poseidon of Greek myth, was a sort of metalsmith who invited passersby to spend the night on their route to Athens. His bed, which he offered to the travelers, never seemed to adequately fit their requirements. It did not occur to Procrustes to adjust the bed. Instead he preferred to adjust the travelers. He used his skills as a smith to elongate the shorter travelers or simply amputate the extremities that proved too long. This is the metaphor that we have been using in our organizations. Today we call it thinking outside the box. Malcolm Gladwell, in *What the Dog Saw*, says, "If everyone had to think outside the box, maybe it was the box that needed fixing." Questioning reality is a tradition in philosophy since Plato's Cave. Gladwell is also the author of *Blink*, which deals with what he calls thin slicing, or interpreting multiple phenomena by one brief experience. This is the reality of what it means to be human in the twenty-first century. Gladwell focuses on the intuitive shortcuts that we take to perceive reality. No doubt our perception of myth informs our thousands of tiny decisions that allow us to function on a daily basis. Leadership, however, cannot take the same trajectory.

Marshall Goldsmith, in *What Got You Here Won't Get You There*, believes, like Jeffery Pfeffer, that narcissism in our leaders has been an effective quality, at least for individual success. In Goldsmith's view, it has been an ingrained delusion that up until now has worked remarkably well. Perhaps, says Goldsmith, the measurement of narcissism in leaders is just earned self-esteem through years of navigating and conquering the levels of hierarchy. Great leaders minimize failure and overestimate wins. They project themselves as central to those wins and distance themselves from losses. Their skill is offering a rhetoric that ensures glorification regardless of its merit or virtue. Salim Ismail has introduced the notion of exponential organizations. The market cap to $1 billion for the average Fortune 500 company has traditionally been twenty years. Google took half that time and still Facebook half of that duration. Amazingly, Snapchat reached $1 billion in half the time of Facebook. The vast reorganization of business models calls for leadership that is not inherent to the slow structural change of the traditional leadership gospel. The trouble with success, according to Goldsmith, is that success can be easily misattributed. Gladwell's *Blink* is insightful, but paired with Goldsmith's message, leaders can often project their success on the wrong causes. Confidence in their decision-making has been heightened due to past successes, which may have little to do with the current environment. Also, in the midst of the exponential world, the route to success is not paved in past glories. Past is prologue only through adherence to the two-headed symbol of Janus that looks to the future while acknowledging the past and not living by it.

The notion of leading from behind has become a ridicule often attributed to President Barack Obama's foreign policy. In the mainstream, this meme is a contemptuous indictment demonstrating a lack of coherent leadership strategy. Linda Hill of the Harvard Business School coined the term after reading a passage from Nelson Mandela's 1994 autobiography. He said, "A leader . . . is like a shepherd. He stays behind the flock, letting the most nimble go ahead, whereupon the others follow, not realizing that all along they are being directed from behind." So essentially, it is the masterful tactic of empowering a team to unleash their individual strengths and then persuade the rest of the team that leadership can be distributed, which is a counterintuitive reversal of traditional leadership models. Electrical engineers Gerardo Beni and Jing Wang developed the term *swarm intelligence* in artificial intelligence to understand behavior of self-organized systems. James Haywood Rolling Jr. of Syracuse University has written a book by the same name that identifies the modern leader as an orchestrator of the natural intelligence of a system. In an economy that requires creativity, innovation, openness, and collaboration causes leadership to follow a more networked, nonlinear, and dynamic trajectory. Command and control authority, which worked exceptionally well for decades, if not centuries, is no longer a valuable strategy.

Strong leadership as we know it will still have its time and place. Coercive systems, like the procedural checklist on a flight manual, do not require the dynamism of the human spirit. As we head into a more entrepreneurial, creative, and irrational "experience" economy, innovation, problem-solving, and question-asking are the skills in high demand. The advanced problem-solving required to identify and solve what have come to be known as wicked problems, or highly interdependent and misunderstood issues, requires not a structure of compliance and predetermined initiatives but highly educated and deep thinkers who can build an environment that fosters excellence and imagination. So leading from behind is essentially servant leadership, as proposed by AT&T executive Robert Greenleaf in 1970, using soft skills to allow others the freedom to maximize an attack of a problem in a multitude of ways from different perspectives. A traditional leader creates an inspiring vision and rallies a team to follow based on the pathos, ethos, and logos of the problem. The swarm leader uses mythos to allow complete flow and maximization of individual attributes. Like a judo master, the new leader uses the energy of the natural systems, which has replaced the coercive systems to find a new apex of human possibility. Only a leader from behind can attack the antifragile because only they have identified the decentralized Zen required of modern power.

Brian J. Robertson, in *Holacracy*, says, "Markets are dynamic, while companies are not." Organizations as we know them are losing their relevance along with their power structures. We are applying what we knew about the world in the twentieth century to the twenty-first century, and it is not working. According to Robertson, in the world, there have always been two choices. The first is the "benevolent dictator," known as the heroic and charismatic motivator who was essential to unleash potential within the rigid confines of a closed system. The second choice is the fear of economist Joseph Schumpeter when he wrote *Capitalism, Socialism, Democracy* in 1942. Schumpeter feared the idea of bureaucratic collectivism replacing the lone entrepreneur. Robertson calls it the "tyranny of consensus," which is nothing but a societal norm making a decision that leads to mediocrity. The third way, as proposed by Robertson, is called holocracy, which dictates that the role rather than the position has the power. Leadership is only authentic when the natural system distributes power to the most responsible, accountable, and creative. The role, not the position has authority. In a world of simultaneous projects, interdependencies, and the need for situational applications, the leadership muscle can be flexed by the flow of the system, giving authority to a leader of a process across departments and organization levels. The role of the leader is to "lead from behind" and follow the process to its maximization. This is called simplicity, but it is also chaotic and difficult to understand. It requires a release of central control and a flattening of an organization. It is highly unlikely a seasoned veteran of the old guard would even consider this a possibility, much less cede power to a natural process they do not even believe exists.

This is the post-efficient world. Uber efficiency of 6 Sigma has brought the asymptote closer to perfection. Our isolated processes have been scientifically engineered to produce maximum results. The problem is that the next great feat of mankind is to not master the independent problems but the interdependent ones. The wicked problems of interdependency live in the natural world of chaos. Attacking wicked problems linearly as one problem, as would a traditional leader, with a show of force, banishes the problem to arise in another form in another realm. Leading from behind allows us to attack the problem from multiple perspectives. One leader, eschewing a narrow definition of the requirements of one perspective of leadership cannot compare to a hive of equally talented leaders driven by authentic internal motivation. In a more complex world, the virtue of the lone leader is less significant; however, the inner directed nature of the individual is still the most important component. In 1950, sociologists Nathan Glazer, David Riesman, and Reuel Denney published *The Lonely Crowd*. They claimed that individuals are directed by three main components. Motivation arises from either tradition, group dynamics in our lives, or our own internal moral and spiritual compass. They prophesized the imbalance of the traditions of the past and the pressures that conformity would command in competing against a true personal nature. The conundrum of Janus as a representation of the metamodern ethic requires collaboration above all else in a time where the virtue is based on adherence to, once again, the inner directed.

In *Reinventing Organizations*, Fredric Laloux assigned colors to the particular values that he claims have been the evolution of organizational development of mankind. The toddlerlike chiefdoms were red, the city-state civilizations were amber, the industrial multinationals were orange, and green was the destruction of hierarchy represented by the postmodern period of "group consensus." The green organization is fading before any of its leaders had a chance to enact the values of the era. The new organization, according to Laloux, is the teal organization. In *Ulysses*, we saw Leopold Bloom from various perspectives. He was a mentor, a man who had lost a child, and even a deviant, each for which we pass judgement. The perspective of the teal organization as a leader demands a perspective of a wholeness, which transcends personal judgement of an individual yet still seeks and believes in personal truths. Laloux says, "In green we rebuke judgement for tolerance," and finally, teal loses both while still believing in and striving for truth. Laloux is explaining the developmental and evolutionary psychology behind evolving to the point, in an organization and as a human, where truth is real but control is counterproductive. The journey toward leadership then is a stoic journey inward. Reaching for myth in our own personal truths within natural systems will lead to leadership as nature intended.

Clare Graves was the father of the scientific inquiry into psychological development. He organized groups together based on their inherent views of the world. Essentially, he organized groups into not personality types but what he considered to be deep-seated worldviews or psychological perspectives. Laloux aligned the perspectives of the teal group with what Graves considered to be his most evolved group of participants. It turned out that this equivalent, which was essentially Laloux's teal group, solved problems and displayed coping skills better than all the other groups put together and in less time. This group required less concrete requirements of traditional organizations such as directions, policies, budgets, and benchmarks. The negative byproducts of the group dynamics of hierarchy, including fear and power struggles, never developed. Higher-level values, including trust, purpose, community, growth, and wholeness, emerged. If a traditional manager were to measure the quality of this group, they would rate it exceptionally low. As we enter the experience economy, true quality is irrational by traditional measurements but the most effective. Tasks to increase productivity become invisible, and searching for efficiency becomes counterproductive. These ideas have entered the mainstream only via the idea of agile software development, which takes a cross-functional and systematic approach depending on the needs of the live and organic system, which requires adaptation. Software is the only facet of business that absolutely demands pace with modern culture. The mythology has again shifted. The power structures have realigned. Leadership must adjust to the new interdependencies of relationships. Lao Tsu might have explained modern power best 2,500 years ago in perhaps the most concentrated collection of wisdom ever assembled. Chapter 51 of *Tao Te Ching* claims in one translation, "To have without possessing, do without claiming, lead without controlling, this is mysterious power."

CHAPTER 15

GLOBALIZATION AND DEMOCRACY (PLANETARY SHIFT)

We have lived as humans for five hundred generations since the Neolithic revolution. Prior to this period, mankind lived 97 percent of its existence as a nomad, walking the earth for the next meal and conserving energy for the next kill. For the great majority of our existence, there was no need to understand the world as a whole. The world was nothing more than the immediate earth surrounding us and the small classless tribes that flourished only through killing its next meal. It has only been five hundred generations since we realized that planting a seed, leveraging the inherent benefits of a plot of land, taming an animal, and working together could the infinite wandering end. So the hunters became farmers. The fear of starving, which kept the hunters agile, became the fear of conquest due to the richness of the land they had been traversing. It was here that freedom first ended. Material wealth was the ability to meet our most basic needs of food, water, and shelter. Once mankind stopped moving, the collection of these things posed a target for potential conquerors. Morality, therefore, rested in the violent gods through myth. The discovery of ethics was a way for the new ruling classes to limit the inevitable violence. The new organization of humans, called society, required replacing unbridled freedom with the security that the new ruling class was providing. The modern human brain, now fully developed and capable of empathy, could justify atrocities but had not yet offered a coherent and socially acceptable argument for peace.

Joseph Campbell declared that nature was feminine but society was unmistakably masculine. Gilgamesh was the model of the ruling class in the Agrarian society. He was "the strongest of men . . . but . . . arrogant like a wild bull." It was said that "the people suffer from his tyranny." Karen Armstrong, in *Fields of Blood*, outlines this period as a world before any understanding of morality, ethics, or especially, democracy. "Work," she says, "and even trade was not noble—you took what you wanted if you were nobility." The Old Testament of the Bible resonated so profoundly because it was a collection of ideas that challenged the status quo of theft and warfare inherent in humankind at the time. The Old Testament of the Bible in the modern context is a violent book yet was the antithesis of violence for its time and place. The Bible ensured that even the aristocracy must answer to a hierarchy. Still, the warrior is the metaphor for goodness. In the Hindu tradition told in the Bhagavad Gita, Arjuna "rides into battle," which depicts a metaphor for life. Buddha, like Jesus, seeks peace among turmoil. The Abrahamic religious tradition is continued in the Middle East in the seventh century as the prophet Muhammad sought to unite the Middle East under a single religion and end the continuous raiding of caravans, which were a way of life. The basis of the major religions was to give a voice to those unheard. Jesus drew the ire of the ruling class of Palestinians as well as Roman authority. Muhammad sought to overthrow the privilege of aristocracy on the Arabian Peninsula.

Both men sought to redefine the potential for human empathy beyond the narrow constructs of mankind's allegiance to the blood ties of the hunter/gatherer society. By the Middle Ages, religion was the central creed of human existence. The tie that bound had evolved to the central tenet of society called religion. It may have no longer been noble to raid or conquer neighboring tribes, but evolution in thought warranted the expanded notion of raiding neighboring religions called Holy Wars. The circumference of our civility had expanded from the family unit to the religious like-minded.

In 1492, Columbus discovered the New World, but perhaps, more importantly, an epoch had ended. Queen Isabella had declared victory over the Muslim kingdom. The Holy Wars, which had been a Christian versus Muslim battle for hundreds of years, reintroduced the savagery that their respective religions originally opposed. By the sixteenth century in the west, the world was changing. Progress in the arts and sciences was seen as a possibility for the first time in centuries. Freedom, which had been relinquished to a ruling class for protection, had the possibility of revitalization. Feudalism and theocracy, which had served a purpose in the conservative era known as the Middle Ages, gave way to the Renaissance to bridge the humanism indicative of the Enlightenment. By the mid-fifteenth century, the printing press was being utilized in the west. The Ottoman Empire, which was a loose organization of the Muslim world, however, did not fully adopt the technology for another three hundred years. There were only eight years between 1450 and 1700 where the empire itself was not at war. The "Great Divergence," as it is called, is usually identified as the economic separation of the west from the advanced Chinese economy of the fifteenth century can also apply to the cultural transition that left the near east behind until the early nineteenth-century reforms.

Natural law, handed down from the ethics of Aristotle, the virtues of Cicero, and the faith of Aquinas, was resurrected by John Locke and applied to politics in the form of life, liberty, and property in the eighteenth century. Perhaps not obeying the constructs that unfolded in the evolution of civilization was what should have been natural! These constructs up to that point were government and religion. James Madison said, "Religious bondage shackles and debilitates the mind and unfits it for every noble enterprise, every expected prospect." Just as severe a limiter in this period was the effects which nationalism would bring. The intense ligament of religion gave way to the shared experience of rallying around the common nation-state with the fall of empire. The rise of the state displaced religion as the sole divider of humankind. The American founding fathers of Madison and Jefferson understood the virtues of the separation of church and state because even within Christianity itself could it be classified and condensed into infinite sects. The idea of the modern nation, united under the democratic consent of the people, could only be universally accepted absent any coherent interpretation of religion. The pioneers of democracy understood that the very unifier of the western world for 1,500 years would be the divider. In its place would be the state, ruled not by the heredity of the monarchy or the privilege of aristocracy but the will of the people and the individualism and meritocracy of natural law.

Democracy and capitalism merged into the most benevolent existence mankind had ever known. Liberalism, which in its finest form is the enfranchisement of all who take part in democracy, has the goal to dissolve the influences of all forces outside the individual. Thirteen colonies overthrew the tyranny of imperialism to form a new ideal in the possibilities of humankind. The idea of America itself was an intentional combination of ideas that the old world deemed impossible but yielded immeasurable results, including the defeat of the world's foremost empire. Alexis de Tocqueville wrote of the melding of ideas that combined seamlessly in the United States but may have been met with disdain in other parts of the world. To be an American was not to eschew your personal religion but to understand that your religion was personal. The world had finally known a society where the rule of law was given consent by the governed. Leaders served at the behest of the electorate. Fiefdoms had been replaced by communities. The "ends" of security would no longer justify the "means" of tyranny. Natural law dictated that new mixtures of humans and the sharing of ideas previously distributed had been collected to quite literally see humanity as a technology in progress. The classic liberal transcended political party. As the modern period approached, its only enemy was the fundamentalist.

Conservatism as the antithesis of liberalism treats nostalgia as a rational ideal, but fundamentalism mandates dogmatism of any form as the single source of truth. It is simply the lack of empathy to understand different points of view. Anthony Giddens in *Runaway World* calls fundamentalism an extreme ideology, which believes the world has progressed beyond its limits. In early nineteenth-century England, a clandestine group of textile workers, called the Luddites, would meet to destroy the machines that were taking their jobs. The same fundamental angst could be found nearly two hundred years later as Ted Kaczynski, better known as the Unabomber, chose to critique industrialization through death and destruction. Every form of fundamentalism throughout history has been the effect of a society's or an individual's ethnocentrism, bigotry, or xenophobia out of fear of the future. It manifests in predictable patterns, which may be difficult to comprehend by modern standards. British novelist L. P. Hartley opens *The Go-Between* with his most famous line: "The past is a foreign country: they do things differently there." The human rationalization of violence had shifted from religion through the Holy Wars to the nation-state through the Thirty Years' War. From the mid-seventeenth century to the mid-twentieth century, all empires had been divided into states. This new paradigm instituted nationalism, a new construct to human identity.

The year 1492 also marked what Thomas Friedman has called the beginning of Globalization 1.0. The next three hundred years of imperialism and migration allowed humanity to travel to the far corners of the earth. These new patterns found yet another division between humanity. Again, these differences invariably surrounded the new intermingling of ethnic groups. The dominant group did not see the marginalized group as their equal. The result was usually ethnic cleansing, genocide, or slavery. Steven Pinker, in his book *The Better Angels of Our Nature*, documents the decline of violence over time. He says, "The shocking truth is that until recently most people didn't think there was anything wrong with genocide, as long as it didn't happen to them." From Australia to Africa to the Americas, genocide was just an extension of natural rights of the purveyors. Pinker estimates that twenty million Native Americans alone were exterminated to allow for the European immigrants to sprawl across the continent. Even by the end of the nineteenth century, future president Teddy Roosevelt, known for his progressivism, said, "I don't go as far as to think that the only good Indians are dead Indians, but I believe that nine out of ten are, and I shouldn't like to inquire too closely in the case of the tenth." Genocide was generally seen as a virtuous undertaking to rid the world of a subhuman population.

Meanwhile, a plantation economy was rising in the American South, supported by slave labor imported from Africa.

The justification for racism was a remnant of the Great Chain of Being, which designated a God-given hierarchy to all heavenly and earthly beings since the Middle Ages. By the time of the Spanish Inquisition, religion, sexual orientation, behavior, bloodlines, and ideas were tested against the status quo. The next few hundred years required intellectual theories to justify the inferiority of races. According to Robert Wald Sussman, in *The Myth of Race*, there were two theories that the dominant group, which happened to be white Europeans, used to dehumanize other ethnic groups. The Degenerative Theory assumed that the purity of the white race was somewhere tainted by sects of lesser humans known as Asian, Indians, and Africans. The Polygenic Theory, embraced by many Enlightenment thinkers including Hume, Kant, and Locke, saw the white man as simply a higher-level species of human, born of another birth line other than Adam. Voltaire said, "The negro race is a species of men different from ours as the breed of Spaniels is from that of greyhounds." As philosophy merged into science, a period of pseudo-science emerged, which was attempting to scientifically justify racial superiority. Whether the monogenic theory of racial degeneration or the polygenic theory of different ancestry was valid, the takeaway was certainly that the white race had the monopoly on the attainment of advanced human intellect. The Great Chain of Being was being subjected to new and modern quasi-scientific methods.

Sir Francis Galton, the nineteenth-century polymath, coined the term *eugenics* in 1883. The goal of Eugenics was continuation of the "well-born" to continue to reproduce at higher proportions and the elimination and sterilization of those who were not genetically pure. By the early twentieth century, eugenics was nearly universal in high school textbooks and was a class in as many as forty-four American universities. In 1912, four hundred of the most prestigious minds from around the world, including Winston Churchill, Alexander Graham Bell, George Bernard Shaw, and H. G. Wells, attended the International Eugenics Congress. The goals included not only who should or should not breed based on race but it also highlighted the intellectual deficiencies of the races and lobbied for a scientific justification to end immigration and eliminate the mixing of races. By 1924, the Johnson-Lodge Act was passed, which banned immigration from the east and disenfranchised southern and eastern Europeans to "preserve the homogeneity of Americans." One year before the Eugenics Congress in 1911, Franz Boas wrote *The Mind of the Primitive Man*. He said, "There is no difference in mental capabilities between savage or civilized or black or white." Even though Boas was doing the real scientific work regarding race, no one listened until Nazism seized eugenics in the 1930s. Twenty-five years after his scientific breakthrough, in 1936, Boas finally found the cover of *Time Magazine*. By 1942, anthropologist Ashley Montagu proclaimed race, "man's most dangerous myth." In 1950, the United Nations Educational, Scientific, and Cultural Organization (UNESCO) declared that geneticists, psychologists, anthropologists, and sociologists all agreed that there is "no scientific basis for race." The human race is 99.9 percent the same. Eugenics was just another fallacy to divide mankind, this time by race.

Thomas Friedman associates Globalization 2.0 as the physical connecting of the earth. In the span of two hundred years, the Industrial Revolution began and ended. The infrastructure and hardware that defined our lives had been built, if not in relative prototypical fashion. We revolutionized energy, reorganized commerce, and personalized communication and transportation. Most of the twentieth century was spent fighting capitalism's one and only enemy, communism. When the Berlin Wall fell in 1989, the world had literally opened up. Just months prior to the wall coming down, a symbol of a barrier to freedom eroding, the "evil empire" of the Soviet Union retreated from Mujahedeen engagement in Afghanistan. The west had lost an enemy and gained three billion potential customers and competitors. Meanwhile, a resurgence of fundamentalism in the form of Wahhabism attempted to destroy secularism in many parts of the Muslim world. Islam itself is sometimes unjustly identified as the culprit of the rage manifested as terrorism, but India and Turkey are two countries with large Muslim populations that do not have fundamentalist views and, therefore, little need for terror tactics. The

Arab world, however, among other places, began to justify violence through jihad as a means to regain dignity. The subjugation of race, religion, sexual orientation, and gender, which the west had at least addressed, reverted to the dogma of Sharia Law, a religious justification of ancient laws, which are seen as barbaric to most of the western world.

Sam Harris, in *The Moral Landscape*, understands that religious conservatism, especially at the extremes, demands that science is a perverter of truth, morality is filtered through scripture or dogma, and homogeneity is the beneficial to preserve the ideal state. The opposite end of the spectrum is the secular liberal who espouses moral relativism, which seeks no ultimate truth, sees cultural relativism as perspective developed through experience, and is tolerant of societies which contrast with classical liberalism. Harris says that these are false choices. "Human knowledge and human values can no longer be kept apart." Respecting the methods of flogging, stoning, and beheading as relative punishments based on societal differences is something that we can no longer tolerate. The social sciences have progressed, especially in the last couple of decades, to give us insight into what is ultimately good for humanity. Harris's contention is that values and facts are merging. There are states of human nature that are universally bad, which include loneliness, poverty, illness, and helplessness. Human well-being provides a continuum of states that can be at least qualitatively ranked. There are objective truths in the world called science. If systems are put in place that counter humanities attempt at freedom, hope, and self-empowerment, then the well-being of the individual is compromised. A society that allows hunger, sickness, anger, and destruction in return for obedience is not moral. We need to encourage a society that can replace fundamentalism with human principles. This is the liberal trajectory of progress.

In Adam Smith's *Theory of Moral Sentiments*, Smith identified the flow of information and ideas that was looming for the future. Inevitably, this would lead to economic progress as specialization and innovation met in a world which was shrinking. The world was opening to new technologies and new ideas that had been previously inaccessible. In *The Rational Optimist*, Matt Ridley describes the fact that King Louis XIV had 498 people assisting in preparing his dinner. A dinner in the modern world, he describes, has a lineage of much more than 498 people. Today we can thank the farmers, distributors, salesmen, sanitation workers, and manufacturers. The lights are provided by the electric company rather than candlelight. The serving staff may include management, hosts, bartenders, food servers, as well as various cooks. Each spice itself may have come from different parts of the world. Specialization is the economic structure that has allowed us to raise our living standards above that of a king from just a few centuries ago. The exchange of ideas, however, is the human factor and precursor to economics. Regression and fundamentalism is a symptom of a society that refuses to exchange ideas. Today, the Middle East is the best example of a society that retreats toward fundamentalism for fear that its ideas will be overshadowed and dissolved within the progress of humanity.

The English economist David Ricardo, early in the nineteenth century, defined the advantages of Industrial era globalism by the fact that "two countries who trade will both benefit   even if one has advantage over production." Ricardo identified a magical economic formula derived of Plato's dialectic. If two parties converge to unite their own specialization, they can leave with something that neither could have obtained on their own. Plato understood the benefit to be ideas and discourse, but Ricardo said that the world can attach economic benefit. The world was ready for the idea that civility and trade could take the place of conquest. It was, in fact, a more reliable method for long-term success and security. The newly opened world also introduced the inevitable transfer of cultural ideas in the physical world. Philosophers began studying the idea of materialism, as physical items of trade began changing lives. Then the new materials began, for the first time, changing large patterns of human behavior. The Industrial Revolution was in full swing. By 1857, the English politician Richard Cobden declared, "Free Trade is God's diplomacy, on there is no other certain way of uniting people in the bonds of peace." Security itself turned economic and was cloaked under the national economic policy of the state.

Thomas Friedman introduced the world to Globalization 3.0 in 1999 by his work *The Lexus and the Olive Tree*. He outlined the global economic philosophy heading into the twenty-first century in very metamodern terms. The Lexus represented human desire for prosperity, technology, and progress, and the olive tree represented the clinging to the traditions of the past. This was Friedman's portrayal of Janus on a global scale. In terms of peace and prosperity, he introduced the Golden Arches Theory, where he claimed that no two countries with a McDonald's had fought a war against each other. In his next book, *The World is Flat*, he updated this theory and applied it to Dell's global supply chain. The idea is that the deep integration of economies balances geopolitical power in systematic methods beyond our understanding of diplomacy. Rogue states, or nations still under authoritarian rule, removed from the global supply chain and modern methods of information exchange, are most likely to be susceptible to war and destruction. These places, because of religion or government or the combination of the two, have removed themselves from the systems of the modern world. Centuries of knowledge about the evolution of human connection are absent, and integration and progress is the enemy.

Human integration is called immigration. Europeans came to the new world and brought their culture. St. John de Crevecoeur, in *Letters from an American Farmer*, wondered, "What then, is the American, this new man?" It was a nation of immigrants that from its beginning could assimilate in a large new land, "united by the silken bands of mild government." It was "this great metamorphosis . . . [which] extinguishes all of his European prejudices; he forgets that mechanism of subordination, that servility of disposition which poverty had taught him." In 1903, a sonnet by Emma Lazarus was etched into the lower pedestal of the ancient symbol of libertas, called the Statue of Liberty, a gift from France to guide immigrants to America's shores. "The New Colossus" read, "'Keep, ancient lands, your storied pomp!' cries she with silent lips. 'Give me your tired, your poor, your huddled masses yearning to breathe free, The wretched refuse of your teeming shore. Send these, the homeless, tempest-tost to me, I lift my lamp beside the golden door!'" Immigration was the basis for civilization in the new world, but by the 1920s it was severely limited. The twentieth century organized and progressed with technologies and economies, which seem local in comparison to today's global climate. The twenty-first century calls for a stark contrast to our strategies and sensibilities regarding immigration.

Ben Wattenberg and Richard M. Scammon wrote *The Real Majority* in 1970, which paraphrased Heraclitus's ancient message that "character is destiny" into the modern version, "Demography is destiny." Over the past few decades, we have seen as an exponential amplification of identity. 2011 marked the first year that the birth of minority babies outpaced the birth of white babies. Interracial marriage is a phenomenon that has only been recognized since 1970. The United States Census did not even acknowledge that the union could lead to offspring until the year 2000. New migration patterns find greater numbers of Hispanic and Asian immigrants, which are heterogeneous groups as compared to the Western groups who had been previously assimilated for hundreds of years. We may have learned to accept different faiths and different ancestry in recent years, but these new mixtures fractured identities into smaller and smaller pieces. Each of these identities is assigned a level of importance to character as we try to assess the virtues in our own lives. In recent decades, we have come to terms with the overarching differences of the human experience, but we are more divided over politics and morality than ever. Connection is at once easier than ever yet more difficult to fully embrace. Technology has allowed us an echo chamber to reverberate our ideas in a manner that is always palatable. We have grown accustomed to believing that the marrying of ideas is dangerous when the only danger is the disregard for progress.

Demographically, we have two large and influential age groups in the United States. There is the Baby Boomer Generation and older, who have lived in a world which has been mostly free of the effects and the requirements of diversity. It is estimated that between the years 2010 and 2030, the white labor force will decrease by fifteen million and the minority labor force will increase by twenty-six million workers. The economic model that we have set up that includes Medicare, Social Security, and pensions requires future generations to be successful and productive to pay for these programs that they are not guaranteed but are all but sacred for the current eligible generations. Ronald Brownstein has called the new tension in modern society, especially as it pertains to America, as divide between the "Grey and the Brown." Institutional racism decimated the African American population. Even in 1959, more than 50 percent of the population still lived in poverty. By 2010, the average family income for African American was only 56 percent of their white counterparts. Segregation is still the norm in many parts of the country. The white population is aging and not multiplying. A new version of America will soon arrive where the minorities will be the mainstream. Investment in the future means investment in minorities themselves, which happen to be disproportionately poor.

Luckily, if we have learned anything from the exchange of ideas throughout history, our modern predicament is an opportunity. *Fortune Magazine* has said that "America's 50 best companies for Asians, Blacks, and Hispanics" regularly beat the S & P 500 Index. The United States' nonwhite workforce is expected to more than double by 2020 from its 1980 total of 18 percent. According to the Brookings Institute, 92 percent of population growth in the United States between 2000–2010 were minorities even though net immigration has been decreasing. In 2011, over 200 million people lived outside their country of birth, which is a 50 percent increase over the previous two decades. One billion people were added to earth between 2000 and 2013. It is nearly universally agreed that economically, the world requires innovation. Historian William McNeill, who authored *The Rise of the West*, said we must surrender "social cohesion and psychological comfort" from those different than us in return for innovation and novelty. One cannot exist without the other. In poor countries, failure of diversity can have catastrophic ramifications, including fundamentalism, which reacts in antihumanist fashion to prepare for the future. In the developed world, lack of diversity will assuredly lead to stagnation, both economically and culturally.

Friedman suggests not only promoting immigration but "thinking like an immigrant." The low-skilled, unemployed, and working poor draw the ire of Americans across the political spectrum. Whether real or imagined, a large percentage of the population believes that the well-being of a certain percentage of the poor increases by the welfare state, displacing gainful employment. In other words, the poor are lazy and it is the government's fault. Immigrants have no innate understanding of welfare. Their understanding of risk analysis is not a factor because they are too busy working. Many immigrants may come to the United States poor but see a society where opportunity is unlimited. This is what he refers to as paranoid optimism. Immigrants have the passion for seizing opportunity while understanding that success is volatile. Populist narrative states many immigrants have virtually the same skill sets as the poor yet they are despised for the exact opposite reason; they have the motivation to work and will do whatever it takes to provide for their family, even if it means carrying multiple jobs. Menial jobs to an immigrant do not carry the social stigma that it would for an American. For this virtue, the immigrant is at once admired for their work ethic and admonished for taking American jobs.

Diversity and inclusion began as a compliance item mandated through affirmative action constructs. The reason that it was necessary is that humans have an unconscious bias toward those who we believe are similar to us. A 2012 "Ladders" study detailed hiring habits of recruiters. Each resume was browsed for an average of six seconds. The first and many times the only item which was noticed was the name. The idea of meritocracy assumes that all individuals at every step were given an equal chance. Meritocracy is a noble idea to which we must always strive, but bias hinders the selection process. Like-mindedness is an attractive quality when filling a position, even when what is required is diversity. Diversity may be one of the most important strategies in the modern world for long-term value. It is not limited to sex, skin color, or religion but expands to point of view. Homogeneity is a comforting quality, but diversity is the precursor to innovation. Purposeful diversity is also important so as to mirror society as a whole. If power structures refuse inclusion, we would find a ruling class or a business class that has no connection to the masses. The minority will become the masses in the near future.

In *The Difference*, Scott Page details the fact that in many of the world's most pressing issues, diversity now trumps ability. If systematic thinking is truly the best way forward, we need to include all parts of the system. The narrow constructs of the lip service of diversity are no match for the possibilities of human potential and growth in the twenty-first century. The understanding of diversity itself derives from the fact that we see large differences in humans for various reasons. We can only transcend the idea of diversity by seeing difference without passing judgement and doing so without contradicting our own principles. Global leadership expert Mark Gerzon outlines the evolution of civic consciousness. The nation state gave us what he calls a sociocentric perspective, and the postmodern era that highlighted our multiple differences was called a multicentric point of view. Humanity, he says, has the capacity to become geocentric. That is the ability to take a holistic approach to the earth and all its population. Jeremy Rifkin calls the multicentric period, which treats diversity as a task rather than an intuitive understanding, a psychological period of human consciousness. Human technology, for the first time ever, has the capability to connect all humankind and the earth itself. Rifkin calls this consciousness understanding the biosphere. In this context, evolution is nothing but broader understanding of empathy. Technology has given humanity the capacity to discount diversity as difference at all.

A new wave of cosmopolitanism is accessible. This is the very opposite of fundamentalism. The traditional idea of cosmopolitanism sought universal values, although that ideal is difficult when considering the whole world. The goal is always toward openness rather than restriction. Harvard Professor Anthony Appiah has called for "rooted cosmopolitanism." Identity has expanded to demand the most evolved to be a world citizen but also attached to our time and place. G. Pascal Zachary calls this idea "roots and wings." This is the metamodern application of the global identity. To have ethnic pride is important, but identity must not detract from openly embracing differences. The ability to individually identify has been expanding for some time. The pride that we take in identity has been a slippery slope to division. Our religion, heritage, political affiliation, level of education, field of work, and hobbies, to name a few, are all possible dividers. Even allegiance with our favorite sports team is a potential psychological divider. It is human nature to seek attachments to many different affiliations. The choice to attach does not denigrate those who made the opposite choice. Twentieth-century philosopher and theologian Albert Schweitzer said, "Until he extends his circle of compassion to include all living things, man will not himself find peace." Cosmopolitanism of the twenty-first century then goes well beyond corporate strategy and beyond humanistic ethics and contends with the spiritual solace of the soul.

So we find a new generation of humanity quite different from any that came before. Canadian nationalism academic and politician Michael Ignatieff has called for a "postnational consciousness," just as presidents as diverse as Ronald Reagan and Barack Obama has called for global citizenry. Former billionaire Eric Greenberg wrote *Generation We* in 2008 to describe the values of the millennial generation. He sees their values as crystallizing in a world that is postpartisan, postideological, and postracial, but their unique mystique is that they are the only ones who can recognize it. They are not Liberal and not Conservative mostly because they do not know what those terms represent. Intelligence, education, and technological savvy are now simply requirements of youth. Independence, open-mindedness, tolerance, and diversity are less noble traits than metaphors for existence. Civic-mindedness, environmentalism, and responsibility allow for the continuation of the species. Creativity, innovation, goodness, problem-solving, optimism and pragmatism are the traits that can lead to differentiation and progress once they gain control of our institutions and organizations. Friedman defined Globalization 3.0 as the technological capability of the world, filling with enough bandwidth, software, data storage, devices, and human customers to shrink the world into one global marketplace. The next project would be for business to restructure to account for this new global phenomenon. The last piece of the puzzle would be the skills transformation for the global workforce, which could ultimately take a generation. The irony is that the millennial generation already has the required skill set intact.

The global metaphor for the postmodern world was humanity spreading physically, emotionally, and spiritually. A world of new opportunities and narratives proved to humanity that the shared experiences which had brought people together, even in the atrocities of war, was subsiding. The urban sprawl to the suburbs kept expanding, and the middle hollowed out, represented best by the fleeing of the core of the city, which no longer had a need for manufacturing and industrialization. Social capital, the imaginary glue that held communities together, was eroding. American sociologist Robert Putnam called the phenomenon "bowling alone," representing the depletion of group activities. Polish sociologist Zygmunt Bauman called it "liquid modernity," wherein man has been left free to wander the earth again as a nomad. We became a tourist in our own lives, trying on various identities and momentary allegiances that value exclusion and change over civics and support networks. Privatization had caused the individual to view a new global world in all its chaos. Four hundred years of the Enlightenment had been spent on creating the individual, and in just a few decades in the latter half of the twentieth century, the freedom of the individual had become the burden of individual responsibility. Economic freedom and prosperity had created a melee of postmodern philosophical ponderous, which has never been succinctly articulated. Somehow the ideals of historical liberalism, which had won for centuries, had created an atmosphere where the hard won principles themselves were questioned. Human identity had become so fluid that it had lost its meaning.

All the while, the virtues of democracy, capitalism, and technology were driving down global poverty. The West could wrestle with the existential ramifications of abundance, but the developing world still required the requisite constructs of infrastructure. The United Nations reports that extreme poverty is down 80 percent in the last thirty years. Steven Pinker's grand thesis in *The Better Angels of Our Nature* is that despite two devastating world wars in the twentieth century, the trajectory of mankind is the promise of diminishing violence. All over the world, authoritarian rule is dying, precipitated by new information sources that will not concede to the blockades for very much longer. As humanity rises to shed the ghosts of oligarchy in the far corners of the world, the metamodern ethic represented by Janus will embrace the literal representation of the past with the promise of the future. The capabilities of new technologies, global opportunities, and planetary empathy will shine lights unto the possibilities of humanity. A new understanding of millennial modernism needs to be distributed throughout the world regardless of the learned patterns of differences mastered in the postmodern period and still practiced today. Understanding that just as the middle class in the West live as kings of the Renaissance, technology provides the opportunity for the poor in the developing world to at least meet the necessities required to spark the hope of progress. One billion people still live on less than two dollars per day, but that is an opportunity for mankind to practice the virtues of a new century. The global/technical convergence deemed it possible for the middle class on earth to double in just a decade.

The systems theorist Kenneth Boulding said that a "society that loses a positive image of the future can't deal with present problems." The Organization for Economic and Cooperation Development (OECD) did a study of the twenty advanced industrial democracies and found that the United States, despite an astounding military and GDP, had the highest inequality of income, poverty rate, child poverty rate, infant mortality rate, homicide rate, healthcare expenditures, prison population, and healthcare unaffordability. Unwillingness to deal with the future of the past has left the most powerful and respected nation on earth embarrassingly behind on crucial areas of well-being. Politically, the ramifications of each individual "bowling alone" did not offer us leadership by the way of the grand narrative of universal human progress. We have spent decades contemplating a risk-management strategy of political and apolitical conservatism. The overarching sentiment of the postmodern period was the loss of political power to the subtle but effective big–business themes of consumerism fed by the privatization of the media as entertainment, rather than civic responsibility. Fear was the product that was sold. Even though Pinker spent 832 pages of *Better Angels* documenting the fact that humanity has never been safer and freer, we have spent thirty years raising children and living as the trend were the opposite.

Winston Churchill said, "For myself I am an optimist—it does not seem to be much use being anything else." Byron Auguste, former deputy to the president for economic policy, gave a speech to Harvard Business School in 2011. He said, "We face big challenges . . . but . . . I'd rather be us than anyone else. Compared with other rich countries we have youth, openness, dynamism, best minds from around the world, enormous human capital, the deepest capital markets, unparalleled institutions of innovation, and a market no global business can ignore. Compared to big developing countries, we have high social trust, low corruption, and a historic link between effort and achievement, and democracy, as messy as it is sometimes." There are more reasons than ever to be an optimist. Opportunity in the developed world is partnership with new markets to assist with their huge capability for growth. Opportunity in the developing world is the very same, comparative advantage of which Ricardo spoke nearly two hundred years ago. The Indians and the Chinese are racing to the top. That momentum is allowing for the expansion of the global economic pie. Symbiosis between humanity is expanding to what Al Gore calls the global mind. This is another metaphor for a new version of cosmopolitanism, which Anthony Appiah has described as "shared commitment—not shared values." The virtue of the locomotion is coming together as we move forward while respecting infinite individual perspectives of humanity.

Perhaps one of the most tangible examples of the pragmatism of materialist philosophy can be found in another Churchill quote, which says, "We shape our buildings; thereafter they shape us." A more eloquent definition of design cannot be applied to the way that we live. Over a hundred years ago, we would have found an urban utopia where the streets were clean and the houses were dirty. Nineteenth-century Paris and Vienna, for instance, was designed for life to be lived out in the open. It was eerily similar to a mixture of the New Urbanism found in many American cities as well as its virtual domain called Facebook. One hundred years ago, W. B. Yeats warned that the "center cannot hold." Although he may have been referring to the period of peace between the world wars, it fits the trajectory and the timeline of the slow defection of the urban landscape. As if on cue, the symbolic nature of the decimated inner city, which had been fled in favor of the safety, security, and isolation of the far suburbs out of fear and comfort, is no longer the equation for stability. Urban planning expert Robert Fishman identifies five great migration patterns in American history. First we went west to explore the frontier and then left the farms for the factories. By the twentieth century, we had fully entered the cities only to decentralize to the outskirts of the suburbs. As Yeats was writing *The Second Coming*, Americans began realizing that noise, crime, congestion, and smells of the city was not conducive to raising families, especially if automobiles and public transportation provided for their commuting needs.

The fifth migration pattern is what Alan Ehrenhalt calls the Great Inversion. Signs of affluence allowed families to move from the center of the city, but new patterns in American life are reversing that pattern. Traditionally immigrants settled directly in the center of the cities, but by 2005, 4.4 million immigrants moved directly to the suburbs as compared to 2.8 million in the cities. Urban landscapes are being reborn across the country under the guise of gentrification. The term *gentrification*, as the negative connotation of the displacement of a native population, may not be a myth, but it has been a good storyline for those who fear progress. Cities are once again fashionable for the youth. It is estimated that 77 percent of the millennial population prefer to live in an urban area. Not only are cities a microcosm of the increasingly diverse global climate but they are also the physical representation of the openness of the information age. Economist Richard Florida identifies a group of urbanite youth, which he calls the creative class, as the key to our economic future. Tony Hsieh, the innovative Zappos CEO, has said, "Every time a city doubles in size- innovation and productivity per resident increase by 15 percent." The same growth rate of companies seems to have the opposite effect. The distributed system of the city, which is codified and imbedded with a natural openness, automatically embraces diversity. It lives in contrast to the centrally planned company, which prioritizes risk over productivity and innovation.

The urban historian Peter Hall, in *Cities in Civilization*, talks about the role of cities throughout history as it pertains to human progress. The global trend is the return to the cities. Already 80 percent of all global production happens in the cities. By 2050, it is estimated that 70 percent of the world's population will live in cities, many of which will grow to combine in just a few dozen "megacities," which will flourish under a fast-paced and cosmopolitan idea of capitalism. In 1942, economist Joseph Schumpeter revolutionized economics by stating that capitalism "is by nature a form or method of economic change and not only never is but never can be stationary." If we are to live in a messy, complex, and fast-paced world of capitalism and democracy, coming together for the common good— once called dialectics of philosophy, comparative advantage of economics, or transcendence of religion—all finally have the opportunity for unity. Generations of humans were born only to live exactly as those before them. As the epochs of history unfolded, generational identities grew more pronounced. As the lengths of the great cultural eras diminished, simultaneously technology grew more exponential, and a single birth cycle presented increasingly distinguishable characteristics. The twenty-first century arrived amid a digital world of exponential progress. Simultaneously, a generation of candor and stealth works within the constructs of a natural system reminiscent of the stoic ideal, which leads from behind. The value system is complete yet ill-defined as it waits for a world qualified to adhere to its new enlightenment.

BIBLIOGRAPHY

INTRODUCTION

Boudieu and Habitus. "Understanding Power for Social Change." http://Powercube.net/other-forms-of-power.

Bury, J. B. *The Idea of Progress*. Echo Library, 2006.

Harford, Tim. *Adapt: Why Success Always Starts with Failure*. New York: Little, Brown Young, 2011.

Howe, Neil and Strauss, William. *Generations: The History of America's Future, 1584 to 2069*. New York: William Morrow and Company, Inc., 1991.

Schwartz, Barry. *The Paradox of Choice: Why More is Less*. New York: Harper Perennial, 2004.

Schwartz, Barry. *Practical Wisdom: The Right Way to Do the Right Thing*. New York: Riverhead Books, 2010.

St. John de Crevecoeur, J. Hector. *Letters from an American Farmer*. Whitefish: Mt. Kessinger Publishing, 2004.

Taleb, Nassim Nicholas. *The Bed of Procrustes*. New York: Random House, 2010.

Wilson, E. O. *Consilience: The Unity of Knowledge*. New York: Vintage Books, 1998.

Wagner, Tony. *Most Likely to Succeed: Preparing Our Kids for the Innovation Era*. New York: Scribner, 2015.

Young, Alex Trimble. "Andrew Sullivan Is Wrong Again: His Mainstream Liberalism Has Become Scarily Anti-Democratic." Salon.com, May 8, 2016.

Zakaria, Fareed. *In Defense of a Liberal Education*. New York: W. W. Norton & Company, 2015.

CHAPTER 1

Abbott, Andrew. *Chaos of Disciplines*. Chicago; London: The University of Chicago Press, 2001.

Aristotle. *Nichomachean Ethics*. London: Penguin Classics, 2004

Aurelius, Marcus. *Meditations*. Amazon Digital Services, 2012.

Bejan, Adrian and J. Peder Zane. *Design in Nature*. New York: Penguin Random House, 2012.

Burstein, David D. *Fast Future: How the Millennial Generation Is Shaping the World*. Boston: Beacon Press, 2013.

Capra, Fritjof. *The Systems View of Life: A Unifying Theory*. Cambridge: Cambridge University Press, 2014.

De Caritat Condorcet, Jean-Antoine-Nicolas. *Sketch for a Historical Picture of Progress of the Human Mind*. New York: Noonday Press, 1955.

Foucault, Michel. *The Archaeology of Knowledge*. New York: Pantheon Books, 1972.

Gay, Peter. *Modernism: The Lure of Heresy*. New York: W. W. Norton & Company, 2007.

Gleick, James. *The Information: A History, a Theory, a Flood*. New York: Pantheon Books, 2011.

James, William. *Pragmatism*. New York: Prometheus Books, 1991.

Kant, Immanuel. *A Critique of Pure Reason*. Retrieved from http://eBooks@Adelaide.edu, 2014.

Keay, Douglas. "Woman's Own." Retrieved from Margaretthatcher.org., Sept. 23, 1987.

Kirby, Alan. *Digimodernism: How New Technologies Dismantle the Postmodern and Reconfigure our Culture*. New York: Continuum, 2009.

Klein, Julie Thompson. *Interdisciplinarity: A History, Theory, & Practice*. Detroit: Wayne State University Press, 1990.

Laszlo, Ervin. *The Systems View of the World*. New Jersey: Hampton Press, 1996.

Lemert, Charles. *Postmodernism Is Not What You Think*. Oxford: Blackwell Publishing, 1997.

Lucretius. *On the Nature of Things, 49 B.C.* Indianapolis: Hackett Publishing, 2001.

Meadows, Donella. *Thinking in Systems*: A Primer. River Junction, Vermont: Chelsea Green, 2008.

Menand, Louis. *Pragmatism: A Reader*. New York: Vintage Books, 1997.

Nietzsche, Friedrich. *On the Genealogy of Morality*. Indianapolis: Hackett Publishing, 1998.

Redrum, David and Nicholas Stavris,. *Supplanting the Postmodern: An Anthology of the Writings on the Arts and Culture of the Early 21st Century*. New York; London: Bloomsbury Publishing, 2015.

Ridley, Matt. *The Evolution of Everything*. Sausalito, California: Polipoint Press, 2010.

Robertson, Donald. *Stoicism and the Art of Happiness*. London: Hodder and Stoughton, 2013.

Sarup, Madan. *An Introductory Guide to Post-Structualism and Postmodernism*. Athens, Georgia: The University of Georgia Press, 1993.

Seneca, Lucius Annaeus. *Letters from a Stoic*. London: Penguin, 1969.

Timberg, Scott. *Culture Crash: The Killing of the Creative Class*. New Haven: Yale University Press, 2015.

Turner, Luke. *Metamodernist Manifesto*. Metamodernism.org, 2011.

Van Doren, Charles. *A History of Knowledge: The Pivotal Events, People, and Achievements of World History*. New York: Ballantine Books, 1991.

Vermeulen, Timotheus and Robin Van den Akker. "Notes on Metamodernism." *Journal of Aesethics and Culture*, vol. 2. aesethicsandculture.net/index.php/jac/article/v.

Wilson, Edward O. *Consilience: The Unity of Knowledge*. New York: Alfred A. Knopf, 1998.

Wilson, Edward O. *The Social Conquest of Earth*. New York; London: Liveright Publishing Corporation, 2012.

CHAPTER 2

"2010–2011 Graduation Rates for Area Districts in Missouri." *St. Louis Post*. Dispatch Nov. 21, 2011. Retrieved from stltoday.com.

Brynjolfsson, Erik and Andrew McAfee. *The Second Machine Age*. New York; London: W. W. Norton & Company, 2014.

Clifton, Jim. *The Coming Jobs War*. New York: Gallup Press, 2011.

Cooper, Anderson. On *The Howard Stern Show*, Mar. 31, 2014.

Covey, Stephen R. *The 7 Habits of Highly Effective People*. New York: Simon and Schuster, 2013.

Covey, Steven, et. al. *The Leader in Me*. New York: Simon and Schuster, 2008.

Dawkins, Richard. *The Selfish Gene*. Oxford; New York: Oxford University Press, 2006.

Goleman, Daniel. *Emotional Intelligence*. New York. Bantam Books, 2011.

Heldman, Caroline. "Hurricane Katrina and the Demographics of Death." *The Society Pages*. Aug. 29, 2011. Retrieved from the-societypages.org.

Wilson, E. O. *Consilience: The Unity of Knowledge*. New York: Vintage Books, 1998.

Wilson, E. O. *The Social Conquest of Earth*. New York; London: Liveright Publishing Corporation, 2012.

Kamenetz, Anya. *Generation Debt: How the Future Was Sold Out for Student Loans, Credit Cards, Bad Jobs, No Benefits, and Tax Cuts for Rich Geezers—and How to Fight Back*. New York: Riverhead Books, 2006.

Lanier, Jaron. *You are Not a Gadget: A Manifesto*. New York: A. A. Knopf, 2010.

Costa, Rebecca D. *The Watchman's Rattle: A Radical New Theory of Collapse*. New York: Vanguard Press, 2010

Deaton, Angus. *The Great Escape: Health, Wealth, and the Origins of Inequality*. Princeton: Princeton University Press, 2015

Liu, Eric and Nick Hanauer. *The Gardens of Democracy: A New American Story of Citizenship, the Economy, and the Role of Government*. Seattle, Washington: Sasquatch Books, 2011.

Mullainathan, Eldar and Eldar Shafir. *Scarcity: Why Having Too Little Means So Much*. New York: Times Book, Henry Holt and Company, 2013.

Murray, Charles A. *Coming Apart: The State of White America, 1960–2010*. New York: Crown Forum, 2012.

Piketty, Thomas and Arthur Goldhammer. *Capital in the 21ˢᵗ Century*. Cambridge, Massachusetts: The Belknap Press of Harvard University Press, 2014.

Pink, Daniel H. *A Whole New Mind: Why Right-Brainers Will Rule the Future*. New York: Riverhead Books, 2013.

Schwartz, Larry. "35 Soul Crushing Facts About American Income Inequality." Jul. 15, 2015. Retrieved from Salon.com.

Selingo, Jeffrey J. *College Unbound: The Future of Higher Education AND What It Means for Students.* Boston; New York: New Harvest, 2013.

Szalavitz, Maia. "How Economic Inequality is (Literally) Making Us Sick." *Time Magazine,* Oct. 19, 2011. Retrieved from health-landtime.com

Vaughn, Richard. "Sugata Mitra: Schools Should Scrap the 3Rs." Jan. 20, 2016. Retrieved from Tes.com.

Wolfer, Justin. "The Economics of Happiness, Part 2: Are Rich Countries Happier Than Poor Countries?" April 17, 2008. Retrieved from freakonomics.com.

CHAPTER 3

Fitzgerald, F. Scott. *The Crack-Up*. Retrieved from esquire.com/features/the-crack-up.

Howe, Neil and William Strauss. *Generations: The History of America's Future, 1584 to 2069*. New York: William Morrow and Company, Inc., 1991.

Palfrey, John and Urs Gasser. *Born Digital: Understanding the First Generation of Digital Natives*. New York: Basic Books, 2008.

Putnam, Robert D. *Bowling Alone: The Collapse and Revival of the American Community*. New York: Simon and Schuster, 2013.

Strauss, William and Neil Howe. *The Fourth Turning: An American Prophecy*. New York: Broadway Books, 1997.

Williams, Roy H. and Michael R. Drew. *Pendulum: How Past Generations Shape Our Present and Predict Our Future*. New York: Vanguard Press, 2012.

Winograd, Morley and Michael D. Hais. *Millennial Momentum: How a New Generation Is Remaking America*. New Brunswick; London, 2011.

CHAPTER 4

De Tocqueville, Alexis and Arthur Goldhammer. *Democracy in America*. New York: Library of America, 2004.

Diamandis, Peter H. and Steven Kotler. *Abundance: The Future is Better Than You Think*. New York: Free Press, 2012.

Forscher, Bernard K. "Chaos in the Brickyard." *Science Magazine*. Oct. 18, 1963. Retrieved from science.sciencemag.org.

Friedman, Thomas and Michael Mandelbaum. *That Used to Be Us: How America Fell Behind in the World It Invented and How We Can Come Back*. Waterville, Maine: Thorndike Press, 2011.

Friedman, Thomas L. *The World Is Flat: A Brief History of the Twenty-First Century*. New York: Farrar, Straus, and Giroux, 2005.

Gleick, James. *The Information: A History, A Theory, A Flood*. New York: Pantheon Books, 2011.

Johnson, Steven. *The Case for Progress in the Networked Age*. New York: Riverhead Books, 2012.

Kelly, Kevin. *What Technology Wants*. New York: Penguin, 2010.

Morris, Ian. *Why the West Rules—For Now: The Patterns of History, and What They Reveal About the Future*. New York: Farrar, Strauss, and Giroux, 2010.

Parry, Marc. "The Shape of History: Ian Morris, Historian on a Grand Scale." *The Chronicle of Education*. Feb. 25, 2013. Retrieved from chronicle.com.

Potter, David M. *People of Plenty*. Chicago: University of Chicago Press, 1958.

Schmidt, Eric and Jared Cohen. *The New Digital Age: Reshaping the Future of People, Nations, and Business*. New York: Alfred A. Knopf, 2013.

Standage, Tom. *A History of the World in 6 Glasses*. New York: Bloomsbury, 2005.

Taylor, Paul. *The Next America: Boomers, Millennials, and the Looming Generational Showdown*. New York: Public Affairs, 2014.

Toffler, Alvin. *Future Shock*. New York. Bantam, 1984.

Toffler, Alvin. *The Third Wave*. New York: Bantam, 1984.

Whyte, William H. Jr. *The Organization Man*. New York: Doubleday Anchor Books, 1957.

CHAPTER 5

Anderson, Chris. *The Long Tail: Why the Future of Business is Selling Less of More*. New York: Hyperion, 2006.

Ariely, Dan. *Predictably Irrational: The Hidden Force That Shape Our Decision*. New York: Harper Collins, 2008.

Brynjolfsson, Erik and Andrew McAfee. *The Second Machine Age*. New York; London: W. W. Norton & Company, 2014.

Cowen, Tyler. *Average is Over: Powering America Beyond the Age of the Great Stagnation*. New York: Dutton, 2013.

Cowen, Tyler. *The Great Stagnation: How America Ate All the Low Hanging Fruit of Modern History, Got Sick, and Will (Eventually) Feel Better*. New York: Dutton, 2011.

Dugger, William M and James T. Peach. *Economic Abundance: An Introduction*. Armonk, New York; London: M. E. Sharpe, 2009.

Ford, Martin. *Rise of the Robots: Technology and the Threat of a Jobless Future*. New York: Basic Books, 2015.

Gorbis, Marina. *The Nature of the Future: Dispatches from the Socialstructed World*. New York: Free Press, 2013.

Hanauer, Nick. "Beware, Fellow Plutocrats, the Pitchforks Are Coming." TED Talk. Aug. 2014. Retrieved from ted.com.

Hoffman, Reid and Ben Casnocha. *The Start-Up of You: Adapt to the Future, Invest in Yourself, and Transform Your Career.* New York: Crown Business, 2012.

Jones, Daniel Stedman. *Masters of the Universe: Hayek, Friedman, and the Birth of Neoliberal Politics.* Princeton: Princeton University Press, 2013.

Kishtainy, Niall and George Abbot. *The Economics Book.* New York: DK Publishing, 2012.

Smith, Adam. *An Inquiry into the Nature and Causes of the Wealth of Nations.* New York: Modern Library, 1994.

Sinclair, Upton. *The Jungle.* New York: Penguin Books, 2015.

Reich, Robert B. *Saving Capitalism: For the Many, Not the Few.* New York: Alfred A. Knopf, 2015.

CHAPTER 6

Bruni, Frank. "Dear Millennials, We're Sorry." *The New York Times.* Jun. 7, 2014. Retrieved from mobile.nytimes.com.

Eisenhower, Dwight D. "The Farewell Address." Retrieved from Eisenhower.archives.gov.

Ferguson, Niall. *The Great Degeneration: How Institutions Decay and Economies Die.* New York: Penguin Press, 2013.

Fraser, Steve. *The Age of Acquiescence: The Life and Death of American Resistance to Organized Wealth and Power.* New York: Brown and Co., 2015.

Haidt, Jonathan. *The Righteous Mind: Why Good People Are Divided by Politics and Religion.* New York: Pantheon Books, 2012.

Larson, Erik. "Why College Costs Too Much." *Time Magazine.* Jun. 24, 2001. Retrieved from content.time.com

Laurent, Cliff. *Tomorrow's World: A Look at the Demographic and Socio-Economic Structure of the World in 2032*. Singapore: John Riley and Sons, 2013.

Lilley, Sasha. *Capital and Its Discontents: Conversations with Radical Thinkers in a Time of Tumult*. Oakland, California: PM Press, 201.

Lipset, Seymour Martin. *The First New Nation: The United States in Historical and Comparative Perspective*. New York: Basic Books Inc., 1963. Retrieved from archive.org.

Piketty, Thomas and Arthur Goldhammer. *Capital in the 21ˢᵗ Century*. Cambridge, Massachusetts: The Belknap Press of Harvard University Press, 2014.

Politics Book, The. New York: DK Publishing, 2013.

Robin, Corey. *The Reactionary Mind: Conservatism from Edmund Burke to Sarah Palin*. New York: Oxford University Press, 2011.

CHAPTER 7

Allenby, Braden R. and Daniel R. Sarewitz. *The Techno-Human Condition*. Cambridge, Massachusetts: MIT Press, 2011.

Borges, Jorge Luis, Desmazieres, and Andrew Hurley,. The Library of Babel. Boston: David R. Godine, 2000.

Bostrom, Nick. *Superintelligence: Paths, Dangers, and Strategies*. Oxford: Oxford University Press, 2014.

Brynjolfsson, Erik and Andrew McAfee,. The Second Machine Age. New York; London: W. W. Norton & Company, 2014.

Carr, Nicholas. *The Glass Cage: Automation and Us*. New York: W. W. Norton & Co., 2014.

Diamandis, Peter H. and Steven Kotler. *Bold: How to Go Big, Achieve Success, and Impact the World*. New York: Simon and Schuster, 2015.

Domingos, Pedro. *The Master Algorithm: How the Quest for the Ultimate Learning Machine Will Change Our World*. New York: Basic Books, 2015.

Ford, Martin. *Rise of the Robots: Technology and the Threat of a Jobless Future*. New York: Basic Books, 2015

Grossman, Lev. "Quantum Computing: A Primer." *Time Magazine*. Feb. 7, 2014. Retrieved from science.time.com.

Jazwiec, John. "Speaking of Unemployment—I am a Serial Job Killer." Jun.11, 2011. Retrieved from johnjazwiecblog.com.

Kelly, Kevin. *Out of Control: The New Biology of Machines, Social Systems, and the Economic World*. Reading, Massachusetts: Adison-Wesley, 1994.

Kelly, Kevin. *What Technology Wants*. New York: Penguin, 2010.

Kurzweil, Ray. *The Singularity is Near: When Humans Transcend Biology*. New York: Penguin, 2005.

Mayer-Schonberger, Viktor and Kenneth Cukier. *Big Data: A Revolution That Will Transform How We Live, Work, and Think*. Boston; New York: First Mariner Books, 2014.

Ridley, Matt. *The Rational Optimist: How Prosperity Evolves*. New York: Harper, 2010.

Shelley, Mary Wollstonecraft and Maurice Hindle. *Frankenstein: or, The Modern Prometheus*. London: Penguin Classics, 2013.

Susskind, Richard and Daniel Susskind. *The Future of the Professions: How Technology Will Transform the Work of Humans*. Oxford: OUP, 2015.

Toffler, Alvin. *Future Shock*. New York. Bantam, 1984.

Weinberger, David. *Too Big to Know: Rethinking Knowledge Now That the Facts Aren't the Facts, Experts Are Everywhere, and the Smartest Person in the Room Is the Room*. New York: Basic Books, 2011.

Wolf, Maryanne and Catherine J. Stoodley. *Proust and the Squid: The Story and Science of the Reading Brain*. New York: Harper, 2007.

Wright, Alex. *Cataloguing the World: Paul Otlet and the Birth of the Information Age*. New York: Oxford, 2014.

CHAPTER 8

Crease, Robert P. and Alfred S. Goldhaber. *The Quantum Moment: How Planck, Bohr, Einstein, and Heisenberg Taught Us to Love Uncertainty*. New York: W. W. Norton & Co., 2014.

Dweck, Carol S. *Mindset: The New Psychology of Success*. New York: Random House, 2006.

Hart-Davis, Adam. *The Science Book: Big Ideas Simply Explained*. New York: DK Publishing, 2014.

Johansen, Bob. *Leaders Make the Future: Ten New Leadership Skills for an Uncertain World*. San Francisco: Berrett-Koehler Publishers Inc., 2012.

Kahneman, Daniel. *Thinking Fast and Slow*. New York: Farrar, Straus, and Giroux, 2011.

Lanier, Jaron. *Who Owns the Future?* New York: Simon and Schuster, 2013.

Lindley, David. *Uncertainty: Einstein, Heisenberg, Bohr, and the struggle for the Soul of Science*. New York: Anchor Books/Random House, 2008.

Mankiw, N. Gregory. "Defending the One Percent." *Journal of Economic Perspectives*. Jun. 8, 2013. Retrieved from scholar.harvard.edu.

Neumeier, Marty. *Metaskills: Five Talents for the Robotic Age*. USA: New Riders, 2013.

Packer, George. *The Unwinding: An Inner History of the New America*. New York: Farrar, Straus, and Giroux, 2013.

Rosen, Sherwin. "The Economics of Superstars." *The American Economic Review*, vol. 71, No. 5. Dec. 1981. Retrieved from users.polisci.wisc.edu.

Silver, Nate. *The Signal and the Noise: Why Most Predictions Fail—But Some Don't.* New York: Penguin Press, 2012.

Sommers, Cecily. *Think Like a Futurist: Know What Changes, What Doesn't, and What's Next.* San Francisco: Jossey-Bass, 2012.

Taleb, Nassim Nicholas. *The Black Swan: The Impact of the Highly Improbable.* New York: Random House, 2007.

Taleb, Nassim Nicholas. *Fooled by Randomness: The Hidden Role of Chance in Life and in the Markets.* New York: Random House Trade Paperbacks, 2004.

Tetlock, Phillip E and Dan Gardner. *Superforecasting: The Art and Science of Prediction.* New York: Crown, 2015.

Vielmetter, Georg and Yvonne Sell. *Leadership 2030: The Six Megatrends You Need to Understand and Lead Your Company into the Future.* New York: Hay Group Holdings, 2014.

CHAPTER 9

Anderson, Chris. *The Long Tail: Why the Future of Business is Selling Less of More.* New York: Hyperion, 2006.

Berkun, Scott. *The Myths of Innovation.* Sebastopol, California: O'Reilly, 2010.

Brown, Brene. *Daring Greatly: How the Courage to Be Vulnerable Transforms the Way We Live, Love, Parent, and Lead.* New York: Gotham Books, 2012.

Curtis, Adam. "The Century of the Self: Happiness Machines." Season 1, episode 1. BBC documentary. Retrieved from freedocumentaries.org.

Dweck, Carol S. *Mindset: The New Psychology of Success.* New York: Random House, 2006.

Flood, Gavin D. and Charles Martin. *The Bhagavad Gita: A New Translation.* New York: W.W. Norton & Co., 2012.

Fuda, Peter and Richard Badham. "Fire, Snowball, Mask, Movie: How Leaders Spark and Sustain Change." *Harvard Business Review*. November 2011. Retrieved from hbr.org.

Gladwell, Malcom. *David and Goliath: Underdogs, Misfits, and the Art of Battling Giants*. New York: Little, Brown, and Co., 2013.

Godin, Seth. *Purple Cow: Transform Your Business by Being Remarkable*. New York: Portfolio, 2009.

Guillebeau, Chris. *The Art of Non-Conformity: Set Your Own Rules, Live the Life You Want, and Change the World*. New York: Penguin, 2010.

Hoffman, Reid and Ben Casnocha. *The Start-Up of You: Adapt to the Future, Invest in Yourself, and Transform Your Career*. New York: Crown Business, 2012.

Kirby, David. "What Really Happened the Night Dylan Plugged in His Guitar?" *The Washington Post*, Jul. 24, 2015. Retrieved from Washingtonpost.com.

Pressfield, Steven. *The War of Art: Break Through the Blocks and Win Your Inner Creative Battles*. New York: Black Irish Entertainment, 2012.

Reardon, Kathleen Kelley. *It's All Politics: Winning in a World Where Hard Work and Talent Aren't Enough*. New York: Doubleday, 2005.

Weber, Max. *The Protestant Ethic and the Spirit of Capitalism*. London; New York: Routledge, 1992. Retrieved from d.unm.edu.

Whyte, William H. Jr. *The Organization Man*. New York: Doubleday Anchor Books, 1957.

Young, Neil. On the *Howard Stern Show*. Sirius Satellite Radio, Oct. 14, 2014.

CHAPTER 10

Carnegie, Dale. *How to Win Friends and Influence People*. New York: Simon and Schuster, 1981.

Clinton, Hillary Rodham. *It Takes a Village: And Other Lessons Children Teach Us.* New York: Simon and Schuster, 2006.

Comaford-Lynch, Christine. *Smarttribes: How Teams Become Brilliant Together.* New York: Portfolio/Penguin, 2013.

Girard, Joe. *How to Sell Anything to Anybody.* New York: Fireside, 2006.

Hardin, Garrett. "The Tragedy of the Commons." *Science Magazine.* Dec. 13, 1968. Retrieved from garretthardinsociety.org.

Pentland, Alex. *Social Physics: How Good Ideas Spread—the Lessons from a New Science.* New York: Penguin Press, 2014.

Pink, Daniel H. *To Sell is Human: The Surprising Truth About Moving Others.* New York: Riverhead Books, 2012.

Putnam, Robert D. *Bowling Alone: The Collapse and Revival of the American Community.* New York: Simon and Schuster, 2013.

Read, Leonard E. "I, Pencil." Retrieved from admin.fee.org.

Rifkin, Jeremy. *The Zero Marginal Cost Society: The Internet of Things, The Collaborative Commons, and the Eclipse of Capitalism.* New York: Palgrave Macmillian, 2014.

Rose, Carol. "The Comedy of the Commons: Custom, Commerce, and Inherently Public Property." *The University of Chicago Law Review*, vol. 53, num. 3, summer 1986. Retrieved from digital commons.law.yale.edu.

Surowiecki, James. *The Wisdom of the Crowds: Why the Many Are Smarter Than the Few and How Collective Wisdom Shapes Business, Economies, Societies, and Nations.* New York: Doubleday, 2004.

Tapscott, Don and Anthony D. Williams. *Wikinomics: How Mass Collaboration Changes Everything.* New York: Penguin, 2008.

CHAPTER 11

Arielly, Dan. *Predictably Irrational: The Hidden Forces That Shape Our Decisions.* New York: Harper, 2009.

Burchard, Brendon. *The Motivation Manifesto: 9 Declarations to Claim Your Personal Power*. Carlsbad, California: Hay House, 2014.

Coine, Ted and Mark Babbitt. *A World Gone Social: How Companies Must Adapt to Survive*. New York:

Collin, Catherine. *The Psychology Book*. London; New York: D. K., 2012.

Covey, Stephen R. *The 7 Habits of Highly Effective People*. New York: Simon and Schuster, 2013.

Csikszentmihalyi, Mihaly. *Flow: The Psychology of Optimal Experience*. New York: Harper and Row, 1990.

Galbraith, John Kenneth and James K. Galbraith. *Galbraith: The Affluent Society and Other Writings*. New York: Library of America, 2010.

Gallup. "The State of the American Workplace." 2013. Retrieved from employeeengagement.com.

Greene, Robert. *Mastery*. New York: Viking, 2012.

Herzberg, Fredrick. "One More Time: How Do You Motivate Employees?" *Harvard Business Review*, January 2003. Retrieved from hbr.org.

Johnson, Spencer. *Who Moved My Cheese?: An Amazing Way to Deal with Change in Your Work and in Your Life*. New York: G.P. Putnam's Sons, 2002.

Maslow, A. H. "A Theory of Human Motivation." Retrieved from docs.google.com.

McGregor, Douglas. *The Human Side of Enterprise. From Leadership and Motivation, Essays of Douglas McGregor*. Cambridge, Massachusetts. MIT Press, 1966. Retrieved from kean.edu.

Otto, Shawn Lawrence. "The Democrats Are About to Blow It: This Election is About New Millennials, Not Aging Baby Boomers." *Salon*, Mar. 6, 2016. Retrieved from salon.com.

Pink, Daniel H. *Drive: The Surprising Truth About What Motivates Us*. New York: Riverhead Books, 2009.

Porter, Michael E. "What Is Strategy?" *Harvard Business Review*, November–December 1996. Retrieved from HBR.org.

Rifkin, Jeremy. *The Third Industrial Revolution: How Lateral Power is Transforming Energy, the Economy, and the World*. New York: Palgrave Macmillan, 2011.

Sinclair, Upton. *The Jungle*. New York: Penguin Books, 2006.

Toffler, Alvin. *Future Shock*. New York. Bantam, 1984.

Vygotsky, Lev. *Thought and Language*. Cambridge, Massachusetts: MIT Press, 2012.

Webb, Maynard and Carlyle Adler. *Rebooting Work: Transform How You Work in the Age of Entrepreneurship*. San Francisco: Jossey-Bass, 2013.

Whyte, William H. Jr. *The Organization Man*. New York: Doubleday Anchor Books, 1957.

CHAPTER 12

Deresiewicz, William. *Excellent Sheep: The Miseducation of the American Elite and the Way to a Meaningful Life*. New York: Free Press, 2014.

Gibbon, Edward and David Womersley. *The History of the Decline and Fall of the Roman Empire*. London; New York, Penguin Books, 2011.

Knowledge@Wharton. "Why Good People Can't Get Jobs: Chasing After the Purple Squirrel." Interview with Peter Capelli. Jun. 20, 2012. Retrieved from knowledge.wharton.upenn.edu.

Landau, Cecile, Andrew Szudek, and Sarah Tomley. *The Philosophy Book*. London: Dorling Kindersley, 2011.

Menand, Louis. *Pragmatism: A Reader*. New York: Vintage Books, 1997.

Ozmon, Howard A. and Samuel M. Craver. *Philosophical Foundations of Education*, 6th edition. Upper Saddle River, New Jersey: Prentice-Hall Inc., 1999.

Ripley, Amanda. *The Smartest Kids in the World: And How They Got That Way*. New York: Simon & Schuster, 2013.

Scheuer, Jeffrey. "Critical Thinking and the Liberal Arts: We Neglect Them at Our Peril." American Association of University Professors. November–December 2015. Retrieved from aaup.org.

Wagner, Tony. *Creating Innovators: The Making of Young People Who Will Change the World*. New York: Scribner, 2012.

CHAPTER 13

Achor, Shawn. *The Happiness Advantage: The Seven Principles of Positive Psychology That Fuel Success and Performance at Work*. New York: Crown Business, 2010.

Berry, Thomas. "The World of Wonder." Retrieved from creativesystemsthinking.wordpress.com.

Coleman, Mark. *The Sustainability Generation: The Politics of Change and Why Personal Accountability Is Essential Now!* New York: Select Books, 2012.

Collins, James C. *Good to Great: Why Some Companies Make the Leap—and Others Don't*. New York: Harper Business, 2011

"Constitution of the Iroquois Nations, The." The Great Binding Law. Retrieved from indigenouspeople.net

Dennett, Dan. "Let's Teach Religion—All Religion—in Schools." TED Talk. Feb. 2006. Retrieved from ted.com.

Drucker, Peter F. "What Business Can Learn from Non-Profits." *Harvard Business Review*, July–August 1989. Retrieved from hbr.org.

Frankl, Viktor E. *Man's Search for Meaning.* Boston: Beacon Press, 2006.

Hamel, Gary. *The Future of Management.* Boston, Massachusetts: Harvard Business School Press, 2007.

Hanh, Thich Nhat. "The Bells of Mindfulness." Retrieved from moralground.com.

Haque, Umair. *The New Capitalist Manifesto: Building a Disruptively Better Business.* Boston: Harvard Business Review Press, 2011.

Harvey, Fiona. "IPCC Climate Report: Human Impact is 'Unequivocal.'" *The Guardian.* Sep. 27, 2013. Retrieved from theguardian.com.

Kasser, Tim. *The High Price of Materialism.* Cambridge, Massachusetts; London: MIT Press, 2002.

Kumar, Satish. "Three Dimension of Hindu Ecology: Soil, Soul, and Society." Retrieved from qscience.com.

Mackey, John and Rajendra Sisodia. *Conscious Capitalism: Liberating the Heroic Spirit of Business.* Boston: Harvard Business Review Press, 2013.

McGilchrist, Iain. *The Master and His Emissary: The Divided Brain and the Making of the Western World.* New Have: Yale University Press, 2009.

Meister, Jeanne C. and Karie Willyerd. *The 2020 Workplace: How Innovative Companies Attract, Develop, and Keep Tomorrow's Employees Today.* New York: Harper Business, 2010.

North, Anna. "The Fall of Narcissism." *The New York Times.* Jun. 4, 2014. Retrieved from op-talk.blogs.nytimes.com.

Porter, Michael and Mark R. Kramer. "Creating Shared Value." *Harvard Business Review*, January–February 2011. Retrieved from hbr.org.

Rahula, Walpola. "What the Buddha Taught." Retrieved from dhammaweb.net.

Tankersley, Jim. "Baby Boomers Are What's Wrong with America's Economy: They Chewed Up Resources, Ran Up the Debt, and Escaped Responsibility." *The Washington Post.* Nov. 5, 2015. Retrieved from washingtonpost.com.

Savitz, Andrew W. *The Triple Bottom Line.* San Francisco: Jossey-Bass, 2009.

Teilhard de Chardin, Pierre. *The Phenomenon of Man.* New York: Harper Perennial Modern Classics, 2008.

Tolle, Eckhart. *A New Earth: Awakening to Your Life's Purpose.* New York: Plume, 2006.

Melville, Herman. *Moby-Dick.* New York: Harper Perennial Classics, 2011.

Twenge, Jean M. "Generation Me: Why Today's Young Americans Are More Confident, Assertive, Entitled—and More Miserable Than Ever Before." New York: Atria Pbk, 2014.

Twenge, Jean M. and W. Keith Campbell. *The Narcissism Epidemic: Living in the Age of Entitlement.* New York: Free Press, 2009.

Urban, Tim. "Why Generation Y Yuppies Are Unhappy." Retrieved from waitbutwhy.com.

Warren, Rick. *The Purpose Driven Life: What am I Here for?* Grand Rapids, Michigan: Zondervan, 2012.

Whiteman, Gail, Chris Hope, and Peter Wadhams. "Climate Science: Vast Costs of Artic Change." *Nature Magazine,* Jul. 25, 2013. Retrieved from nature.com.

CHAPTER 14

Boyer, Pascal. *Religion Explained: The Evolutionary Origins of Religious Thought.* New York: Basic Books, 2001.

Brafman, Ori and Rod A. Beckstrom. *The Starfish and the Spider: The Unstoppable Power of Leaderless Organizations.* New York: Hudson, 2006.

Campbell, Joseph. *The Hero with a Thousand Faces*. Novato, California: New World Library, 2008.

Campbell, Joseph and Bill Moyers. *The Power of Myth*. New York: Doubleday, 1988.

Coelho, Paulo and Alan R. Clarke. *The Alchemist*. San Francisco: Harper San Francisco, 2013.

Gladwell, Malcolm. *Blink: The Power of Thinking without Thinking*. New York: Back Bay Books, 2005.

Gladwell, Malcolm. *What the Dog Saw and Other Adventures*. New York: Little, Brown, and Co., 2009.

Godin, Seth. *The Icarus Deception*. New York: Portfolio/Penguin, 2012.

Goldsmith, Marshall and Mark Reiter. *What Got You Here Won't Get You There: How Successful People Become Even More Successful!* New York: Hyperion, 2007.

Holy Bible, the. King James Version. Peabody, Massachusetts: Hendrickson Publishers, 2007.

Homer. *The Odyssey*. New York: Farrar, Straus, and Giroux, 1998.

Ismail, Salim. *Exponential Organizations: Why New Organization Are Ten Times Better, Faster, and Cheaper Than Yours*. New York: Diversion Books, 2014.

Joyce, James. *Portrait of an Artist as a Young Man*. New York: Barnes and Noble Digital Library, 2002.

Joyce, James and Stuart Gilbert. *Ulysses*. New York: Vintage Books, 1955.

Kellerman, Barbara. *The End of Leadership*. New York: Harper Business, 2012.

Laloux, Frederic. *Reinventing Organizations: A Guide to Creating Organizations Inspired by the Next Stage of Human Consciousness*. Brussels: Nelson Parker, 2014.

Pfeffer, Jeffrey. *Leadership BS: Fixing Workplaces and Careers One Truth at a Time*. Harper Business, 2015.

Robertson, Brian J. *Holacracy: The New Management System for a Rapidly Changing World.* New York: Henry Holt and Co., 2015.

Saval, Nikil. *Cubed: A Secret History of the Workplace.* New York: Doubleday, 2014.

Schumpeter, Joseph A. *Capitalism, Socialism, and Democracy.* London; New York: George Allen and Unwin, 2003. Retrieved from dl4a.org.

Taleb, Nassim Nicholas. *Antifragile: Things That Gain from Disorder.* New York: Random House, 2012.

Thorpe, Christopher. *The Sociology Book.* New York: DK Publishing, 2015.

Tsu, Lao, Gi-Fu Feng, and Jane English. *Tao Te Ching.* New York: Vintage Books, 1997.

CHAPTER 15

Armstrong, Karen. *Fields of Blood: Religion and the History of Violence.* New York: Knopf, 2014.

Ehrenhalt, Alan. *The Great Inversion: And the Future of the American City.* New York: Alfred A. Knopf, 2012.

Florida, Richard L. *The Rise of the Creative Class: And How It's Transforming Work, Leisure, Community, and Everyday Life.* New York: Basic Books, 2002.

Friedman, Thomas L. *The Lexus and the Olive Tree: Understanding Globalization.* New York: Farrar, Straus, Giroux, 1999.

Friedman, Thomas L. *The World is Flat: A Brief History of the Twenty-First Century.* New York: Farrar, Straus, Giroux, 2005.

Gardner, John and John Maier. Gilgamesh. New York: Vintage Books, 1985.

Gerzon, Mark. *American Citizen, Global Citizen: How Expanding Our Identities Makes Us Safer, Stronger, Wiser, and Builds a Better World.* Boulder, Colorado: Spirit Scope, 2010.

Giddens, Anthony. *Runaway World*. New York: Routledge, 2010.

Gore, Al. *The Future: The Six Drivers of Global Change*. New York: Random House, 2013.

Greenberg, Eric and Karl Weber. *Generation We: How Millennial Youth Are Taking Over America and Changing Our World Forever*. Emeryville, California: Pachatusan, 2008.

Harris, Sam. *The Moral Landscape: How Science Can Determine Human Values*. New York: Free Press, 2010.

Hartley, L. P. *The Go-Between*. New York: New York Review Books, 2002.

Kaplan, Mark and Mason Donavan. *The Inclusion Dividend: Why Investing in Diversity and Inclusion Pays Off*. Brookline, Massachusetts: Bibliomotion, 2013.

Page, Scott E. *The Difference: How the Power of Diversity Creates Better Groups, Firms, Schools, and Societies*.

Pinker, Steven. *The Better Angels of Our Nature: Why Violence Has Declined*. New York: Viking, 2011.

"Keeping an Eye on Recruiting Behavior." Retrieved from cdn.ladders.net.

Putnam, Robert D. *Bowling Alone: The Collapse and Revival of the American Community*. New York: Simon and Schuster, 2013.

Ridley, Matt. *How Prosperity Evolves*. New York: Harper, 2010.

Sussman, Robert W. *The Myth of Race: The Troubling Persistence of an Unscientific Idea*. Cambridge, Massachusetts: Harvard University Press, 2014.

Zachary, Z. Pascal. *The Global Me: New Cosmopolitans and the Competitive Edge*. New York: Public Affairs, 2000.

INDEX

A

C

D

G

H

N

Q

R

S

T

Z

ABOUT THE AUTHOR

James Surwillo, MA, SSGB, CAPM, is a speaker, author, and leader in a Fortune 15 company. He is an advocate for the possibility of progress of youth and an authority on the critical theory and history of the Millennial Generation. His goal is to help business, government, and nonprofit organizations adopt strategies based on the inevitable human resources and leadership transformation. He received his BA from the University of Missouri and his MA from Webster University in St. Louis where he currently lives.

CPSIA information can be obtained
at www.ICGtesting.com
Printed in the USA
LVHW040353311018
595214LV00008B/758/P